EARTH ANGELS

The Short Lives and Controversial Deaths of Three R&B Pioneers

STEVE BERGSMAN

FOREWORD BY TOM BIALOGLOW

Texas A&M University Press
College Station

Copyright © 2023 by Steve Bergsman
All rights reserved
First edition

∞ This paper meets the requirements of ANSI/NISO Z39.48-1992 (Permanence of Paper).
Binding materials have been chosen for durability.

Library of Congress Cataloging-in-Publication Data
Names: Bergsman, Steve, author.
Title: Earth angels : the short lives and controversial deaths of three R&B
   pioneers / Steve Bergsman ; foreword by Tom Bialoglow.
Description: First edition. | College Station : Texas A&M University Press,
   [2023] | Includes bibliographical references and index.
Identifiers: LCCN 2022042614 | ISBN 9781648431258 (cloth) | ISBN
   9781648431265 (ebook)
Subjects: LCSH: Belvin, Jesse, 1932–1960. | Guitar Slim, 1926–1959. | Ace,
   Johnny, 1929–1954. | African American singers—Biography. |
   Singers—United States—Biography. | Rhythm and blues musicians—United
   States—Biography. | Rhythm and blues music—History and criticism.
Classification: LCC ML400 .B46 2023 | DDC 782.42166092/2
   [B]—dc23/eng/20220913
LC record available at https://lccn.loc.gov/2022042614

Frontispiece: Portraits commissioned by Demar Douglas

Contents

Foreword, by Tom Bialoglow		vii
Introduction		1
Part One: Jesse Belvin		
Chapter 1	Dream Girl	9
Chapter 2	Earth Angel	25
Chapter 3	Goodnight, My Love	35
Chapter 4	You Cheated, You Lied	43
Chapter 5	Guess Who	51
Part Two: Guitar Slim		
Chapter 6	Black Snake Moan	71
Chapter 7	Feelin' Sad	85
Chapter 8	The Things That I Used to Do	104
Chapter 9	If I Had My Life to Live Over	118
Part Three: Johnny Ace		
Chapter 10	I Wonder	135
Chapter 11	My Song	147
Chapter 12	The Clock	159
Chapter 13	Saving My Love for You	171
Chapter 14	Pledging My Love	187
Epilogue		197
Acknowledgments		201
Appendix: Selected R&B Hits, 1952–1955		203
Discography		205
Sources		209
Index		221

Foreword

Sometimes you don't realize how intrinsically connected you were to individual performers remembered from youth until you embark on that trip down memory lane. Take the singers featured in this book: Jesse Belvin, Guitar Slim, and Johnny Ace. I didn't know them personally, and I never shared a stage with them, but somehow they were apparitions in my younger years.

Take, for example, Guitar Slim. My father owned a print shop in Jersey City, and one of his commissions was to produce a poster for an upcoming show at a local venue. The featured performer I remember as being Fats Domino. There were two supporting acts, one of which was a young girl called Little Anne. The other was Guitar Slim. My dad's job was to print these posters and hand them off to the guys who would staple or tape them to telephone poles. That was how shows were promoted back then.

It was at the end of 1954 when I first heard about the passing of Johnny Ace. Alan Freed made the announcement when I was listening to his show on the radio. It was a time of ducktail haircuts, pegged pants, chinos, cherry cokes, beautiful cars, and rock 'n' roll. My father used to call early rhythm & blues race music (*Billboard* used this term until 1950) but I really didn't dwell on the wording or know what he was talking about.

When I went to my first rock 'n' roll show, I found out. It was at the Fabian Theater in Hoboken, New Jersey. I went to hear the Heartbeats, Valentines, El Dorados, and Paragons. I arrived with a few other teenage boys. When the curtain came up, I was surprised and astounded. All of the performers in all the groups were Black. I didn't know that in advance, but my father must have known. So the music that I loved was being performed by African Americans. And they became my heroes. I wanted to sing like them. I wanted to imitate them. And that's what I did.

One of the first groups that my friend Joey Vann and I sang with was a mixed-ethnicity group. The three other members of the group were Willie Washington, "Flea," and "Food." In those days in Jersey City, everybody had a nickname; mine was Bomb.

After Johnny Ace's death, and after "Pledging My Love" was such a big song, I bought what became known as *The Johnny Ace Memorial Album.* There was a nice picture of him on the cover, so I knew that he was Black. I was crushed by his passing. That such a young man, who made the music of the day so memorable, should die was heartbreaking. Prior to his recording of "Pledging My Love," he recorded a song titled "Anymore." I loved that song. I wish I still had that album.

At night, my cousin who lived in upstate New York used to be able to receive the signal from radio station WJW in Cleveland, where a disc jockey named Alan Freed had a show called *The Moondog House* that played a lot of rhythm and blues. I couldn't pick up that show in Jersey City, but in 1954 Freed moved to WINS in New York, and I was a devoted listener. Freed would end his shows with Jesse Belvin's "Goodnight My Love."

Belvin wrote a song called "Earth Angel," which was very popular, although I really liked the B-side, "Hey Senorita." Belvin would also sing with a number of groups like the Shields, which had a big hit with "You Cheated." One of my favorite Belvin numbers was the one he recorded under the group name the Cliques. It was called "The Girl of My Dreams," and I believe "the Cliques" was actually just Jesse Belvin.

When I got to be a teenager, my friends and I would go to school dances and congregate around the record player or the speakers and sing along to the music. We had a good time doing that and thought we sounded "real fine," so we continued, performing our own renditions of doo-wop songs. Joey Vann (Joey Canzano) and I formed a group called the Utopians, and we practiced at the gazebo in Jersey City's Hamilton Park. We started out singing on the benches, but a lot of kids, especially the girls, would come and gather round. It got to be a distraction, so we moved to the men's room, which had a good echoey sound. The men's room had a green door, which was always locked, but one day it opened, and a cop came out. We took off. The cop yelled after us, "Hold on, I want to talk to you guys." We stopped and came back. He said to us, "I've been listening to you guys all summer, and I think you sound good." He introduced us to another policeman, who was known as Bob, the Singing Cowboy. The first cop had told Bob about the guys singing in the park, so Bob wanted to hear us. He liked our sound, and they gave us our first two gigs: at Catholic Youth Organization event in Jersey City and at a canteen at Greenwood Lake, New Jersey.

FOREWORD

This would have been about 1959, when we were singing "A Fool in Love," "One Summer Night," and "Sincerely." We dug very deep into doo-wop tunes from esoteric groups such as the Charts, Jesters, Channels, and Paragons. I would do all the falsettos, which was unusual. Most of the white guys in groups wouldn't do falsetto.

By the early 1960s, my group became known as the Parisians, and we had put together a demo of "My Own True Love," a vocalization of "Tara's Theme" from *Gone with the Wind*. One place we dropped a copy of the demo was Coed Records, which eventually invited us back to audition. We probably sang "My Own True Love," which was our first hit under our new name, the Duprees. We wanted our next record to be "As Time Goes By" but Coed preferred "You Belong to Me." It was our biggest hit, going to number seven on *Billboard's* Hot 100 chart in 1962.

I read at one time that the Duprees were referred to as "the last of the Italian singing groups." That made me chuckle, because I was the ringer. The last names of all the originals were Canzano, Santollo, Arnone, Salvato, and Bialoglow. My name sounds Italian, doesn't it? But "Bialoglow" is Polish. My father's business was called the Whitehead Printing Company. If you were to ask anyone who understands Polish, they would tell you that "Bialoglow" means Whitehead in English. When our first album came out we all received four complimentary albums apiece. They spelled my name wrong on the first 4,000 albums. On the back of the album my name was "Tom Bialoblow." George Paxton, the CEO of Coed Records, laughed when I called his attention to the fact. Boy, did that piss me off. I can laugh now when I think about it, but I didn't find it funny back then.

The Duprees had two major hits in 1962, and I was expecting a big royalty check, but the money for everything we did as a singing group —the recording sessions, hiring musicians, even our outfits—was taken out of our royalties. Instead of $25,000 each, we got $800. I had gotten married in January 1963, and my wife quickly got pregnant. She said to me, "You have to get a regular job, because there is not enough money coming in." So I left the group. I was loading tires in a truck terminal when the mechanic and I took a break. On the radio, the DJ introduced a new song by the Duprees. It was "Have You Heard," and it was beautiful. The mechanic looked at me and said, "What the fuck are you doing *here*?" Tears started running down my face.

That music was so important to me—and still is today. I'm thrilled to be a part of a book that remembers guys like Johnny Ace, Guitar Slim, and Jesse Belvin.

Tom Bialoglow

EARTH ANGELS

Introduction

So in between shows we drank. We drank, and we were drunk when we went out before the audience, but we always managed to stand up straight. Nobody could tell we were drunk. . . . Guys like Jesse Belvin, Johnny Ace, Guitar Slim, we had drinking sessions with a gallon of Italian-Swiss colony Muscatel wine, and we'd sit in the hallways of the Teresa Hotel, which is very famous in Harlem, or the Cecil Hotel, which is another famous one on 118th Street and Lennox Avenue. And we would sit there, and after we got about half way down the gallon I would say, "we've got a show tomorrow." And while I'm talking, I'm pulling off my clothes, and the next thing I know I'm sitting in the hallway naked, and Slim's naked . . . then somebody wakes us up early in the morning and says, "you can't lay in the hallway naked, and, besides, it's time to go back to the theater and do the show."

—"SCREAMIN' JAY" HAWKINS

Screamin' Jay Hawkins, the man who sang "I Put a Spell on You," was never a reliable witness to events. His personal stories resembled tall tales more than actual histories. However, even his most outlandish myths had a basis in reality, and by 1983, when he told a story during a London radio interview, saying he'd gotten drunk and naked withy Guitar Slim, there really was no reason to embellish. In mentioning drinking with Jesse Belvin, Johnny Ace, and Guitar Slim, he invoked the names of three bluesmen from the early to mid-1950s who were mostly forgotten. It's not as if he was saying, "hey, I got drunk and naked with Little Richard, Chuck Berry, and Elvis Presley," so we'll give him this one. Not a million-dollar quartet but maybe a dollar-a-quart quartet.

Hawkins escaped a marriage and his hometown of Cleveland to play in a band fronted by Tiny Grimes, one of the two headliners for the first great rock 'n' roll concert (and the first to cause a near-riot situation), the Moondog Coronation Ball in 1952, which was hosted by Cleveland disc jockey

Alan Freed. Hawkins came east and played first with Grimes and then with a host of other fine musicians centered around New York and Philadelphia. At the time, much of the United States was still segregated land, and many hotels didn't allow African Americans as guests, and that gave rise to accommodations just for nonwhites, such as the Teresa and Cecil Hotels in Harlem. So we can assume that part of the story is reliable.

The Hotel Teresa was constructed on the corner of 125th Street and Seventh Avenue in Harlem, opening for business in 1912. (It still stands.) At thirteen stories, it was the tallest building in Harlem. Ironically, in its early years it only catered to a white trade, but in the twentieth century Harlem became a mecca for African American culture, and in the 1940s the whites-only policy ended, and the clientele became almost exclusively black. Everyone who was everyone in the African American celebrity world stayed there, from sports figures such as Sugar Ray Robinson to entertainers like Louis Armstrong and Josephine Baker. As the 1950s arrived with a new kind of music, younger singers such as Little Richard and Ray Charles stayed there. In the 1960s, the hotel could claim Jimi Hendrix as a guest.

As for the Cecil Hotel on 118th Street, it was home to Minton's Playhouse, a famous jazz club founded by tenor saxophonist Henry Minton in 1938. (This building too still stands.)

As for the drinking sessions described by Hawkins, he could have met Johnny Ace and Guitar Slim in New York between 1952 and 1954, but Jesse Belvin would have been harder to place there during those years since he was drafted into the military in 1953 and served for two years. We do know Belvin was in New York in 1956, because he was a performer at the Alan Freed Christmas Jubilee at the Brooklyn Paramount. The singer closing the show that night was Screamin' Jay Hawkins. Belvin would likely have stayed in Harlem, not Brooklyn.

Either hotel would have been comfortable and accepting of up-and-coming R&B musicians looking for a place to stay while performing, recording, or just hanging out and visiting clubs in the Big Apple. Long-term stays at the hotels were not unusual.

Assuming Hawkins correctly remembered his drinking partners, a good question for the interviewer to ask would have been, "When did this bacchanalia take place?" Since that wasn't asked, we have to try figure it out when it could have happened if it happened at all, and the best guess would be early in 1954 because by the end of the year one of the three singers mentioned by Hawkins would be dead. What makes this story so remarkable is that Hawkins, two years before he would make a name for himself with "I

EARTH ANGELS

Put a Spell on You," had hooked up with these three young singers who had already become rhythm and blues stars and seemed to have had a future that was clear and as bright as the yellow brick road.

Then that future it didn't happen. Death came calling for them all except Hawkins.

Born in Greenwood, Mississippi, blues guitarist Eddie Jones, known to his audience as Guitar Slim, boasted a monster hit in 1954 called "The Things I Used to Do." It sold a million records at a time when an R&B song selling in the hundreds of thousands was considered a big deal.

John Marshall Alexander Jr. came out of Memphis with a new name, Johnny Ace, and had become the most popular R&B singer in the country, with songs such as "My Song" and "Cross My Heart." Almost everything he recorded became a hit, including his great crossover tune of 1954, "Pledging My Love."

Finally, Texas-born Jesse Lorenzo Belvin had a hit record, "Dream Girl," in 1953 singing in the duo Jesse and Marvin. Later that year, he cowrote the doo-wop classic "Earth Angel." He followed that song with "Goodnight My Love," another wonderful and cherished tune he wrote. He also sang with the Shields on "You Cheated, You Lied."

Hawkins >would outlast all his southern drinking pals. He would live until the year 2000, dying at seventy. As for those three great singers with whom he drank in Harlem, they would all be dead by early 1960. Johnny Ace would die first, in 1954, at age twenty-five. Guitar Slim was next, passing away at the ripe old age of thirty-two in 1959. Jesse Belvin made it to February 1960, and then he too was gone, at age twenty-seven.

To paraphrase Chuck Berry, there were a whole lot of good women shedding tears for a brown-eyed handsome man, and there were many young African Americans who shed tears for these three good-looking guys who were buried too young. It is said that five thousand fans showed up for Johnny Ace's funeral in Memphis. He was to African American teenagers what James Dean, who died less than a year after Johnny Ace, was to many white teens.

The three singers were in their prime right when rhythm & blues was turning into rock 'n' roll, although none of the three were moving in that direction. They were more crooners constructing a sound that in the 1960s would become soul music, although all were thoroughly copied by rockers ranging from Elvis Presley to Frank Zappa.

The earliest to break out of the box were Johnny Ace and Guitar Slim, each finding the top of the R&B charts in the early 1950s. Guitar Slim offered a blues sound that was very basic except for something subtle and exceptional, his strum with distortion on his electric guitar, a sound that would become a hallmark for many future guitar players. Johnny Ace was a pianist, and if one were looking for a precursor to the likes of Smokey Robinson or Sam Cooke or Jerry Butler then Johnny Ace would be a good place to start. Jesse Belvin not was far behind, but he would make a name for himself writing lush romantic melodies that became some of the finest songs of the doo-wop era.

Some old R&B singers and bluesmen like Big Joe Turner (who passed away at the age of seventy-four in 1985), Howlin' Wolf (who departed in 1976 at sixty-five); and Muddy Waters (who died at sixty-eight in 1983) would have a renaissance of appreciation during the 1960s. Johnny Ace, Guitar Slim, and Jesse Belvin too might have eventually been recognized as pioneers of R&B and eventually ensconced in the Rock 'n' Roll Hall of Fame. Instead, they had the bad luck to die young and be forgotten by the music industry.

The three also share something else: lack of clarity as to just how they died. Did Guitar Slim drink himself to death or simply die of pneumonia? Was Johnny Ace's gunshot to the head self-inflicted or an accident? And did Jesse Belvin meet his end in a common automobile accident, or did the KKK force him off the road after an integrated concert appearance in Little Rock?

With this book I investigate these questions and hope to give each one of the singers his due.

Part One
JESSE BELVIN

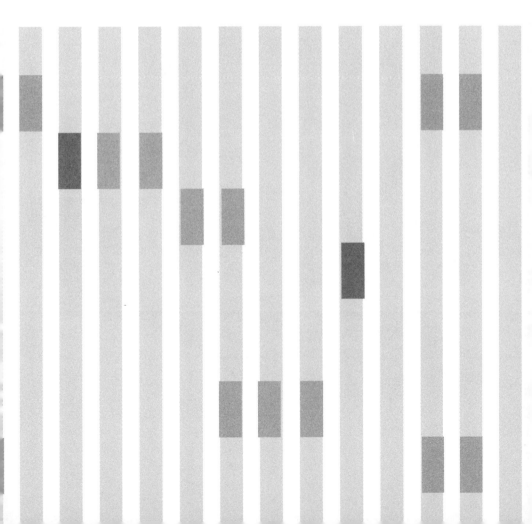

C
H
A
P
T
E
R

Dream Girl

Long before rock 'n' roll – South Central LA, a hothouse of talent – Black families from Texas and Oklahoma migrate to LA – Jesse Belvin in the studio – Rise of independent record labels in LA – "Dream Girl" – All cherries for "Cherry Pie"

1

This is how myths are created: just mix aggressive public relations with compliant mass media. Take the case of Jesse Belvin, the man who cowrote some of the most cherished songs of the early 1950s, including "Earth Angel" and "Goodnight My Love."

In the spring of 1959, Jesse would have another hit record, "Guess Who," and *Billboard* magazine, which ran a helpful column for deejays called "Artists' Biographies for Jockey Programming," spotlighted him:

Jesse Belvin was born in Texarkana, Ark., December 15, 1933, but moved to Los Angeles with his family when he was five. He attended Jefferson H. S. and Compton Junior College in L. A. Belvin's singing career began at the age of seven in a church choir directed by his mother. At 16, he joined Big Jay McNeely's [orchestra] and made his first recording. In 1953, the artist enlisted in the US Army and served at [Fort] Ord and in Germany. Following his stint in the service he enjoyed several hit records both as a singer and songwriter. . . . Belvin's current RCA Victor single, "Guess Who," was written by his wife, Jo Ann. They have two children and a French poodle named Francoise.

DJs all over the country would take this column and talk up the Jesse Belvin background as if Jesse was right there in the studio. A loquacious but lazy disc jockey would chatter into the microphone something like this: "Jack Spratt here on radio KOOL. That's right, we are the coolest of the cool, so don't be a fool, listen to this next jewel of a record by Jesse Belvin. This cat made his first record with Big Jay McNeely at just sixteen, and now he's swinging "Guess Who," which was written by, guess who, his wife."

The trouble was that the article was almost all made up, including the last "fact." Maybe Jesse had a premonition about what the near future held for him when he put his wife's name, "Jo Anne Belvin," (correctly spelled "Jo Ann") on "Guess Who" as the songwriter instead of his own, as a form of estate planning. No matter what, royalties would go directly to her. It was nothing unusual for Jesse not to be credited as songwriter. Many of his songs were credited to producers and record business moguls who then made big money off his best efforts.

As for "born in Texarkana, Ark., on December 15, 1933," the day is right, but the year is wrong. He was born in 1932 – and not in Texarkana but in San Antonio. As for enlistment, yes, he joined the US Army in 1953, but he was drafted. The difference between being drafted and enlisting is two years. If you enlist, it's four years, and in 1956 he was out in the world being a recording star.

Finally, the capsule bio says that at sixteen Belvin joined Big Jay McNeely's band and made his first recording. Jesse cut early-career records with Big Jay's orchestra in 1950, and computing from the accurate birthdate of December 15, 1932, he would have been seventeen. Nevertheless, McNeely is a good place to start when considering Jesse Belvin, because this much is true in the article. Big Jay gave Jesse his big break.

Now, let's turn the clock back to the prehistory of rock 'n' roll.

Rock 'n' roll first stormed the popular record charts in 1955 with "(We're Gonna) Rock Around the Clock," by Bill Haley and His Comets. The rowdy tune was the theme song from the teenage-juvenile-delinquent movie *Blackboard Jungle*, which opened that year. Yet the groundswell of rhythm and blues that would contribute directly to the creation of rock 'n' roll began in the late 1940s, and pre–rock 'n' roll songs were already charting by 1949. The top ten R&B songs for 1949 included John Lee Hooker's "Boogie Chillin,'" which would have made Woodstock band Canned Heat swoon; Wynonie Harris's "All She Wants to Do Is Rock," which could have been sung by any band from the 1960s through the 1980s; and Big Jay McNeely's "The Deacon Hop," an instrumental showcasing a rough, monster saxophone performance by Big Jay himself. ("Big Jay McNeeley's Blue Jays," the label read, misspelling his name.) It was a sound that would define rock 'n' roll through the 1950s.

Before Big Jay was Big Jay, he was Cecil McNeely. He was born and raised in the Watts area of Los Angeles and began his musicianship by stealing time on his older brother Bob's saxophone. He formed a band with another saxophonist, Sonny Criss, and pianist Hampton Hawes, both of which became significant bebop musicians. A few short blocks from Cecil's house stood the Barrelhouse Club, run by Johnny Otis, and legend has it that Cecil won an amateur contest at the club and shortly thereafter joined Otis's house band. That gig didn't last long because record producer and talent scout Ralph Bass discovered him and got Cecil a contract with Savoy Records. Herman Lubinsky, the head of Savoy, didn't think the name Cecil was jazzy enough and dubbed his new talent Big Jay. In December 1948, Big Jay walked into the studio and recorded "The Deacon Hop," which became a big hit the next year. In that session Big Jay recorded "Wild Wig," which also hit the R&B charts.

McNeely was a flamboyant showman, perfecting the art of lying on his back and honking the sax, hard and raw, always a crowd-pleasing performance. As Big Jay told an interviewer about his time in the "The Deacon Hop" spotlight, "I had a great band then, but nobody was responding. . . . I got on my knees; nothing happened. I lay on the floor and that did it. And that's how come I started lying on the floor."

Something else happened on the R&B charts that would have importance going forward. Larry Darnell, a rail-thin young singer with a flamboyant pompadour, boasted the third-biggest single of 1949, "For You My Love." The song was backed by a saxophone-led band playing straightforward blues, but this was not jump-blues in the party sense, it was a blues-based ballad, a sound that only became more popular as the 1940s rolled into the 1950s. As successful as he was as a saxophonist, Big Jay realized he could give depth to his recordings, if not his live performances, by adding a vocal group to sing the slower ballads.

He didn't have to look far. Big Jay grew up in the South Los Angeles area, and when he needed singers he just looked around his old neighborhood of Watts to see who was available.

In the history of popular music there have always been geographic nodes that produced for a limited period of time an outsized effect. Think Detroit and Liverpool in the 1960s and Seattle in the 1990s. One of the first nodes in the modern era was South Central Los Angeles, home to a sizeable African American population, many with Texas or Oklahoma roots. Here in South Central Jesse Belvin lived a few houses down from Gaynel Hodge, who cowrote "Earth Angel."

Hodge recalled his neighborhood: "I had a piano in my house, and Mel Walker [lead singer in the Johnny Otis band, which had a couple of number one R&B hits in 1950] was in and out of my house all the time. Arthur Lee [lead singer for sixties rock group Love] was in the same grade as me, and he would come over to play baseball. On my first day of high school I met Richard Berry [writer of "Louie Louie"] on the bus and then Johnny Guitar Watson in class. He was trying out for the choir."

Arthur Lee would come to Hodge's house, bringing with him Johnny Guitar Watson and Curtis Williams (the third cowriter of "Earth Angel"). Sometimes they would show up with someone new. One day Cornell Gunter, an original member of Platters, came with his sister Shirley, who, as lead singer for Shirley Gunter and the Queens, boasted the first charting doo-wop tune, "Oop Shoop," by a female group.

"There were about seventeen or eighteen boys in the neighborhood that all ended up as singers," Hodge said.

Big Jay graduated from Jefferson High School, itself so rich in music talent that an alumni roster of famous singers, songwriters, and musicians dwarfs a football team. Some of the more prominent names include Barry White, Johnny Guitar Watson, Richard Berry, Art Farmer, Dexter Gordon, Gaynel Hodge, Etta James, Merry Clayton, and Don Cherry.

In her autobiography, *Rage to Survive: The Etta James Story*, Etta wrote, "I was ten or eleven when I met Alex Hodge. Alex and his brother Gaynel Hodge could sing. Along with Eugene Church, who became another close chum of mine, they formed the Fellas and then the Turks. Richard Berry . . . was also part of our crowd."

The other local school known for producing singers was Fremont High School, also drawing from the surrounding African American population. "If you didn't go to Jefferson, you went to Fremont," Hodge noted. "A lot of my friends went to both places, and journalists writing about singers got confused. Cleve Duncan, an original member of the Penguins, went to Jefferson, but I've read where he attended Fremont. Dexter Tisby, another original member, went to Fremont. The singing group the Blossoms, they came out of Fremont."

Gloria Jones, an original member of the Blossoms, confirms Hodge's memory: "We all attended Fremont High, but we didn't know Jesse or Marvin (Phillips) from the neighborhood. They were older, and at the time we only knew them from shows."

The Dootone record label was formed in 1951. According to Arnold Shaw in his book *Honkers and Shouters: The Golden Years of Rhythm and Blues*, founder Walter "Dootsie" Williams garnered much of his talent from street-corner singing groups in Watts. Shaw writes that that Williams "invaded the R&B market in the mid-1950s with five groups," and at least three of these originated at Fremont High: the Penguins, Dootones and

Medallions. Williams started his first label, Blue Records, in 1949 before changing the name to Dootone in 1951. According to the label discography by Both Sides Now Publications (bsnpubs.com), the address of the company was 9512 South Central Avenue, which was Williams's home. For many years the label was run out of an enclosed front porch of his house. One might say that Williams could literally see or hear the local talent from his front yard. Eventually the Williams family moved out, and Dootsie's business took over the whole structure.

There were so many singers in South Central that they were always bumping up against each other, as singing groups formed and then disbanded, formed again, and then reformed once more under a different name. It was roundelay of harmonic voices. Take Cornel Gunter, who sang backup on Big Jay McNeely's recording of "Nervous Man Nervous." As a young teenager in the early 1950s, Gaynel Hodge was playing with the Hollywood Flames (whose "Buzz-Buzz-Buzz" would reach number eleven on the pop charts in 1957) and a couple of other groups and doing very well, and his mother asked him if he could help his brother Alex get a group together. Gaynel introduced Alex to Gunter, and, with the addition of Herb Reed and Joe Jefferson, a new group called the Platters was formed. That was in 1952. A year later, Gunter left to become a member of the Flares (whose "Foot Stompin,' Pt. 1" would be a top twenty-five hit in 1961). That group was formed in 1952 as the Debonairs and included Richard Berry. Gunter left the Flares and eventually joined the Coasters during that group's most successful and prodigious years at the end the 1950s.

That was still in the future. Big Jay had a scorching 1949, with "The Deacon Hop" a number one hit on the R&B charts and "Wild Wig" getting as high as number twelve. He also charted with "California Hop." These were Savoy recordings, but Big Jay decided to move on that year and signed with Exclusive, a Hollywood recording company. After Exclusive folded in 1950, Big Jay moved on to Imperial, where he decided to record with a group of singers. The first person he looked for was another Jefferson High School alum, Jesse Belvin.

Jesse Lorenzo Belvin was born in San Antonio in 1932 to Jack and Selena Belvin. His mother boasted a slew of family in the northeastern corner of state around the small burgs of Nash and Texarkana, Texas. There is much confusion as to Jesse's birthplace, owing to Jesse Belvin Jr. and two Texarkanas located across the state line from each other. Jesse Belvin Jr. in an interview would say that his father was born in Texarkana, Texas. Since he was only four (his and younger brother just eighteen months old) when his parents Jesse and Jo Ann were killed in an automobile accident, Jesse Jr. would have gotten that information from his grandmother, who raised him and his brother. This canard goes back to the 1950s as seen in the *Billboard* magazine bio, so even Jesse Sr. would have been told this bit of misinformation. If Jesse, the singer, for example, had asked his mother where in Texas he came from, she would have answered Texarkana. Since Texarkana, Arkansas, is a bigger city and much better known than Texarkana, Texas, that would be the first assumption of most people – and it was incorrect.

Selena was an Allen before marrying a Belvin, and the Allens lived in the Texarkana, Texas, and area including what is now called Nash, Texas. In the early 1930s, Texarkana, Texas, boasted a population of about sixteen thousand to seventeen thousand folks, while less than one thousand people lived in Nash. Selena was one of ten children, and some ended up remaining in the area, including Jack Belvin and Selena Allen Belvin. Her father, Jesse's grandfather, still lived there during Jesse's last visit in 1960. According to Billy Allen, Jesse's cousin who saw Jesse a few weeks before the accident that took his life, the Belvins lived in the area before taking off for California. But not all the Belvins moved away. By the time Selena took the kids to California, she was separated from Jack. Why Selena gave birth to Jesse in San Antonio, well over four hundred miles away, is unknown.

Sometimes Jesse's birthplace is listed as Hope, Arkansas, probably because it makes for a good story, as he died near Hope in a car accident. According to San Antonio government records, Jesse Belvin was born there on December 15, 1932.

The family moved to Los Angeles around 1937. This family journey was akin to that of Depression-era Okies who moved from Dust Bowl farms to work the agricultural fields of California. The Belvins and many other African American families in Texas migrated west at the end of 1930s and into the mid-1940s for better jobs in the burgeoning war industries of South California. Gaynel Hodge, who was five years younger than Jesse, was born in Los Angeles, but his family also came from Texas, the San Antonio area. Hodge's bandmate in the Hollywood Flames, Bobby Day (originally Robert James Byrd), who also sang "Rock-in Robin," a number two record in 1958, was born in Fort Worth. His family moved to Los Angeles in 1945 when Bobby was fifteen. Marvin Phillips, Jesse's singing partner in the duo Jesse and Marvin, later teamed up with Emory "Johnny" Perry for another duo, Marvin & Johnny, who had a big R&B hit in 1954 with "Cherry Pie." While Marvin was from Oklahoma, Johnny was Sherman, Texas.

The first time Gaynel met Jesse was when he was five years old, which would have been in 1942. Jesse was about ten and walking his dogs. Gaynel's house was only four houses away from Jesse's, but railroad tracks ran between. Gaynel stepped out of his house and witnessed Jesse in an altercation with small group of Mexican boys about the same age. "I started walking toward the tracks, but the other boys started throwing rocks, so Jesse and I departed," Gaynel said.

A few years later, Gaynel was in a singing group at the nearby Santa Barbara Mission, and Jesse came to him and said, "You got a group. I'll come by and sing with you on Sunday if you come with me to sing at my mother's church. And we'll feed you all." At that time he was maybe twelve or thirteen years old and already the junior choir director at his mother's church. She led the choir. Jesse would sing with Gaynel's group at the Santa Barbara Mission, and then they would go to Jesse's mothers church to sing again.

"I was the youngest in the group," Gaynel said. "I just had a natural ear for harmony, so when I was eight I got drafted into the glee club at my elementary school. Jesse was always encouraging me – and not just me, all the guys in the neighborhood. We idolized him."

In 1951, Jesse Belvin scored a hit record with Big Jay McNeely's band. Gaynel said, "They all came to our high school to sing: Jesse, Big Jay, and another local boy, Marvin Phillips." To Gaynel's surprise they called him up to the stage. "From that moment on, Jesse and I just connected. I mean, Jesse was the man," Gaynel recalled.

Lou Rawls is another one who confirmed Belvin's significance. Singer, songwriter, and producer Billy Vera recorded four albums with Rawls, who told him that when he (Rawls) and Sam Cooke first came to Los Angeles they had hung out in a clique with Johnny Guitar Watson, Gene McDaniels, Les McCann, and Jesse Belvin. "Jesse was our leader," Rawls told Vera. "We all bowed to Jesse, even Sam." In Vera's words, "Jesse was so well thought of, even by the guys who went on to greatness."

It was no different for the opposite sex. If anything, the idolization of Jesse was even more passionate. Etta James wrote:

I was surrounded by talented boys – Richard [Berry], Eugene [Church], Alex [Hodge], Gaynell [sic]. But I do believe the most gifted of all was Jesse Belvin. He lived one block over on Thirty-Second Street. Jesse was something else – the golden boy, everyone's idol. He was five or six years older than me and a legend in our neighborhood. . . . Jesse spoke Spanish and hung with Mexicans. He could hang with anyone. Every girl in the world loved him, me included. His hair was half good – straight but wavy – worn slicked back in a ducktail. He had the most beautiful body of any boy in the city. He was buff before buffed was in. I can still see his muscular chest popping all out of his white slingshot. Lord, Lord, Lord! Jesse wore his jeans tight, and had these huarache sandals with taps on the soles so you hear him coming. He had strong legs, walked bowlegged, and smiled with these big ol' juicy soup-cooler lips. When he peered into your eyes, you melted. This was when every guy, black or white, wanted to look as cool as James Dean. But Jesse, well, he was beyond cool.

In a neighborhood bursting at the seams with talented musicians, there were good reasons Jesse was so venerated. First of all, he was a bit older than the wave of doo-wop and R&B singers that would arrive in the early 1950s, so he was successful before any of the others and thus the one every young, aspiring dude and chick wanted to be. Secondly, he was talented and prodigious.

According to Jesse Jr., Bumps Blackwell (Robert Alexander Blackwell), an important songwriter and record producer from the 1950s through 1970s, told him that Jesse Sr. could compose a song by just "snatching it out of the air."

Jesse Jr. liked to retell this anecdote from his grandmother: One day, she sent young Jesse Sr. to the store for a carton of milk. When he came back, Jesse had written four songs, one on each side of the carton. Later that day he sold all the songs.

Jesse Jr.'s grandmother had many stories such as that one. Once she was cooking, and a door fell off the oven. In less than three hours, Jesse arrived home on the back of a truck along with a new oven. He had written a song and sold it in Hollywood. Jesse probably didn't have to go so far. By the end of 1940s and into the early 1950s, record companies were popping up all over Los Angeles, from the ritzy streets of Hollywood to the very heart of Watts. Indeed, as Nelson George in his book *The Death of Rhythm and Blues* noted, from 1942 through 1952, the largest number of significant R&B labels originated in Los Angeles. Of the thirty companies George listed, nine were formed in LA: Excelsior (Exclusive), Modern, Philco-Aladdin, Bronze, Four Star, Super Disc, Specialty, Imperial, and Meteor.

As Gaynel Hodge recalled, with obvious exaggeration, "Suddenly, we had thousands of record companies all over Los Angeles. The city was bursting wide open with them. Everyone who had $100 had a record company. Many were in it just for a moment. If they were lucky, they would have a hit and retire."

DREAM GIRL

One of the earliest in this burst of entrepreneurism was Modern Records, opened by the three Bihari brothers, Saul, Jules, and Joe. In the 1970s, when he was researching *Honkers and Shouters*, Arnold Shaw went to Modern to interview Joe Bihari. He would write: "Situated in Los Angeles' Watts district, the two-story red-brick buildings squat alongside the railroad spur that crosses South Normandie Avenue. A wide stairway takes you from the street level up to a long hallway with offices on both sides. . . . Several freight trains stand on the railroad tie. You can imagine some of the down-home bluesmen riding in from Texas or Oklahoma."

While the Bihari brothers did record bluesmen coming from the middle of the country, they also recorded artists such as Etta James from the local neighborhoods. They didn't record Jesse as a solo artist in those early days, but they knew of him. He was a well-known prodigy, becoming a fine musician and songwriter while working with his mother on the church choir.

As a teenager, he got a contract with Big Jay McNeely when he went to Johnny Otis's Barrelhouse, probably at an amateur night where he sang, Gaynel Hodge said. Jesse Jr. noted in an interview that his father at that time was underage and that his grandmother had to sign the contract for Jesse. This would have been in 1948 or 1949. At the end of 1950, McNeely brought in Jesse and three others to sing because he wanted vocals on his next recording.

According to one discographer, Jesse's first appearance in a record studio came earlier in 1950. Richard Lewis had been fronting a band and recording since in the late 1940s, first as Dick Lewis and His Harlem Rhythm Boys. By 1950 he was performing as Richard Lewis and the Barons, and that's the name he used when he and his bandmates rolled into the Biharis' Modern Records studio to record "Believe in Me" (and "Forever," the B-side). Carl Green and Richard Lewis handled the vocals on "Believe in Me," but Marvin Phillips took over the vocals on "Forever," a song he cowrote with Lewis. Jesse is said to have participated in this recording session, which makes sense because he and Marvin Phillips would launch their careers together.

Big Jay discovered Jesse Belvin at the Barrelhouse in his old neighborhood and signed him because he knew he needed to diversify his act with vocalists. At the end 1950, Big Jay, for Imperial Records, came into the studio with a group of singers led by Jesse and three other LA singers, whom he called Three Dots and a Dash. The Dash was Bettye (sometimes "Betty") Jean Washington, and the Three Dots were Jesse, Marvin Phillips and Jimmy

Huff. The latter was also Big Jay's drummer, according to Gaynel, and cowrote the first of Big Jay's records featuring the singers.

Released in 1951, "All That Wine Is Gone" was a response to the wildly successful Stick McGhee recording of "Drinkin' Wine Spo-Dee-O-Dee," a top five R&B recording in 1949. The record misspells Big Jay's name as "McNeeley," and such misspelling was a common and intentional practice: a record company could withhold royalties to an artist on grounds that the person wasn't the one whose name was on the record. Otherwise the disc has Belvin's name spelled correctly: "Vocal By: Jesse Belvin & Three Dots & A Dash." The same credit was printed on the B-side, "Don't Cry Baby."

"All That Wine Is Gone" was Imperial 5115. Subsequently, "Sad Story," Imperial 5130, credits Jesse Belvin and Three Dots and a Dash. Jerry Osborne and Bruce Hamilton's record collector guides in the 1980s listed Imperial 5164: "I'll Never Love Again," with "Let's Do It" on the B-side, credited to Three Dots and a Dash featuring Jesse Belvin.

America's teenagers had increasingly tuned to rhythm & blues stations since the start of the 1950s. Established record companies fought a rearguard action by recording cover versions of the exciting new R&B songs and doing the same in country and western, formerly known as "hillbilly." However, conservativism in popular music began to win out, and, as academic author Philip Ennis pointed out, the number of crossover records declined in 1952 and 1953. It was the calm before the storm.

If one looks at the top songs on the pop charts of 1953, there is almost no progressive development, nothing new in regard to musicality. The conservative stream held sway with the likes of "The Song from Moulin Rouge," by Percy Faith (number one); "How Much Is That Doggie in the Window," by Patti Page (number three); "I'm Walking Behind You," by Eddie Fisher (number four); and "You, You, You," by the Ames Brothers (number five), followed by such mainstream singers and bandleaders such as Les Baxter, Perry Como, Julius La Rosa, Ray Anthony, Pee Wee Hunt, and the Hilltoppers.

Yet Ennis, who wrote *The Seventh Stream: The Emergence of Rocknroll in American Popular Music*, called 1953 a seminal year for rock 'n' roll because of one song, "Crying in the Chapel," by the Orioles. It was the rare case of an African American group successfully covering what was originally a country song. Although June Valli's version of the song was the big seller on the pop markets, the Orioles version was number one on the R&B charts and crossed over to the pop charts, where it reached number eleven spot. It stayed on the chart for two months. Ennis wrote, "This record was

DREAM GIRL

important mainly because it showed . . . an explicitly black-styled, young vocal group could bring a song appealing to the teen-aged audiences directly to the pop market."

In 1953, the R&B charts continued to showcase pre–rock 'n' roll badass numbers such as "Hound Dog," by Big Mama Thornton, but there was also that sweet R&B sound that Larry Darnell tapped into back in 1949 with "For You My Love." By the early 1950s, that soft blues beat had broken into two distinct strands, the harmonic group sound of doo-wop and the blues crooner, as seen in the popularity of Johnny Ace. Whereas "Crying in the Chapel" was the number R&B one song of 1953 and the Five Royales had two lush doo-wop songs ("Help Me Somebody" and "Baby, Don't Do It") in the top twenty-five songs of the year, so too did blues crooner Johnny Ace have two in the top twenty-five ("The Clock" and "Saving My Love for You").

One of the most interesting R&B songs in the top twenty-five for 1953 was a tune that bridged the crooner and group doo-wop sound. Number twenty-two was "Dream Girl," by the first successful doo-wop duo, Jesse and Marvin. As European music writer Dik de Heer stated, by the early 1950s, "duos were fairly common in country music, but black singers had traditionally worked in trios, quartets and larger groups." Indeed, in the waning weeks of 1952, when Marvin Phillips joined with Jesse Belvin to record "Dream Girl," Marvin was also recording with his own five-piece band, the unlikely named Marvin Phillips and His Men from Mars. The band's name was unique, but Marvin's Men from Mars couldn't let go of Stick McGhee's undying "Drinkin' Wine Spo-Dee-O-Dee" and recorded "Wine Woogie," a response penned by Marvin. On a solid blues beat and a traditional honking sax break, Marvin sings about wine "woogie," repeating the word three times, followed by a statement that the "woogie" makes him feel so fine.

♪♪♪♪♪

Marvin was a year older than Jesse, and he and his family moved to Los Angeles from Oklahoma in the mid-1940s. Also a fine musician, he took up the saxophone and ended up playing with Richard Lewis when he was still trying to make it as Dick Lewis and his Los Angeles-based band, the Harlem Rhythm Boys. Marvin, like Jesse, had the energy, talent, and openness that attracted other musicians, and, in his few years with Richard Lewis, Marvin befriended Jesse Belvin, Carl Green, and Emory Perry, all of whom would be important to Marvin's career.

Friendships and connections in the quickly evolving West Coast R&B world were important. Jesse left Three Dots and a Dash due a dispute said to be over money—disputes with exploitive record companies and band leaders were almost always about money—but when Marvin took over the lead singing duties there were no hard feelings.

"Dream Girl" was written by Jesse and Marvin, and that's how the act was billed: Jesse and Marvin. "Daddy Loves Baby," a Marvin tune, made the B-side of the record on Art Rupe's Specialty label. "Dream Girl" was a highly romantic, slow stroll of a song, with Jesse and Marvin playing off against each other very effectively. When Marvin, in his deep baritone, confesses his love and sings that no one else in this whole wide world will ever do, Jesse, a tenor, comes in behind, begging her to say that she'll be true, adding for emphasis that she's his little dream girl. Marvin does a nice job tricking out the words with a mock stammer while Jesse elongates syllables of the most precious words in the flow, ru-uu-hun-un-ning away. The key instrument setting the tone is a tinkling piano.

An impatient Jesse was so unhappy that Rupe didn't put out the Jesse and Marvin record right away that he went over to John Dolphin, who recorded him as a solo artist singing "Dream Girl" for his Recorded in Hollywood label.

The song was finally released by Specialty early in 1953, and in just a few weeks many a teenage girl was sighing and crying while watching the record spin round and round.

The record made inroads here and there across the country. As reported by *Cash Box* magazine, on January 17, 1953, "Dream Girl" was the number two R&B song in St. Louis and number ten in San Francisco, but it was nowhere to be found in Los Angeles, Milwaukee, or Dallas. Two weeks later, "Dream Girl" was number one in St. Louis and number two in San Francisco but still not charting in the other cities. The hot song at that moment was "I Don't Know" by Willie Mabon, which "Dream Girl" was pushing to replace.

In February, though, the song hit the R&B top ten in Chicago, New Orleans, Philadelphia, Newark, and Atlanta. On February 21, *Billboard* had "Dream Girl" as number seven in R&B record sales in the nation and number eight among most-played R&B songs on jukeboxes across the country. Willie Mabon's "I Don't Know" was still the leading R&B song on the nation's jukeboxes, but the Five Royales' "Baby, Don't Do It" was the number one best seller.

By March, Ruth Brown's "(Mama) He Treats Your Daughter Mean" was tearing up the R&B charts, but "Dream Girl" was hanging in, number eight in the country in both R&B record sales and jukebox plays. At the beginning of April, *Billboard* was still showing "Dream Girl" as a top ten record in Washington DC, Baltimore, and Cincinnati. That was a long run, actually out-lasting Jesse and Marvin's time together.

A month after recording "Dream Girl" for Specialty, Jesse visited with Dolphin, an African American entrepreneur who had a famous record store on Central Avenue called Dolphin's of Hollywood, which specialized in jazz records and was frequented by jazz musicians. In 1950, Dolphin started a record company, Recorded in Hollywood (RIH), and hit paydirt the following year with a song penned by Jessie Mae Robinson, another Texan, whose family migrated to Los Angeles, where she grew up. The song was "Once There Lived a Fool," and everyone from Tony Bennett to Tommy Edwards recorded it, although the big hit on the R&B charts was sung by Jimmy Grissom, a vocalist in the Duke Ellington band. As noted above, Jesse recorded a solo version of "Dream Girl" for RIH, and it was put out with a song called "Hang Your Tears Out to Dry." The songwriting credit on both is "Jacques," the pseudonym of John Dolphin, but "Hang Your Tears" was probably written by Jesse, who sold the song rights to Dolphin.

Specialty, the record company behind the original "Dream Girl," was founded by Art Rupe (Arthur Goldberg), a native of Pittsburgh who attended UCLA and eventually went to work for Atlas Records. In 1944, he and partners founded Jukebox Records in Los Angeles, but when he felt he was losing control of the company he branched out on his own, founding Specialty. The "specialty" alluded to: music by black artists. Rupe recorded Roy Milton and Lloyd Price early in the 1950s and eventually Little Richard, among many others. In 1953, with the success of "Dream Girl," Rupe wanted to quickly get Jesse and Marvin back in the studio to record a follow-up. He just wasn't fast enough. The military was faster.

Gaynel Hodge remembers, "One day, after our rehearsals I said to Curtis Williams, 'let's go to Jesse's house.' Of course, Curtis thought that was a great idea because we were infatuated with Jesse."

They got there, Jesse let them in, and they saw that he had been working with an old friend from Texarkana, Texas, Peppermint Harris (Harrison Demotra Nelson Jr.), who had a monster hit in 1951 with "I Got Loaded." They had the phone book open to record companies and were actually singing on the phone. There was one song Jesse was particularly proud of, and he said to Gaynel, "See what I just wrote." Gaynel looked at a piece of paper. The words "Earth Angel" were written at the top, and below was what looked the like the first verse to a song. That night they all went with Jesse, and that's when Gaynel learned that Jesse had been avoiding the draft.

"We went to a club on Central because Johnny Otis was performing with Little Willie Littlefield, another Texan. Willie's family moved from El Campo, Texas, to Houston in the 1940s, and that where Jules Bihari of Modern Records discovered him and signed to a contract. It was fortuitous because in 1949 Littlefield recorded "It's Midnight," which reached number three on the R&B chart. Little Willie played a peculiar triplet piano style and in 1952 recorded the original version of "Kansas City" (Wilbert Harrison's 1959 recording of the song would be a number one pop hit). During the early 1950s, Little Willie was active on the West Coast, playing with musicians in Los Angeles, which was where Jesse and his posse found him.

"We were outside the club drinking wine when Jesse said to me he was going to turn himself in to the draft board come Monday morning," Gaynel said. "When Jesse joined the service, my brother Alex came around to my classroom and tapped on the classroom window. He said to me, 'we are all going join the service with Jesse.' There were six of them that joined up. Jesse got sent to Germany."

This was the Etta James memory of the time:

I remember how Jesse and Alex Hodge would protect and encourage me when I was just a kid. At the hamburger stand next to Modern Records, some of the cats would give me a hard time, make fun of me, call me fat, question my ability to make records. "Don't do her like that, boys," Jesse would always say. "She's a young girl, but she can sing." Things were going great for him until he got drafted into the Korean War. Seems like a dragnet came down and swept the best black boys off the street. They all disappeared at once. But Jesse was the one who left a mess of weeping girls behind. We prayed he wouldn't be hurt and couldn't wait till our baby came home.

With Art Rupe pushing for another record, Marvin invited Carl Green from his Richard Lewis days to record with him. Marvin didn't think a duo called Marvin and Carl was cool enough, so the two went by "Marvin and Johnny." The first song they released was Marvin's "Baby Doll," with "I'm Not A Fool," also a Marvin tune, on the B-side. In December 1953, it broke into the top ten on the R&B charts, and it was number twenty-two R&B song of the year.

Then everyone got sloppy. There were a few more Marvin and Johnny records on Specialty, such as "Day In-Day Out," written by Marvin, with a Carl Green tune, "Flip," on the B-side. But there were also Marvin and Johnny and the Marsmen records. The magic of "Baby Doll" dissipated, and Rupe let the Bihari brothers sign Marvin to their Modern label. Marvin took the name Marvin and Johnny with him, but he didn't take Carl Green. He was replaced by another old friend from his Richard Lewis days, Emory Perry, who became the new Johnny.

Whatever one might think about record producers in the mid-1950s in regard to being exploitive, probably no group had a worse reputation than the Bihari brothers, who turned exploitation into an art form. The most common way record companies (and important disc jockeys such as Alan Freed) would take advantage of songwriters was to claim, or sometimes purchase, coauthorship of songs, thus securing royalties, which could be very lucrative if a song became a hit. Record producers understood that the big money was not in performing, it was in the songwriting royalties.

In 1954, the first Marvin and Johnny release was "Tick Tock," with "Cherry Pie" on the B-side. Both songs were written by Marvin Phillips. Modern let Marvin have the songwriting credits for the B-side while Joe Bihari, who was not a songwriter, took credit for the A-side under his nom de plume Josea. As it turned out, it was bad guess on Joe Bihari's part. The record was a two-sided hit. In a year when the R&B charts rippled with greatness – "Work with Me Annie" (the Midnighters), "Hearts of Stone" (the Charms), "The Things That I Used to Do" (Guitar Slim), "Shake Rattle and Roll" (Joe Turner), "Sh-Boom" (the Chords), "Gee" (the Crows), "Saving My Love for You" (Johnny Ace), "Goodnite Sweetheart, Goodnite" (the Spaniels), and "White Christmas" (the Drifters) – Marvin & Johnny boasted one of the top forty records.

Although both "Tick Tock" and "Cherry Pie" received substantial airplay, it was the B-side that was more popular at the time. No doubt, this was partly due to the double meaning of the word "cherry" in the title. Not too many male teenagers in the 1950s ever heard the word "hymen," but they knew "cherry" referred to that part of a girl's body. And they may well have used the phrase "bust her cherry," which meant "have intercourse with a virgin." The few actual lyrics in the song could be interpreted or misinterpreted any which way. "Cherry Pie. Ooh so good" and "eatin' his cherry cherry cherry pie," can mean anything depending on how salacious one wants to be.

However, what made this song great were not the few lyrics but the beautiful harmony of Marvin Phillips and Emory Perry. If anyone ever wondered what the attraction of doo-wop music was, this is one of the best songs to listen to. Mostly doo-wop is a group sound, generally with lead ahead of background singers vocalizing rhythm. "Cherry Pie" uses the same structure with just two male vocalists. Six years later, two white boys, Skip and Flip, would have a top twenty hit with the record, and in decades going forward "Cherry Pie" would be remembered as one of the classic songs of the doo-wop era. Joe Bihari guessed wrong in putting his name on "Tick Tock," a song now forgotten.

Earth Angel

CHAPTER 2

Bobby Day and the Flames – Gaynel Hodge and Curtis Williams take over "Earth Angel" – South Central cross-fertilization of the Flames, Platters, and Penguins – "Earth Angel" breaks big – Jesse Belvin returns from service – Lawsuits fly – Selling songs

Bobby Day (Robert James Byrd) was two years older than Jesse Belvin, but they were both Texas boys whose families ended up in Los Angeles in the long quest for better jobs. Bobby was born in Fort Worth on July 1, 1930. He grew up there until he was fifteen, when his family made the migration west. Jesse and Bobby probably knew of each other since they lived in the same part of Los Angeles as all the other African American families who migrated from Texas, were musicians vying for the same audience, and knew all the same people. They also boasted the same excellence in regard to performing and songwriting. As a singer Bobby is best known for "Rock-in Robin," a number two hit in 1958, and as a songwriter, for "Little Bitty Pretty One," a number six record in 1957 for Thurston Harris, and "Over and Over," a number one song for the Dave Clark Five in 1965. But that was all in the future.

In his book *The Sound of the City*, Charlie Gillett repeatedly asserted that Bobby Day worked Clyde McPhatter's sound. Gillett wrote that "among the other West Coast performers who were better than the boys-next-door" was the black singer-composer Bobby Day, who had a high, nasal tone evidently modeled on Clyde McPhatter's style and wrote several novelty songs that introduced birds and insects as characters. Gillett, however, was writing about Bobby as a recording star in the late 1950s. Bobby had been singing professionally for almost ten years before that, and if he was modeling anyone it would have been his neighbor, Jesse Belvin, who got to grab the brass ring of success before him.

At the tail end of the 1940s, Bobby got together with a group of friends from Watts, Los Angeles, to form a quartet called the Flames. The other members were David Ford, Curlee Dinkins, and Willie Ray Rockwell.

As with Jesse Belvin, the group's first playing gig was at the Barrelhouse Club around 1949. The group recorded first for Fidelity Records in 1951 with a song called "Tabarin," with "Wine" on B-side. The songwriter for "Tabarin" was a machinist-salesman named Murry Wilson, who lived less than ten miles away in Hawthorne. "Tabarin" was one of only a handful of songs Murry would ever sell (the Flames would record a second of his songs), but his sons Brian, Dennis, and Carl would sell millions of records as the core of the Beach Boys. At the time of this first recording, Bobby's group billed themselves as the Hollywood Four Flames. By the time the group finally scored a big hit, "Buzz-Buzz-Buzz," a song cowritten by Bobby, the name had evolved into "the Hollywood Flames." Finally attaining success with a Flames group, Bobby quickly abandoned the name altogether.

The lead singer on "Buzz-Buzz-Buzz" was Earl Nelson, whose family migrated to Los Angeles in 1937 from the South. After military service, he and Bobby hooked up through a number of iterations of Flames groups. In 1957, he and Bobby shuffled into a combo, Bob and Earl. Bobby left in 1962, and another Fremont High School grad and doo-wop group veteran named Bob or Bobby (Robert Nelson) Reif took his place. Together with Earl he wrote "Harlem Shuffle," a moderate hit at first but one of those songs that just gained more esteem as time moved on.

Bobby's flaming quartet came over to Specialty Records, which in February 1952 pushed out a platter by the Four Flames with "The Wheel of Fortune" on the A-side and "Later" on the B-side. That was months before Jesse and Marvin walked into the company's recording studio to try out the tune "Dream Girl."

Meanwhile Gaynel Hodge and his buddy Curtis Williams had formed their own singing group and were playing on demo records. Gaynel was all of fifteen years old at the time and also teaching Curtis and Richard Berry how to play the piano.

After Jesse had come home on leave and then departed again for military service, Curtis came by his house because he was trying to complete the song "Earth Angel," which had been left unfinished by Jesse. Gaynel looked over to his friend and said, "What are you doing; that's Jesse's song." Curtis waved him off: "Nah, we traded songs. I gave him my song. I liked his song, and he liked mine." This was a very loose interpretation of what really had gone on before Jesse left town, when a bunch of friends were hanging out at Jesse's house playing everybody's songs and jamming around for fun. "Hey, what's that song you're playing? Sounds good." "This is one of mine that I've been working on." "Let me come in on your song." Gaynel

EARTH ANGEL

was skeptical of Curtis's claim, but Curtis really liked "Earth Angel" and begged him, "C'mon, help with the song. How did it go?" Gaynel touched the keys of the piano.

The Flames were dying down, with Curlee Dinkins and Willie Ray Rockwell leaving. At the same time, Gaynel's little group with Curtis Williams, Richard Berry, and Cornell Gunter was doing well, winning a talent show and performing at the Lincoln Theater. Bobby Day and Dave Ford watched them intently at the Lincoln, and, after Gaynel and his group's performance was complete, the two Flames sauntered over. After eyeballing Gaynel and Curtis, Bobby said, "We would like you to join our group. You'll fit our suits." Gaynel and Curtis were a little amazed by the offer and didn't know what to do. Then Bobby said, "We need you two to make a gig tonight, and we will pay you $25 apiece."

"We thought that was big money," Gaynell recalled. "So we did it. Bobby and Dave were in their twenties, and they were like adults to me. I was all of sixteen years old, and Curtis was nineteen. They had another gig the next week and another gig the next week, and another and another. In 1954, the group, as the Hollywood Flames, went to Swing Time Records to a record "I Know," which oddly doesn't list a songwriter, just the notation "with Rhythm Arrangement." Swing Time was another Los Angeles independent record producer focused on rhythm and& blues. It was formed in 1947, but the company was headed for the corporate graveyard by the time the Hollywood Flames recorded for it.

On the creative side, Gaynell and Curtis made a serious effort to finish Jesse's "Earth Angel," filling it out with bits and pieces of short-term musical memory, including an arrangement that sounded a whole lot like "I Know."

"That little don, don, don, don," I put that in there," Gaynel said. "Clarence and I were putting a demo record together for one of our neighbors, Jessie Mae Robinson. It was called "I Went to Your Wedding," which became a number one record for Patti Page. I had written the bridge for that song and used that as well in "Earth Angel."

Larry Birnbaum, who wrote *Before Elvis: The Prehistory of Rock 'n' Roll*, described the various pieces of "Earth Angel" this way: "The melody resembles that of Jesse and Marvin's 1953 R&B hit 'Dream Girl,' written by Jesse Belvin, a mentor to Williams and Hodge, while the bridge is adapted from 'I Went to Your Wedding,' which The Hollywood Flames [actually Gaynel and Curtis] recorded as a demo for its composer Jessie Mae Robinson. The piano introduction is taken from the Flames' 1953 recording of 'I

Know,' and the chord structure reflects that of the 1934 Rodgers and Hart standard 'Blue Moon.'"

The song called "Earth Angel" would follow a devilishly twisted path to success.

It all began innocently enough. While Gaynel was still in high school he was the best man at Curtis's wedding. This was in 1954, and Curtis and Gaynel were still gigging with the Hollywood Flames while hanging with their old group. The problem was that Bobby Day and Dave Ford were older and really took the music business seriously, always rehearsing. It was a commitment that required Gaynel and Curtis to be available for practice sessions at least once or twice a week. Even being in high school, Gaynel stuck with the discipline. Curtis, who had just gotten married, preferred to spend his spare time in newlywed bliss. This didn't go down smoothly with Bobby and Dave, who cornered Gaynel. "Your buddy is not coming to rehearsals so much," Bobby said.

"Well, give him a chance, he just got married and has a wife," Gaynel responded.

"Nah," Bobby said. "You tell him if he doesn't come to rehearsal tomorrow night he is out of the group."

"That's kind of cold," Gaynel said.

"You need to tell him."

Gaynel didn't want to give that kind of bad news to his friend. "Why don't you tell him?"

"He's your best friend, you do it."

Curtis didn't come to rehearsal, and Gaynel had to be the one to inform him that he was out of the group. To Curtis this was the ultimate betrayal, a stab in the back by his best friend, and they never spoke to each other again on friendly terms.

At that time, Gaynel and Curtis had been refining "Earth Angel," trying to get the Hollywood Flames to sing it. Indeed, the group had practiced the song, but, with Curtis gone, Bobby and Dave didn't want any part of it. Unbeknown to Gaynel, Curtis, in a sense, took the song with him. He hooked up with Cleve (Cleveland) Duncan, a former classmate from Jefferson High, and decided to form another singing group. They brought in friends, two other local guys, Dexter Tisby and Bruce Tate, to fill out the quartet.

Cleve's story goes like this: He was singing at a talent show at the California Club on Santa Barbara Avenue, and afterward Curtis came up to him, explained that he just left the Hollywood Flames, and asked if he wanted to

EARTH ANGEL 29

get together and form a group. Cleve said yes and gets his high school friend Dexter Tisby to join, while Curtis recruited his old high school buddy Bruce Tate.

Since bird names were very popular at the time for R&B groups (the Orioles, Robins, Crows, and other) they decided to call themselves the Penguins. Cleve told interviewer Marv Goldberg a different story as to how the group was named. According to Cleve, one of the members of the group smoked Kool cigarettes, which in the early 1950s had Willie the Penguin as its cartoon advertising character. Since the group considered itself the acme of cool, they decided on "the Penguins."

When doing the demos for Jessie Mae Robinson, Curtis and Gaynel used a jerry-rigged studio that Ted Brinson, a former bass player in jazz bands and a relative of Curtis, had built in the garage of his home on West Thirtieth Street in South Los Angeles. The one big attraction at Brinson's studio was a single-track Ampex tape recorder. The Ampex Model 200 was first shipped in 1948 and used to record Bing Crosby's shows. It was a revolutionary machine because of ease of operation compared to the old audio disc-cutting lathes. By the early 1950s, the company began marketing one- and two-track machines like the one Brinson incorporated into his garage-studio.

Brinson's studio was also used by another Los Angeles record entrepreneur, Dootsie Williams (Walter D. Williams Jr.). A former band leader, he founded in 1949 a recording company called Blue Records, which two years later he would rename Dootone. Brinson did Curtis a favor and recommended his new group to Dootsie.

In an interview before he died in 1991, Dootsie recalled: "He [Brinson] had a backyard studio over on 30th Street between Arlington and Western that was very economical, so I recorded there. My stuff was mostly songwriter demos then. They'd pay me $300 and I'd record their song. So I heard the group [the Penguins] and liked them." After a number of years in the record business, Dootsie figured out where the profits were. It wasn't so much that he considered the Penguins a talented group but that they came with original songs never recorded before, and this was a stream of revenue (publishing and royalties) that a record label could exploit. In the spring of 1954, the Penguins recorded a few songs, some of which Dootsie could put his name on as artist and songwriter.

Dootsie was not the only one playing fast and loose with songs. In the next recording session, the Penguins recorded "Hey Senorita," with "Earth Angel" as the B-side. Curtis put his name on both songs as the songwriter.

Not only wasn't "Earth Angel" his to promote as his own composition, but "Hey Senorita" was originally created by another old friend, Carl Green. "We all got burnt," Gaynel said. "Carl Green wrote 'Hey Senorita,' and we used to sing that song with our group. Back then Cornell Gunter would sing the melody, and Curtis would sing the second bridge, but he got Dexter to sing the bridge on his recording for Dootone."

"Hey Senorita" may have been the A-side, but Los Angeles DJs, who were always willing to help out local talent, flipped over the record – because they pretty much flipped over "Earth Angel." Not only were popular deejays like Huggy Boy and Charles Trammel giving the record exposure, Johnny Otis did them a good turn too, putting them in the lineup for his October 2, 1954, Hep Cap Ball, which was like a "friends of Jesse and Gaynel" show without Jesse Belvin, who was still in Germany, and without Gaynel. On the bill that night besides the Penguins were Cornell Gunter and Alex Hodge's new group the Platters, Richard Berry and the Dreamers, and Marvin and Johnny.

Gaynel went to one of the Penguins' Los Angeles gigs. From the stage Curtis saw him and panicked. Taking the mic, Curtis told the audience, "There is a guy down here named Gaynel, who said he wrote 'Earth Angel.' I'm going to go right down to the floor and kick his ass." Curtis then jumped off the stage, grabbed Gaynel, and dragged him out of the club to the back stairs. As Gaynel recalled, "He kept saying to me 'shut up, shut up, shut up, I'm going to buy you a Cadillac.' I said 'I want my name on that song.' He just couldn't face up to that fact he stole the song." Curtis didn't know it, but his moment as the solo writer of "Earth Angel" was about to be history.

After scorching Los Angeles radio play, the Penguins' "Earth Angel" broke nationally in December 1954. A look at the *Billboard* record charts for the last week of the month shows "Earth Angel" number two on the R&B charts behind "Hearts of Stone," by the Charms, and number nine on the list of most-played songs on America's jukeboxes in its first week on that chart. How did the song break nationally? For the last week in December, it was number two in Atlanta, number one in Los Angeles and New York, number three in Baltimore-Washington and Philadelphia, number four in New Orleans, and number eight in St. Louis. It fared poorly in the rest of the Midwest, not yet near the top of the charts in Chicago, Cincinnati, or Detroit.

In January 1955, the Penguins' recording rolled onto the pop charts, rising as high as number eight. Meanwhile the white Canadian group the Crew-Cuts, who'd had a number one song the year before, a cover of the

Chords' "Sh-Boom," released a version of "Earth Angel" that would reach number three on the pop charts. The Penguins' "Earth Angel" was the first R&B record from an indie label to hit the pop charts.

By early February, the Penguins' "Earth Angel" was number one on the R&B charts in Chicago and Cincinnati, and number two in Detroit and New Orleans, and number three in Charlotte and Atlanta.

At the same time, Johnny Ace's posthumous hit "Pledging My Love" was being played everywhere. It was a time of really strong R&B, with the likes of "Sincerely" (the Moonglows), "I Got a Woman" (Ray Charles), "Tweedle Dee" (LaVern Baker), "Teach Me Tonight" (Dinah Washington), and "Ko Ko Mo" (Gene and Eunice). Varetta Dillard's ode to Johnny Ace, "Johnny Has Gone," was also getting huge airplay. Despite all those, "Earth Angel" was still the number two R&B song in February 1955, number two on the list of R&B songs played by DJs, and number one R&B song played on jukeboxes.

In April, after sixteen weeks, the recording was still number five in R&B sales, number two in R&B songs on jukeboxes, and number three among R&B tunes played by DJs.

"Earth Angel" begins prosaically with a doo-wop chorus that sounds like *oh-oh-oh-oh, wah-ah-ah, oh-oh-oh-oh* before we hear the phrasing "earth angel, earth angel." The lyrics are simple, nothing more complicated than the lead singer admitting he's just a fool, a fool in love with a woman, or, as it is sung, "a fool in love with you-ou." The most complicated rhyme is that of "loveliness" and "happiness."

The song was actually recorded in a garage, technically making the Penguins the first garage band to score a major hit. In May that spring, Dootsie Williams was awarded a gold record signifying one million copies sold. What made the record so successful? When Cleve Duncan died in 2012, the *Guardian* noted: "The dogged piano triplets, rudimentary four-chord harmonic structure, goofy woh-woh backing vocals and the muffled quality of a garage recording were typical of early doo-wop music . . . But perhaps the most distinctive feature of a record that sold more than 1m [one million] copies and became a classic of its genre was the pleading tenor voice of Cleve Duncan." That's a good summation as any.

If Curtis thought he would be able to buy Gaynel a Cadillac with the proceeds from "Earth Angel," the truth was that he would barely be able to fill up the tank of an Oldsmobile 88. The success of "Earth Angel" overwhelmed Dootsie Williams's tiny label. One apocryphal story notes that the company ran out of paper and had to press additional copies with different colored labels. The real problem was the lag time between pressings and payments. After pressing, the records would go to a distributor, but monies didn't come back to Dootsie's label quickly enough. Dollars went out to the actual manufacturers immediately, otherwise they would stop pressing records, but proceeds from sales came back slowly. Meanwhile, Curtis and the rest of the Penguins were seeing booming sales and radio station play and thought some of that should come back to them. They asked for advances from royalties and were continually stiff-armed by Dootsie, who, Gaynel said, "was getting all the money and giving The Penguins peanuts."

A disgruntled group with a successful record caught the attention Buck (Samuel) Ram, a songwriter-publisher who had decided to also become a talent manager. The first act he picked up was the group Gunter and Alex Hodge originally founded: the Platters. Gunter had already left to join another group, the Flairs, and in 1953 been replaced by Tony Williams. Then, in 1954, Alex Hodge left and was replaced by Paul Robi. The Platters had recorded first with Federal Records without much chart success, and Buck wanted to get them to a major label. If he could land the Penguins, then his plan could fall into place. He approached Curtis, who was so unhappy with Dootsie that he jumped ship immediately. Quickly all the Penguins came around, and Buck bundled his two groups and took the package to Mercury Records, which was the label for the Crew-Cuts. It did not go unnoticed by Mercury that the Penguins' version of "Earth Angel" had generated a lot of excitement with teen record buyers, so the record company leaped at the chance to sign them, even though it reluctantly had to take on the unknown Platters at the same time.

Years later, Dootsie told a journalist, "I told them [the Penguins] they'd lose all their royalties, but they told me, 'the hell with your royalties, we're gonna make it big.'"

On the opposite side on the discourse, Cleve recalled: "We were impressed with Mercury's large size and distribution." Then he added, "Ram just used us to get the Platters on the label. He actually owned the Platters and paid them a salary. So he used them to push his best songs."

While all that was happening, Jesse Belvin returned from Germany and discovered his original composition of "Earth Angel" was now a major hit record. He also found himself thrust into the middle of slew of lawsuits. Dootsie was suing Mercury and Buck Ram for inducing the Penguins to break their contract. He claimed his contract with the Penguins was for three years, but a judge decided the contract was null and void because three of the four members of the group were underage. Curtis Williams sued for damages as a result of his underage signing. He also sought an injunction against Dootsie, claiming authorship of the song.

After interviewing three surviving members of the Penguins, Marv Goldberg summed it up: "Buck Ram wanted to take the Penguins away from Dootsie, including the publishing rights to 'Earth Angel'; the ensuing lawsuit was really about the rights to the song." Initially, Jesse and Carl Green wanted to sue Dootsie, claiming ownership of their songs and a share of royalties. Dootsie had a better idea. He thought Jesse and Carl should sue the Penguins for not receiving credit for their songs. Dootsie then went to the court claiming that "Earth Angel" was the creation of Jesse Belvin. That put Jesse and Dootsie on the same side of the most important legal issue, ownership of the rights to the song. When the lawsuit was finally settled in 1957, Jesse was established as the full and exclusive author of the song, and he promptly signed his rights over to Dootsie Williams. This allowed Dootsie to put his own name on the record as songwriter.

The stories that Jesse's mother told to her grandson had a germ of truth to them. Due to his early success in selling his songs, Jesse couldn't shake the habit of hawking his songs when he was low on funds, which in the mid-1950s seemed to be a constant. Even when he was discharged from the military and landed back in Los Angeles, he needed money because he wasn't yet earning any. "Jesse came to me and said Dootsie gave him $50 for the rights to 'Earth Angel,'" said Gaynel.

Sometime later, with a lot of money accumulated through all the recordings of the song, Jesse teamed up with Gaynel and Curtis to force a settlement. "Curtis had gotten back with the Hollywood Flames, and he would come with them into court drunk. The judge scolded them," Gaynel said. "The whole thing tuned out to be a mess. Dootsie offered $50,000 to the three of us. We jumped at the chance to get the money. Jesse's one-third of the take was gone by the weekend."

Summing it up, Gaynel said, "The Penguins were making one-twelfth of a cent on [each sale of] 'Earth Angel.' Dootsie got everything. He had no heirs. When he died, the rights went to his cousin's wife. Then she sold the rights. It took me twenty-nine years to get the authorship straightened out. I didn't get anything from BMI for twenty-nine years."

Writing credits for the song are today split between Jesse, Gaynel, and Curtis. In 2013, as the last surviving member of the trio of writers, Gaynel was given an award from BMI for the song having been played on the radio one million times.

Jesse hit the ground running on his return to Los Angeles and quickly went back to his old friends such as John Dolphin to do some recordings, but things had changed in the two years he'd been gone. Dolphin sold his

34   CHAPTER 2

Recorded In Hollywood label to Don Pierce, who was also president of Starday Records. Dolphin kept the even smaller Money label (also sold to Don Pierce around 1956 or 1957), and Jesse made one his first post–military service recordings there, a song called "I'm Only a Fool," with "Trouble and Misery" on the B-side. He also did a couple of recordings for the Biharis on their Modern label, but you won't find Jesse's name on some of those platters since he was selling his songs as quickly as he could write them. Take, for example, Marvin and Johnny's recording of "Sugar Mama" (Modern 959). The songwriters are listed as Ling and Josea, the pseudonyms of Saul and Joe Bihari, two of the owners of Modern Records.

"Jesse thought small," Billy Vera observes. "There was nothing professional about what he did. Sometimes he would record for John Dolphin for $50."

"Producers stole the writing credits back then," said Gary Levingston, Jesse's nephew. "The blacks that were in the music business were truly taken advantage of despite their talent, the gifts they gave us, and musical genius. They just wanted to hear their songs on the radio. It was 'wow, we made it' – but did you really? Jesse had this thing where he could write a song at the drop of a dime, and he would sell his songs for $300, which, back then, seemed like a lot of money. Unfortunately, the guys who were putting their names on the credits were making hundreds of thousands of dollars on songs they didn't write."

However, Vera maintained that not all record producers during the 1950s were untrustworthy. He used Art Rupe of Specialty as an example and said that the only time Rupe would buy songs outright would be after a recording of the song had been out for several years and royalties were hardly coming in anymore. That was because singers or songwriters would come in asking for a loan or advance against royalties, and it wasn't worth doing the paperwork. It was a pain in the neck to have people coming back asking for more money, so Art would say, "Instead of the $100 you need, I'll give you $500 for the rights, and don't come back asking for more."

"I remember talking to Leiber and Stoller, and even with all their hits [the likes of 'Hound Dog,' 'Kansas City,' 'Searchin',' and 'Jailhouse Rock'] they never thought their songs would have value a year later, let alone fifty years later," Vera said. "As Leiber said to me, 'it wasn't as if we were George Gershwins; we were just writing teenage music. Who thought there was a future for that stuff?'"

Goodnight, My Love

CHAPTER 3

Peripatetic Jesse Belvin – Selling songs for chump change – Fake songwriters – Eugene Church gets active – "Goodnight My Love" says hello – The real songwriter for "Goodnight My Love"

It's hard to track Jesse in the mid-1950s since he was often writing songs, recording, and sometimes just singing background under a pseudonym. A discography put together by writer Jim Dawson shows Jesse in 1955–56 recording on such labels as Modern (he signed a long-term contract in 1956), Money, Specialty, Federal, Hollywood, and Cash.

Gary Levingston explains, "A lot of black singers and songwriters, and Jesse was no exception, used aliases so they could sign multiple contracts under multiple names. If they gave their real name, then they wouldn't be able to sign a contract with another company. Stipulations in those contracts basically said, you belong to me, and you can't sign anywhere else."

That said, Jesse got one big promotional push from Art Rupe at Specialty for his recording of "One Little Blessing," with "Gone" on the B-side. Both songs were written by Jesse. "One Little Blessing" sounded like a hit, with Jesse at the peak of his balladeer prowess on a song of unrequited love. No vocal gimmicks, just Jesse crooning, soft and straight, with a subdued doo-wop chorus in the background. His love has left him sad and blue, and he beseeches the heavenly father, asking what he should do: "I've almost lost my-my mind." The attribution on some pressings of the disc: "Jesse Belvin, The Blues Balladeer."

On April 23, 1955, *Cash Box* magazine featured the song in its "Rhythm & Blues Reviews" section. It gave a B+ to "One Little Blessing," saying: "Jesse Belvin does an emotional bit of changing as he tells the slow blues story of his lost love. Moving [and] well done. Could stir up some action." The reviewer gave the B-side, "Gone," a B, writing: "Belvin couples with a similar slow [song]. Another good performance."

Cash Box ran a regular gossip column on rhythm and blues happenings in New York, Chicago, and Los Angeles. The unnamed columnists did an excellent job following the selected markets, and the column called "Rhythm & Blues Ramblings" ran for almost a full page depending on ad layout. In the May 21, 1955, issue, the Los Angeles columnist scoped out Specialty and wrote: "Art Rupe is plenty pleased over his newest artist Jesse Belvin. He says that the boy's waxing of 'One Little Blessing' is proving to be the hottest tune that has come out under the Specialty banner in several months."

In the same column from Los Angeles: "The Jewels have been plenty busy guys these days with club dates and guest appearances on deejay shows to ballyhoo their latest Imperial slicing 'Angel In My Life' and 'Hearts Can Be Broken.' They teamed up with Joe Houston, Marvin & Johnny and Jesse Belvin for three weekend dates at the 5-4 Ballroom May 13 thru 15. The troupe also doubled up for an early evening show at the Torrance Civic Auditorium." This was a West Coast jamboree. The Jewels were a Los Angeles quartet that sang the original version of the doo-wop classic "Hearts of Stone" for R&B Records on Santa Monica Boulevard in Hollywood. The Charms also recorded a version of the song, and that one was the national hit. Joe Houston was another Texan who migrated to Los Angeles. As a saxophonist, he recorded with Amos Milburn and Big Joe Turner before forming his own band, and in 1952 at the age of twenty-six he came to Los Angeles and formed another band, the Rockets.

After two years in the service, it was hard for Jesse to settle down or settle in. He was peripatetic, not just moving from label to label but also dropping in on old friends to form ad hoc singing groups. One of his first efforts, the Sheiks, wasn't successful for him, but one song became a big hit for another group down the road.

Around the summer of 1955, Jesse got together with Eugene Church, an old friend from the neighborhood, and singers Harold Lewis and Mel Williams to form the Sheiks. For the Federal label they recorded a Johnny Otis composition, "So Fine," with "Sentimental Heart" on the B-side. The song got little radio play and disappeared quickly, but four years later a group called the Fiestas cut the record "So Fine," and it became a big hit (number three on *Billboard*'s R&B chart and crossing over to number eleven on the pop chart). Jim Gribble, who was the manager of the Fiestas and a handful of other doo-wop groups, decided to put his name on the record as the writer of the song. Did Gribble think some itinerant R&B singer wrote the song and wouldn't know he took credit? A little research would have told him it was written by Johnny Otis, at the time one of the shrewdest men in the music business. Of course, Otis filed a lawsuit, saying that this was his song as recorded by the Sheiks four years before. He won the case.

GOODNIGHT, MY LOVE

The key lyrics revolve around the long "i" rhyme scheme coming off the key phrase "so fine." The lead singer suggests his baby is "doggone fine" because she loves him "come rain, come shine." Key phrases are repeated three times and then accentuated with a definitive "yeah" before an important phrasing returns. The lead singer testifies that his baby thrills him all the time and sends chills up and down his spine. The song itself is so fine.

For many years in the mid-1950s, Mel Williams of the Sheiks recorded with numerous Johnny Otis band iterations including one called the Johnny Otis Show. After he died, one obituary said: "A commanding presence in the early rock 'n' roll music era in 1950s Los Angeles, Williams was a popular vocalist with bandleader Johnny Otis. He was known as 'Handsome' Mel Williams to the throngs of female fans who came to his performances in droves."

There is no reason to single out Mel Williams in this regard. Guys like Mel, Jesse, and Eugene Church were matinee-idol handsome. This was a time when young men accented their hair by combing it high on their heads, wild pompadours, or combing it back into to ducktails down the back of the neck. Black singers like the Sheiks boasted moderate coifs, slicked back yet still mostly atop the head. The sides were cut shorter. They always wore suits, with white shirts and slim ties. Mel Williams had a mature face with pronounced cheeks, and he often sported a trimmed mustache, as did Eugene Church. The preternaturally young Jesse always looked like he just graduated from high school.

On Jesse's last road trip to Texarkana, Texas, he was traveling in a blue Cadillac with three people, including his wife Jo Ann Belvin. Jesse was visiting his cousin Billy Allen. Chester Jones, a friend of Billy's was hanging out with Billy when Jesse came to town. "Billy was my classmate and Jesse's second cousin," Chester recalled. "He would always tell me about Jesse, and at that time I hadn't met him. Then in 1960, about the latter part of January, Billy called to tell me to come to the road. So, I walked out and there was this two-door, hardtop, 1959 Cadillac with Jesse on the right side, Charles . . . driving, Jo Ann [sitting] on the righthand side, and Kirk Davis, the guitarist, sitting on the left side behind Charles the driver. Kirk told us he wrote the song "Girl in My Dreams" for Eugene Church.

That was partly an accurate memory. In 1956, Jesse teamed up with old friend Eugene Church to form a duo called the Cliques, and the first song they released was "Girl in My Dreams."

In 1954, when Etta James signed with Modern Records, she was all of sixteen years old. She later wrote, "I felt comfortable because my buddies were there, a whole flock of the California kids I'd grown up with. Richard Berry was on staff as a writer and arranger. He'd been hired by Jules Bihari, the slickest of the brothers. Jules also brought on Jesse Belvin, who was back from Korea [actually Germany]. Eugene Church had a group that used two different names, the Klock Klicks and the Fellas."

The "Klock Klicks" morphed into "the Cliques," and the Fellas eventually became Eugene Church and the Fellows. Eugene had moderately successful career in the late 1950s with songs such as "Pretty Girls Everywhere" (a number six R&B and number thirty-six pop hit in 1958) and "Miami" (a number fourteen R&B hit in 1959). This was followed by some rough patches. When Etta wrote about her years of heroin addiction, she told a story of the cops raiding her apartment. She wrote, "I had just copped a little bit of smack from my childhood friend Eugene Church, which I immediately shot up in the bathroom. (Eugene had been running heroin over the Mexican border; I even did a couple of runs for him.)"

Etta was a trenchant observer of people. As to her time with Modern, Etta noted: "None of the Biharis really had any taste in music, but at least Joe Bihari learned to how to engineer. The others couldn't even pat their feet to the beat. So, they hired guys like Maxwell Davis and Johnny Otis to run their music department." Taking all that into consideration, it's amazing how many records the Biharis were credited for writing.

Going back to Kirk Davis's boast that he wrote "Girl in My Dreams" for Eugene Church, the Cliques' recording of the song, Modern Records 987, was printed with a black label with silver lettering. Underneath the title these songwriters are listed: Josea, Ling, Taub and Davis. Each of the Biharis, under their individual pseudonyms, took a piece of the record. The B-Side was a song written by Jesse, "I Wanna Know Why." The listed songwriters were Josea, Ling, and Taub, who probably bought the rights to the song from Jesse for chump change. The Cliques released one more record on the Modern label, "My Desire," another Jesse song. Listed as songwriters were Josea and Ling. On the B-Side was Jesse's "I'm in Love (With a Girl)." The listed songwriters were the very busy Ling and Josea, reversing their names to keep it all interesting.

Jesse didn't have a heroin addiction like Etta or his friend Eugene Church, but he couldn't kick his habit of selling his songs as if they were nickel bags of dope. Black songwriters like Jesse made it easy for unscrupulous record producers such as the Bihari brothers to take advantage of them. A few hundred dollars in hand always sounded a lot better than the promise of royalties in the future. Records like "Girl in My Dreams" and "My Desire"

GOODNIGHT, MY LOVE

were not big hits, so maybe taking the easy money was the right way to gamble. But what would happen when that hit record like "Earth Angel" came around again? Jesse would find out very quickly.

By 1956, Jesse was scatting around, still trying to find his place in the music world. Discographer Jim Dawson has him singing with the Gassers on the Cash Records recording of "Tell Me," with "Ricky" (Richard Berry) on "Baby Please Come Home," with the Youngsters on "Dreamy Eyes" for Empire Records, and with the Dots on "Good Luck to You." Jesse still was under contract with Modern, so when George Motola, one of the company's producers, as legend has it, came to him with a song that just seemed perfect for Jesse's ballad style of singing, he took an interest. The only problem was that the song, "Goodnight My Love (Pleasant Dreams)," wasn't finished. That wasn't an issue for Jesse, who said to Motola he would fill in the missing pieces.

Motola was a first-generation New Englander, his parents having migrated to the United States from Italy. He started out selling used cars but realized he had an abiding interest in writing music and by the mid-1950s found a job with the Bihari brothers as producer. He had married a singer named Rickie Page, and together they wrote a slew of songs, none of which became hits. The closest they ever got was writing "Jeanie, Jeanie, Jeanie" for Eddie Cochran.

The mythology of "Goodnight My Love" is that Motola had written the song a decade before and never finished it, that the song just sat around partly forgotten until he realized it would be perfect for Jesse. According to Bruce Eder (allmusic.com), the oft-repeated story is that Belvin provided the lines for the bridge that completed the song and asked for $400 in lieu of coauthorship credit. Motola didn't have the cash, but a colleague, John Marascalco, did, and he put up the money, receiving cowriting credit in return.

Gaynel Hodge has an important alternative take on what happened.

"I helped Jesse write 'Goodnight My Love,'" he said. "What happened was Jesse and George told me they were going to get some money, and I needed to put in the bridge. They gave me these lyrics, and I finished the song. I met them down around Hollywood and Argyle in Los Angeles, where there were a lot of songwriter shops like in the Brill Building in New York. I was in this office, and, when Jesse and George came in, I said 'here's the song.' They looked it over and went to a pay phone in the hall. They were both good friends with John Marascalco at the time, and that's who they called. They came back and told me I had to go to John's place, and he was going to give me something that I should bring back, which I did. John gave me an envelope that was full of money. I realized John had bought my share of 'Goodnight My Love' (along with Jesse's)."

Jesse and George recorded the song in three days. Gaynel was so upset he didn't even go to the recording session. His brother Alex went and came back and told Gaynel, "That was a bad [i.e., very good] tune." At some point afterward, Gaynel got a call from Jesse saying he had a bunch of "Goodnight My Love" records and that Gaynel should come and get some. So Gaynel went back to Hollywood and Argyle, and who should he meet there but Tony Bennett, sitting around in formal, black-tie attire. Tony had been talking with Jesse. Gaynel and Jesse then headed upstairs for a private chat.

"We got into a big fight, because I wanted to see my name on the record," said Gaynel. "I explained to Jesse that we had just gone through this with 'Earth Angel.'"

"My name is not on the record either," Jesse responded.

"But you are the singer. You are going to get some money from this."

"They sold me down the river," Gaynel concluded.

The first trade-press coverage of the song came on October 27, 1956. That week *Cash Box* magazine for its R&B Reviews page chose three songs for its top picks, "Suffering with the Blues" (Little Willie John), "Juanita" (Chuck Willis), and "Smooth Operator" (Ruth Brown). Also getting a review was "Goodnight My Love." It was given a B+ and described briefly: "Belvin handles a tender ballad lovely with a delicate bit of vocalizing. It is a fragile, melodic love offering that comes off in a manner that beckons spins and sales. Watch this one very carefully."

Cash Box gave a B to the flip side, "I Want You with Me Xmas": "Belvin makes his pitch at the Yule trade with a sweetly tender offering. Love and Christmas trees combine with good results."

Then all went quiet on "Goodnight My Love" until the beginning of December.

On December 1, *Billboard*, in its section on rhythm and blues records, chose "Goodnight My Love" as one of its week's "R&B Best Buys," saying, "This record has been making a lot of noise out on the West Coast the past few weeks – and attracted a cover by the McGuire Sisters [a pop "Best Buy"] this week also. Now it is digging in in the other areas. Philadelphia lists it in its Top Ten this week and it is also one of New York's best retailing discs. This action is bound to be mirrored in many other markets in the next days."

GOODNIGHT, MY LOVE

That did not happen. The song both scored and floundered at the same time. The December 8, 1956, issue of *Cash Box*, for example, listed the top ten R&B records in six cities across America. "Goodnight My Love" was number two in Los Angeles and Philadelphia but not on the lists for Memphis, Cleveland, St. Louis, and Detroit. One month later, "Goodnight My Love" was number one in Los Angeles and Philadelphia but not on the top ten lists for Detroit, St. Louis, Atlanta, or Boston. The song eventually reached number seven on the R&B charts, but it wasn't listed as one of the top one hundred R&B songs in either 1956 or 1957.

What happened?

Two things. Firstly, the song was released at the same time that a host of other wonderful R&B songs were hitting the charts, so the competition was intense. Room had to be made for "Blueberry Hill" (Fats Domino), "Oh What a Night" (the Dells), "Since I Met You Baby" (Ivory Joe Hunter), "A Thousand Miles Away" (the Heartbeats), "Honky-Tonk" (Bill Doggett) to say nothing of "Don't Be Cruel" by Elvis Presley, who managed to crash the R&B charts.

Secondly, the McGuire Sisters immediately released a cover version of the song that became a top forty hit on the pop charts. As Larry Birnbaum wrote in his book *Before Elvis: The Prehistory of Rock 'n' Roll:*

> The McGuire Sisters) made the Top Ten in 1954 with a deracinated cover of The Spaniels' "Goodnite Sweetheart Goodnite." They had a No.1 hit in early 1955 with a cover of the Moonglows' "Sincerely" by scrubbing the song nearly clean of doo-wop flavor. . . . The McGuires' cover of "Hearts of Stone" the same year was not a hit, but their next release, a cover of Ivory Joe Hunter's R&B Ballad, "It May Sound Silly," was. . . . The McGuires had 11 more hits by the end of 1956, when they charted their next R&B cover, Jesse Belvin's ballad hit "Goodnight My Love (Pleasant Dreams)."

Pick up any "Goodnight My Love" record and look at the label: Jesse Belvin will not be credited. As described, he is said to have sold away the rights to the song for $400, allowing the nonmusical John Marascalco to share writing credits with George Motola. Jesse pushed on in his usual manner, John and George laughed their way to the bank, and the song has lived on and on.

The first person to give the song a major boost was Alan Freed, the biggest DJ on the planet at the time. He made "Goodnight My Love" his sign-off, reaching millions of listeners night after night.

"When I was in seventh grade, my friend Charlie and I went to our very first school dance," Billy Vera recalled. "All the girls were on one side of the gym, the boys on the other. Charlie and I decided we would break the ice and asked two girls to dance. They said yes. The song we danced to was 'Goodnight My Love,' and I became a big fan of Jesse Belvin and the way he sang."

According to some, the piano player on Jesse Belvin's 1956 recording of the song was eleven-year-old Barry White, a South Central LA boy who would become a major recording star in the 1970s. He recorded a version of the song, as did an arena full of others, including the Fleetwoods in 1963 and Paul Anka in 1968 (both those versions charted as well).

Dave Marsh in his book *The Heart of Rock and Soul: The 1001 Greatest Singles Ever Made* selected two Jesse Belvin songs, "Earth Angel" and "Goodnight My Love," the latter charting ahead of the former. Marsh wrote:

Jesse Belvin was the king of L. A. doo-wop. A prolific composer, a fabulous mellow balladeer, studio singer without peer . . . Belvin sang just about every kind of fifties R&B but his specialty was crooning. Stylistically, "Goodnight My Love" stands midway between the smooth piano blues of Charles Brown and Nat "King" Cole and the rawer, more gospel-inflected sounds that came from Sam Cooke (upon whom Belvin was a major influence) and his successors. Though the arrangement features strings and full female chorus, the only part that really matters is Belvin's vocal, intoning verses guaranteed to melt any dream date at her doorstep. You don't have to buy a word of it to wither a little yourself.

The highly romantic lyrics begin with Belvin singing the key phrase "goodnight, my love" to the one he adores and telling her to have pleasant dreams and to sleep tight. There is optimism, because tomorrow may be sunny and bright, but the tone changes when Belvin asks whether her love for him is still warm or grown cold. Finally, he whispers that if his adored one awakes "in the still of the night" she should have no fear: he will be there for her.

Gaynel was right about the origins of the song. It was fully a Jesse Belvin tune by the time Gaynel was called in to help by creating a bridge for the melody. As Gary Levingston asserted, "all Jesse's hit records were written by Jesse."

Today more and more music historians and discographers agree and think that George Motola told a whopper in claiming to have written most of "Goodnight My Love." Jesse Belvin wrote the song.

You Cheated, You Lied

Who was Frankie Ervin? – Jesse Belvin signs with RCA – Jo Ann Belvin takes over – "You Cheated" all the way from Texas – Frankie Ervin on the lead – The Shields versus the Slades

Outside of New York, instability was the hallmark of the recording industry in 1950s. Not only did performers flit from record label to record label like the buzz, buzz, buzz of a bumblebee, they also moved frequently from one professional circumstance to another. The record companies weren't much more rooted. Most were tiny independent companies that appeared and disappeared just as quickly.

All this made for great complexity in what should have been a simple process, getting a song recorded. Such was the case of Jesse Belvin's last great collaboration, "You Cheated, You Lied," with a group called the Shields.

Not surprisingly, much of this story has Texas roots.

It begins with an itinerant worker and sometime-salesman named Willie "Charlie" Ervin from Houston, who married a Cherokee woman from Oklahoma and then migrated to California, where their son Frankie Ervin was born in 1926. Soon afterward, Willie ran off with another woman, and the family moved back to Oklahoma. Then in 1944, the Ervin family returned to California, this time to Los Angeles, and by the end of the decade Frankie was scatting about, trying to make it as a performer. Here the story will seem familiar. His brother Jessie Ervin began working with Johnny Otis, and that created the opportunity for Frankie to record. Eventually, Frankie began singing with Johnny Moore's Three Blazers. In 1953, with Frankie on the lead, Johnny Moore's Three Blazers recorded "Dragnet Blues" for the Bihari brothers' Modern Records. The song was a top ten hit on the R&B charts that year. The Bihari brothers then split Frankie from Johnny Moore's Three Blazers, getting him to record as a solo act. That wasn't successful, so Frankie went back to the Three Blazers and recorded for Don Pierce's Hollywood label. The first release of Frankie with Johnny Moore's Three Blazers was a tribute song, "Johnny Ace's Last Letter," in 1955. In interviews with Kate Karp and Marv Goldberg in 1997 and 2009, Frankie said, "I sounded so much like Johnny that I scared myself trying, because of the way he went out. I had a fear of the studio too, so you can really hear that." Either Kate or Marv added to the transcript of that interview, "'Johnny Ace's Last Letter' accents Frankie's talent as a mimic."

Despite a lot of new recordings, not much was happening for Johnny Moore's Three Blazers, and by 1956 Frankie was looking for new opportunities. He hooked up with LA DJ Huggy Boy (Dick Hugg), who had a label called Caddy Records. They recorded Frankie's composition "Baby, I Don't Care," which Frankie said sold 150,000 copies. Regardless of whether or not this number is close to being accurate, Frankie received no royalties from the song. The name of the singer on the label: Frankie Day.

While Frankie was following Jesse's career path, Jesse's career was changing direction. It would take two more years for their paths to merge professionally. Meanwhile, with the success of "Goodnight My Love," George Motola brought Jesse back into the recording studio looking for that a follow-up hit record.

Earlier, Gary Kramer's column in the February 23, 1957, *Billboard*, "On the Beat: Rhythm & Blues – Rock & Roll," reported that Jesse had been inked for a role in an upcoming film biography of jazz singer Billie Holiday. The movie role might have had something to do with Jesse signing a big contract with a major label RCA Records. According to Gary Levingston, "the contract that he signed with RCA equaled that of Elvis Presley at that time because RCA was also going to do five films with him. After all, he was a good-looking young man. It was Jo Ann, his wife, who actually got him to sing with RCA."

Jo Ann Johnson, who Jesse married in 1955 and with whom he had two children, had been working for Dolphin's of Hollywood, which Jesse continue to frequent because the owner John Dolphin would always pay Jesse cash for whatever song he needed to peddle. Although John sold Hollywood Records in 1956, he still had smaller labels such as Cash. In 1957, Cash released "Beware," with "Dry Your Tears" on the B side. The label reads, "Jesse Belvin Sings . . . Beware," with the writer listed as Jo Ann Belvin, although it was a Jesse Belvin composition. John Dolphin was an African American producer who worked with performers such as Sam Cooke, Major Lance, Percy Mayfield, and Illinois Jacquet, but he was no better than the white record producers when it came to exploiting talent. As researcher and blogger Rebecca Miller noted, "Jo Ann worked in a record shop owned by one of the guys ripping off all the young black musicians in the LA area, giving them $50 for a song and taking the rights to it."

Jo Ann saw Jesse (and others) come into the record store numerous times and heard all her boss's conversations about dealing with songwriters, so she knew the songwriters were all being exploited. She pulled Jesse aside and told him what was going on and how he could do better. One thing led to another, and, though Jesse didn't take Jo Ann's advice initially, the two married and started a family, and eventually Jo Ann took over the management of Jesse's career. Apparently, Jo Ann was a good at this, because she got him the big contract with RCA.

The problem with tying a motion picture with Jesse's RCA contract is that he didn't start recording with RCA until about mid-year 1958. He was still tied to a contract with Modern, although there might have been surreptitious discussions about Jesse coming to RCA months and months before it actually happened.

Meanwhile, in the post–"Goodnight My Love" glow, Jesse was striving. The Los Angeles segment of the March 9, 1957, "R&B Ramblings" column in *Cash Box*, noted: "Jessie [*sic*] Belvin, in the midst of a nationwide tour, has taken time off for two weeks in New York City to exploit his two new sides on Modern Records, 'I Need You So' and 'Senorita,' which is breaking nationally." Both songs were arranged by Maxwell Davis, with Jesse getting credit as the songwriter on "Senorita."

Neither song was a big hit, so Modern quickly issued another single, "Don't Close the Door," with "By My Side" on the B-side. Again both songs were arranged by Maxwell Davis, with Jesse penning both. "Don't Close the Door" was burdened by trilling violins, while "By My Side" was more upbeat, almost country-sounding. The April 6, 1957, "R&B Reviews" page in *Cash Box* featured the new single along with a number of interesting other songs. A box at the top of the page, labeled "Award o' the Week," focused on the best new record at the time, "C. C. Rider," by Chuck Willis. The record would become an R&B classic. The reviewer noted that Willis had risen to stardom on the Atlantic label. "[This should] place him in the charts again. Chuck sings the slow, rhythmic 'C. C. Rider' in good voice, milking the tune for all it's worth against a catchy background. Arrangement works in some interesting sounds, instrumentally and vocally."

The rest of the page included fifteen reviews of other new records. A box at the bottom, labeled "R&B Best Bets," selected four for special notice. One was "I Care," by Larry Darnell, the man who helped popularize the R&B crooner sound with his 1949 hit "For You My Love." Another was Jesse's "Don't Close The Door"/"By My Side." The reviewer gave a B+ to both sides. For "Don't Close The Door," the review said: "Jessie [*sic*] Belvin sings a dreamy lovely [tune] with a pop styled arrangement complete with singing strings. Slow beat ballad done with a lush hand. Pretty listening." For "By My Side": "Belvin tries his hand at the country commercial rock-a-billy style. Quick beat bouncer handled extremely well. Belvin has two different approaches to the teener dollar and both are good."

Finally, Jesse's (and Etta James's) old friend, Richard Berry got a mention on the page, a brief review of his single "You Are My Sunshine." Notably, the B-side was a song Berry wrote, "Louie Louie," which would resurface six years later as a monster hit (number two best-selling record in 1963) for Portland garage band the Kingsmen.

Of all the *Cash Box* selections, the one it got right was Chuck Willis's "C. C. Rider," which would become his first record to reach so high on the pop charts, number twelve in sales. "Louie Louie" would have its day in the future, but in 1957 Richard Berry's version and its flip side flopped. The same was true for the Larry Darnell and Jesse Belvin "Best Bets."

As 1958 rolled from spring into summer, Jesse's career would get a couple of bumps upward, particularly with another well-regarded doo-wop classic, "You Cheated, You Lied." While R&B, doo-wop, and rock 'n' roll were percolating in big cities, from New York to Los Angeles, this song was a Texas original.

The city of Austin, Texas, has earned a great reputation as a music town, especially with the show *Austin City Limits*, the longest-running music series in television history. The show was created in the mid-1970s, and up until that time, though it was the state capital and home to the University of Texas, it was still a sleepy town as far as music was concerned. Austin's first shot of music adrenaline came from a group of eleven classmates at a night-school course in music marketing. They all chipped to form Domino Records, with Lora Jane Richardson at the helm. Domino recorded some local rockabilly and blues artists. Exemplifying naivete at the very least, the label's first success was by a white doo-wop group called the Spades, formed by five boys from McCallum High School in Austin. Supposedly the name came from one of the two black suits in a deck of cards, but "spade" was also a racial slur in urban areas in the 1950s. The Domino release of "Baby" with "You Mean Everything to Me" by the Spades looked like it was going to be a home run for the new label, but many big city disc jockeys refused to play the song because of the name of the group. ("You Mean Everything to Me" would be the B-side on the Fleetwoods' number one hit "Mr. Blue" in 1959.)

YOU CHEATED, YOU LIED

Having learned a lesson in both marketing and lexicology, the Spades transformed into the Slades, and the group came back even stronger with a follow-up record composed by bandmember Don Burch, "You Cheated, You Lied." The simple and appealing lyrics work around the accusatory phrase "you cheated, you lied," and it is really a song about the hopelessness of loving someone who might not love you back with the same ardor, with the heartbroken singer wondering what he can do.

The record took off like a spooked jackrabbit in the Texas Panhandle. According to those associated with Domino Records who later in life were interviewed about the company by the *Austin American-Statesman*, the little Domino sold more than ten thousand copies of "You Cheated, You Lied" by the Slades just in Texas. That caught the attention of major labels and anyone else wanting to cash in.

Dot Records, a Tennessee label founded by Randy Wood, moved to Los Angeles in 1956. The following year, Randy sold his company to Paramount Pictures. Dot Records had good success with middle-of-the-road, white male singers such as Eddie Fisher and Pat Boone, so a white doo-wop group from Texas seemed to be a reasonable expansion of interest.

About the same time, a record distributor in Texas caught wind of "You Cheated, You Lied" and also tried to make a deal with Domino for the song. Domino turned down the record distributor, who, according to Frankie Ervin, was named "Shapiro." That man, Frankie claimed, contacted George Motola to cover the song in exchange for a finder's fee of five thousand free records. George, who knew a good deal when he heard one, said sure, why not and "Shapiro" sent him the Slades record. George contacted Jesse Belvin to form a group and cover the song – after all, Jesse knew everyone and could put together four or five great singers and have a band ready in about an hour's time. There was one hitch. Jesse was by then under contract to RCA, and though he might be able to put together a group of singers and hide himself in the pack, he couldn't be the face of the group. Despite each having a decade worth of experience in the music business, Frankie Ervin and George Motola had never met until Jack Carroll, president of BMI, introduced them early in 1958. When George realized Jesse couldn't be the lead for a group covering "You Cheated, You Lied," he immediately called Frankie, an experienced singer from his Johnny Moore's Three Blazers days.

Back in Austin, Domino Records decided to release the Slades version of "You Cheated, You Lied" on its own, striking a deal with a small distributor in Los Angeles.

The *Austin American-Statesman*, in its story about Domino, interviewed

Ray Campi, a rockabilly singer who had signed with Domino that hectic year of 1958. In Campi's recollection, that decision by Domino Records to go it alone led to the demise of the label. As Campi explained, it turned out that the Los Angeles record distributor had exaggerated its capabilities, and the already produced records ended up sitting in a warehouse in Los Angeles because the distributor couldn't distribute on a big enough scale.

The cheating and lying continued unabated.

As Frankie told interviewers, he didn't like the song, but George induced him to record it with the promise of spotlighting him as the sole singer. An uncredited studio group would fill in behind. This was not going to happen, because Jesse had taken control of putting together a singing group. He quickly brought in an old neighborhood buddy, Johnny "Guitar" Watson, along with Buster Williams and "Handsome Mel" Williams. Ironically, for a song that originated in Texas, this group of California singers had largely Texas roots. Besides Frankie and Jesse, Watson was born in Houston and Handsome Mel Williams in Beaumont. Frankie still took the lead and Jesse sang falsetto-tenor. George brought in top-notch musicians to back up the group – session musician Ernie Freeman and his band. (Freeman's remake of the instrumental hit "Raunchy" reached number four on the pop charts in 1957).

According to Frankie, the band had already laid down tracks by the time the group came into the studio to sing. They did the song in three takes, and the final cut was spliced together from the three recordings. "Me and boys overdubbed," Frankie said. "I had one mic, and they had two. . . . They had practiced before they came on the scene, so they had the parts down. I'm sure Jesse controlled what other singers he wanted and what parts they'd sing."

The B-side was "That's the Way It's Gonna Be" with a sound that clearly mimicked Fats Domino. George put his name on that tune as coauthor. The Fats Domino sound may not have been random. The record was initially released on the Tender label, and when Frankie went to sign a contract with Imogene Fadely of Tender, he was led to believe he would become "as big as Fats Domino." Frankie told interviewers that later on he noticed there was a paragraph in the contract giving the label the right to credit the artist anyway it saw fit. When the record came out, the Shields were credited, not Frankie Ervin.

"You Cheated" was so engaging, it hit strongly with DJ and the teen record-buying public almost immediately. Tender, which was a small label, needed to get bigger distribution so it turned to its crosstown neighbor Dot

Records. Owner Randy Wood got the song he wanted, this time by the Shields, not the Slades.

Here's how it all played out. Both the Shields and Slades versions of the song hit the market at about the same time near the end of summer of 1958. At first the different markets split on which version it preferred. The September 27, 1958, "R&B Disk Jockey, Regional Record Reports" for *Cash Box* had the Slades version doing well in the Midwest, but the Shields' version was doing better in New England. Then the strength of a major distributor kicked in. By the next week, R&B retail outlets in such diverse locations as Memphis, Raleigh, Memphis, and Los Angeles were reporting major sales for the Shields version. The next week, retail outlets in Brooklyn, suburban New Jersey, and Detroit were all showing strong sales of the Shields version, and it was getting strong disc jockey play in Florida and Pennsylvania. The only place showing strong disc jockey play for the Slades version was in Texas.

While the Slades version of the song did chart, eventually climbing to number forty-two on *Billboard*'s list of best sellers, the Shields version climbed to number twelve and is the one remembered today.

Since Domino Records owned publishing rights to the song, the company made money off the Shields, but the missed opportunity to break out its top act was demoralizing, says Joyce Webb, who sang backup on the Slades version of "You Cheated" and was interviewed by the *Austin American-Statesman*.

Kitty Karp and Marv Goldberg, who interviewed Frankie Ervin, had their own takes on the record. In Karp's view, "Frankie's lead was heart-wrenching as The Slades' was not, and the group's personnel had very impressive credentials." Goldberg never liked the song. In his opinion, "The Shields' version is almost as boring as The Slades.' Although there's no question that they sound better than the Slades, they can't rise above the material. The one huge difference between the versions is Jesse Belvin's wailing falsetto."

Frankie told Karp and Goldberg that George and Imogene Fadely had put the Shields' name on the record and not his name as a solo artist so they could fire him whenever they wanted to and keep the royalties themselves. "I was so damn mad I went to Imogene Fadely and raised holy hell," Frankie said. "I was told I wasn't entitled to anything, and I couldn't prove that I was."

According to Frankie, George asked him and the Shields to record another single. Frankie asked for $300 for the session, but George beat him down to $150. Jesse and the original Shields came back to record "Nature Boy" along with Gaynel and Alex Hodge's group the Turks. "I'm Sorry" was the B-side.

Despite having signed with RCA, after that session Jesse and Buster Williams skipped over to sing with the Turks. Jesse and Buster also recorded a single on the Los Angeles–based Aladdin label, "Sugar Doll," with a Eugene Church song, "Let Me Dream," as the B-side. They called themselves Jesse Belvin and the Sharptones for that recording. Jesse wrote "Sugar Doll" but once again had the song listed as being written by Jo Ann Belvin.

Guess Who

CHAPTER 5

RCA struggles with Jesse Belvin – "Guess Who" becomes a hit – Adam Wade recalls Belvin – Little Rock concert conflicts – Slashed tires? – Car crash and deaths – Conspiracy theories

In 1956, Elvis Presley left independent Sun Records to sign with a major record company, RCA Victor. Purists would say Elvis was never as good as he was when he recorded "That's All Right" and "Good Rockin' Tonight" for Sun. On the other hand, if he had stayed with the smaller company, he would never have reached millions of new listeners and record buyers, managed to sing over one hundred top forty singles, or recorded almost twenty number one hits, including such rock 'n' roll standards as "Hound Dog," "Jailhouse Rock," "Are You Lonesome Tonight," and "Heartbreak Hotel." Nor, perhaps, would he have also warbled so much tripe as "Viva Las Vegas," "Bossa Nova Baby," "Clean Up Your Own Backyard" or "Do the Clam."

In the 1950s, the independents were out-of-the-box producers, using excellent musicians who were still on the fringe. The sounds were fresh, daring, and often revolutionary. The independents pushed popular music forward, impacting the edges of what was attainable in regard to sound and songwriting. The independents also were rapidly integrating musical genres instead of keeping performers locked into one sector.

Too often the major producers found themselves trying to reach for what the independents were accomplishing, but they did this timidly. A company like Dot Records made millions on the vocal chords of white singer Pat Boone, who would remake dozens of R&B tunes without the rhythms and the blues of the originals. Coral Records, which was formed as a subsidiary of Decca Records in 1949, entered the rock 'n' roll era producing Teresa Brewer, Lawrence Welk, and the McGuire Sisters before discovering there was money to be made with actual rock 'n' rollers such as Buddy Holly and even R&B singers like Jackie Wilson.

After a decade in the music business, Jesse Belvin's train had finally arrived.

Even with two young children, Jesse Jr. (born in 1955) and Jonathan (1958), Jo Ann Belvin decided to take over the management of her husband's career, pulling him away from the financially self-destructive pattern of bartering away his songs for a pittance. She controlled his expenses and focused on the long term. RCA Victor was going to make him the black Elvis Presley, with record and movie deals. Again, according to Gary Levingston, RCA Victor offered Jesse the same contract it had given Elvis. The future looked bright, but the present was obscure. At first, RCA Victor didn't know what to do with Jesse so they tried mainstreaming him to its perception of teen record-buying demographics, which were white kids in cities and the new, fast-growing suburbs of America. Jesse already had a creamy custard sound that crossed the entire teen market from black to white. RCA Victor wanted him whiter, which was almost impossible to attain – unless the company got Jesse into the studio to record already proven hits.

In 1958, one of the most successful records of the decade rose to number one on the pop charts and stayed there for five consecutive weeks. It would become the Grammy winner for Record of the Year and Song of the Year at the very first Grammy Awards ceremony, in 1959. What made it unusual was that the song was Italian and it came to the United States via the still unknown-in-America festival circuit in Europe. It won an award at the San-remo Music Festival and came in third in the prestigious Eurovision Song Contest, and it eventually became one of the most popular Eurovision songs ever, if not the most popular. For fifty years no big Italian wedding could be celebrated without at least one round of "Volare!" The actual name of the record is "Nel blu dipinto di blu," it was sung by Domenico Modugno, and it was his only top forty record in America.

For some unfathomable reason, RCA Victor thought an English version of "Volare" should be Jesse's first release on its label. It probably would have been better, to quote the song, to "leave the confusion and all this delusion behind." (In 1960, a white American singer, Bobby Rydell, took on "Volare" and had a top five hit.) The B-side song was "Ever Since We Met," by Dick Sherman, who with his brother Robert Sherman would become one of the Walt Disney Company's most successful songwriting teams.

None of that worked, so RCA Victor now looked at the R&B market and decided the next release should be a remake of Johnny Ace's greatest hit, "Pledging My Love," with "Funny," which had a piano-dominated, bouncy, Nat King Cole vibe, on the B-side. The single was introduced in the autumn of 1958, and its first coverage came in *Billboard* on October 27 in its column that predicted what new songs would become hits. Seven songs were tabbed "Billboard Spotlight Winners of the Week." Two were by singers who never made it, Billy Dawn and Billy Grammer, and obviously these hot picks didn't make it either. The other five were by musicians and groups that were famous at the time and are still considered some of the very best singers of the 1950s and 1960s. For three of the five, these weren't their best songs: Chuck Berry's "Sweet Little Rock & Roll" (with "Joe Joe Gun" on the B-side), Marty Robbins's "Ain't I the Lucky One" (with "The Last Time I Saw My Heart" on the B-side), and Little Anthony and the Imperials, with "So Much" (and "Oh Yeah" on the B-side). The *Billboard* reviewers did get two of the seven right. The Everly Brothers' "Problems" (with "Love of My Life" on the B-side) went all the way to number two on the pop charts, and Elvis Presley's "One Night"/"I Got Stung" was a disc with two top ten hits, reaching number four and eight, respectively.

Of the magazine's fifteen reviews of other new record releases, it was the same mix of unknowns, such as the Chantones and Cliffie Stone, who never attained stardom or pop music success; known singers such as Buddy Holly ("Heartbeat"/"Well . . . All Right") and Little Willy John ("Why Don't You Haul Off and Love Me"/"It Was Just a Summer Love") who would do very well with other songs; and a handful of well-regarded performers with fabulous new songs that met and exceeded expectations on the pop charts, Eddie Cochran's "C'mon Everybody," Jackie Wilson's "Lonely Teardrops," and the Flamingos' "Lovers Never Say Goodbye."

Two other singers making it to the reviews page were Domenico Modugno, whose "Come Prima" would not have the appeal of as "Volare," and Jesse Belvin, whose "Pledging My Love" would do better than his version of "Volare." The *Billboard* review for "Pledging My Love" read: "The old Johnny Ace hit is undergoing several current revivals. Belvin has a smooth, rockaballad approach on the pretty tune. It could step out." As for "Funny" on the B-side, the reviewer noted: "Funky outing by the artist is given fine chorus and [orchestral] backing. Solid charming effort should draw jock [DJ] spins and loot. Tune is a bluesy ballad." The review hit the nail on the head for "Funny." Radio deejays preferred the B-side song, and it was moderate success, not quite a hit, attaining number eighty-one on the pop charts, giving Jesse a charting under his own name.

The tried and true wasn't working out for RCA Victor, so it bravely decided to attempt a different approach, giving the green light to Jesse recording one of his own tunes, another slow romantic ballad, "Guess Who." Jesse once again put Jo Ann's name on the record as the songwriter, although the label reads "Jo Anne Belvin," which suggests that even the big producers weren't above using tricks such as misspellings to screw songwriters out of royalties.

RCA Victor also couldn't fully commit to its brave new world, so for the B-side it had Jesse sing a Broadway tune, "My Girl Is Just Enough Woman for Me," from *Redhead*, which was then a hit show starring Gwen Verdon.

By 1959, *Billboard* integrated its reviews of new releases, combining R&B records with pop, so its selection of "Guess Who" was in the column "Reviews of New Pop Records" on February 23. This column touted so many acts that would never make it that could have been called "Reviews of Mostly Second-Rate Records." Whatever happened to Jan August and his "Boogie Woogie Cha-Cha," George Kay singing "Daughter of the Desert," the Rituals and their "Gitarro," and Lenny Capello's "Tootles"?

Although *Billboard*'s review process was suspect, the commentary on "Guess Who" was largely accurate: "Belvin gives an emotional reading of a pretty rockaballad that has a salable sound. Smooth chorus and lush [orchestral] support helps. It's worth watching." As for the B-side, "My Girl Is Just Enough for Me," the remarks are brief: "Pretty tune from 'Redhead' is belted smartly by Belvin. Flip appears a bit stronger."

Two months later, on April 30, "Guess Who" climbed to number seven on *Billboard*'s "Hot R&B Sides" after just two weeks on the chart. Number one on the R&B charts that week was Brook Benton's "It's Just a Matter of Time." There were other notable records. Belvin's old friend Eugene Church was number fifteen with "Pretty Girls Everywhere," and Wilbert Harrison's "Kansas City" entered the same charts at number twenty-nine, a remake of "K. C. Loving," originally done by Little Willie Littlefield, the Bihari brothers' Houston discovery. In the same issue, under the "Distributor News" column was a small item out of Philadelphia: "Jesse Belvin's 'Guess Who' is breaking."

A month later, in the June 1, 1959, issue of *Billboard*, Jesse got another mention in the "Distributor News" column: "Raymond Knowles, manager of the RCA Victor Records division of Raymond Rosen & Company, writes that Joe Valino has been signed by RCA Victor and that his initial release 'Gold' has the earmarks of a hit. . . . Other strong sellers [include] 'Guess Who' by Jesse Belvin." "Gold" would never be a hit, and that week "Guess Who" had slipped to number twelve on the "Hot R&B Sides" chart, which was now dominated topped by Harrison's "Kansas City." Old friend Big Jay McNeely was back on the charts at number sixteen with "There Is Something on Your Mind," and Johnny Otis's song "So Fine" was at number four with a remake by the Fiestas.

In April 1959, "Guess Who," which had crossed over to the pop charts, hit number seven, making it Jesse's only top ten pop record under his own name.

The first Grammy Awards were given out May 4, 1959, at the Beverly Hilton in Los Angeles, and the show was hosted by comedian Mort Sahl. As noted, the Record of the Year was "Nel blu dipinto di blu" ("Volare"), by Domenico Modugno. In the category of Best Vocal Performance, Male, Modugno was beaten out by Perry Como for his song "Catch a Falling Star." Among the performers in the same category in the next year's Grammys was Jesse Belvin for "Guess Who"; the winner was Frank Sinatra for "Come Dance With Me." At first glance it looked like it might be an award-winning year for Jesse, as he was also up for Best R&B Performance, but again he was bested, this time by Dinah Washington for "What a Diff'rence a Day Makes."

Even good records need to be promoted, and in the music industry that meant issuing an album and going on the road. In 1959, RCA Victor released *Just Jesse Belvin* to support the single "Guess Who." It's what was expected from RCA Victor, which still didn't know which way to present Jesse, as an R&B artist or as the new Frank Sinatra reinterpreting the classics. As a result the album is heavy on pop standards such as "Zing! Went the Strings of My Heart," "Ol' Man River," and "Love Is Here to Stay." "Guess Who" is on the album, of course, as is the single's B-side, "Funny." The producer was Dick Pierce, and the conductor of the orchestra producing the luxuriant sound behind the songs was Shorty Rogers.

The "West Coast Roundup" column in the January 1, 1960, *Jet* magazine reported: "Every wonder how much money goes behind a recording date? Well, this will give you an idea: RCA-Victor laid out $18,000 for singer Jesse Belvin's upcoming album of ballads, after his current LP, 'Just Jesse Belvin,' went over the 200,000 mark. That's the one which includes his big hit, "Guess Who," which was written by his wife Jo Ann."

Late in 1959, Jesse went back into the studio for three recording dates that yielded a dozen songs. The orchestra conductor this time was Marty Paich, who brought to the recording session a number of pros, including Art Pepper on sax. Whether the songs were finished to Jesse's liking or not is unknown, but after Jesse's death RCA Victor quickly released the cuts in an album titled *Mr. Easy*. The jacket cover depicted a relaxed and resting Jesse Belvin suffused with an eerie greenish-yellow light. It looked like an old summer vacation photo despite the album being released in the chilly winter of 1960. It was the typical Belvin product from RCA Victor, a mixture of pop standards such as "The Very Thought of You" and "Makin' Whoopee" and safe doo-wop tunes such as "In the Still of the Night."

Still, *Mr. Easy* is not without its fans. Bruce Eder of AllMusic wrote, "*Mr. Easy* is about as fine an album as any R&B singer ever cut in search of a mainstream audience and ought to be in every '50s vocal collection. Anyone who owns even one Same Cooke CD should make it his or her business to buy it, and nobody who enjoys Nat King Cole, Frank Sinatra, or Billy Eckstine would be doing wrong, either."

Billy Vera said, "When the *Mr. Easy* album came out, I bought it. I think it is one of the greatest pop-jazz albums ever made. I spoke to Lou Rawls, and he agreed. Nancy Wilson used the same arranger, Marty Paich, and she raved about that album. Then I met Marty's son, David Paich, who sang lead vocals in a band called Toto ('Rosanna,' 'Africa,' and 'I Won't Hold You Back'), and he said his father told him that the *Mr. Easy* album was the greatest he was connected with. Marty Paich arranged albums for the likes of Frank Sinatra and Ray Charles so that was a very big compliment."

RCA Victor Records announced on February, 12, 1960: "Belvin's forthcoming album, *Mr. Easy*, originally scheduled for fall release, is being rushed into production for March release, according to Dick Pierce, West Coast A&R director. Pierce said the album, made up of Belvin material not previously available, is the 'finest example we've had to date of the talent of the man, and of the great things that were so obviously ahead for him.' Belvin's current single, 'The Door Is Always Open,' was released in mid-January, and several unreleased singles are on hand at RCA Victor."

Clearly, RCA Victor was hoping for the Johnny Ace effect. After Ace's death in December 1954, his recording of "Pledging My Love" was a monster hit in 1955.

At the end of 1950s, going on the road almost always meant being part of a package tour with anywhere from a half dozen to a dozen performers, everyone just getting a chance to sing a couple of songs. The tours by sponsors such as radio disc jockey Alan Freed were integrated, but other tours were strictly for African American audiences, and shows took place in African American venues. These tours were sometime called "the chitlin' circuit," but they looked not much different than an Alan Freed tour, with a busload of performers. Sometimes an individual performer could step away from the tour to make some extra money at a local nightclub gig.

In 1959, Patrick Henry Wade was a lab assistant working on the research team of Dr. Jonas Salk at the University of Pittsburgh School of Medicine. Salk was already famous for introducing the polio vaccine, and Wade was one of his tight-knit group of researchers. He had other ambitions, however. Wade and his friend Richard Baugh wanted to sing and write songs, something they did constantly in their spare time. One could see them walking the alley between their homes carrying their precious fakebook, which contained what seemed like hundreds of songs and lyrics, many of which were American standards. One day in 1959, Wade picked up the local newspaper and read where Jesse Belvin was going to be in Pittsburgh, appearing at a nightclub. Although born in 1935, Adam had a memory of seeing Johnny Ace at a record store or record hop when he was a young teenager. Now he and Baugh were going to try to meet another of his recording idols, Belvin.

"Neither of us had nightclub money so we were just standing outside in the rain hoping he would pass by. And there he was," Wade would later remember. "We said, 'Hey Jesse.' And he responded, 'Hey guys, what you doing out here in the rain?' Then he said, 'come on inside with me.'" We followed and sat down with him in the nightclub. Richard and I ordered Coca-Cola because neither of us drank. He was impressed that we had the fakebook. We watched his show. Afterward he came and talked with us. We told him we were thinking of going to New York to try and make it in the music business."

Jesse thought it would be very hard to live in New York trying to make it as a singer or songwriter. He envisioned the two ending up homeless. Wade said,

> He told us the trick is you have to make sure when winter comes you have somewhere to survive, and New York was a lot easier than other big cities because there we so many heating grates and places to hang-out underground. It was best to find a pad, and if you were low on money one could always get a hotdog for fifteen cents. Mostly he stressed that we needed a plan. If we had a plan we wouldn't get lost. You couldn't have asked for a warmer, nicer, more spirited man. He asked me to sing and said I sounded like Johnny Mathis [the similarity would prove to be Wade's big break]. He laid out a path for us to follow.

Soon after, Wade and Baugh made their way to New York, where they had a friend on Long Island, so they didn't have to sleep on grates to stay warm in the cold months. Like thousands before, they made the rounds of songwriters, Broadway denizens, and record companies. Then they arrived at the office of Coed Records, owned by George Paxton and Marvin Cane, on the ninth floor of the Brill Building. When the secretary heard they were from Pittsburgh, she responded, "I'm from Pittsburgh too" and added, "I'm going to make sure George and Marvin listen to you.'"

Paxton and Cane didn't take Baugh's tunes but were instead impressed by Wade's repertoire. "I went to Dr. Salk and said, 'I have this opportunity to sing, what should I do?,' and he said I would be crazy not to follow up," Wade remembered. "And you know, if it works out for you, that's fine, if it doesn't, then you know you always have a job here."

Now known as Adam Wade, he released four songs in 1960 that reached the top one hundred of the *Billboard* pop charts. Then in 1961 he recorded "Take Good Care of Her."

"When Coed first put the record out it died, but for some reason, the deejays in Pittsburgh were mad at Johnny Mathis at this time," Adam said. "They decided to put pressure on him through me because I sounded like Johnny Mathis. The disc jockeys called the record company and said they wanted me to come to Chicago and meet Midwest deejays. That was the launch of my career."

"Take Good Care of Her" shot to number seven on the *Billboard* pop charts, which was quickly followed by two more top ten songs, "The Writing on the Wall" and "As If I Didn't Know." Adam eventually became a television, stage, and screen actor. He also was the first African American to host a television game show, "Musical Chairs," in 1975.

It all started with Jesse Belvin, Adam emphasized. "He inspired us."

♪♪♪♪♪

In the pop music world, inspiration is good, but working is better. The advertisement in the Little Rock, Arkansas, newspaper was a column wide and a few inches vertical. At the top were the words "TONIGHT ONLY," followed by "The First Rock and Roll Show of 1960!" Then the performers were listed, starting with the headliner, Jackie Wilson, followed by Bobby Freeman, Marv Johnson, Baby Washington, Arthur Prysock, Nappy Brown, Jesse Belvin, and Bobby Lewis with Willis Jackson and his Orchestra. A photo of Jackie Wilson appeared at the bottom along with these details: "Robinson Auditorium, 6:50 p.m., $1.75 per ticket; and Tickets Available at Twin City Amusement Co., 1020 Main Street, Little Rock."

All the performers were black, and for the most part the show would have appealed mostly to Little Rock's African American population and secondarily to white teenagers who were tuned into rock 'n' roll music. It is here where the controversies about Jesse's last tour begin.

Some of the media at the time of Jesse's death, occurring within hours of this concert, contend that this was the first integrated concert in Little Rock, but Rebecca Miller found that the same venue hosted an integrated concert the year before. The sticking point is that the term "integrated" is unclearly defined. At that time in US history, concerts that appealed to white and black teenagers often segregated the audiences, not just in the South, with, for example, whites on the ground floor and blacks in the balcony.

Secondly, while the word "auditorium" might imply concert seating, there has always been some disagreement as to whether it was a sit-down-and-listen show or a dance party. Chester Jones, a friend of Jesse's cousin Billy Allen who met Jesse on his travels before coming to Little Rock, said, "Jesse explained to us they were going to play a segregated dance, and there might be some problems. I heard from Billy that they were just going to be playing for black people, but white people wanted them to play a segregated dance and they refused." The one survivor of the automobile collision in which Jesse died was the guitarist Kirk Davis. "He recuperated at our house for a couple of weeks," Billy reminisced. "He didn't say too much about what happened. He said there were two sides [to the audience], whites and blacks."

Kirk was hospitalized in Texarkana, Arkansas, after the accident, and Billy visited him regularly. Afterward, Kirk stayed with Billy until Kirk's wife arrived to drive him back home to Detroit.

Rebecca Miller interviewed Billy a number of years before I did, and the two stories do not entirely match. "Billy did his best to steer . . . conversations away from the accident and its aftermath, but Kirk did tell Billy that he had secured the gig as Jesse's guitarist through his union, and he said that he had been very eager to work with Jesse because Jesse was a rising star. Kirk also spoke of the concert itself, and he did not mention anything amiss or unusual about the performance."

Jesse, along with his wife Jo Ann, guitarist Kirk Davis, and a driver, Charles Ford, arrived in Texarkana, Texas, a few weeks before the concert. Jesse was visiting family, staying with his grandfather, who Chester Jones said lived in Nash, Texas. Rebecca Miller writes, "Billy, a young man who loved cars, was immediately taken with the vehicle that Jesse drove into his driveway – a 1959 aqua-colored Cadillac Sedan de Ville. To his surprise and delight, Jesse tossed him the keys and told him to take it for a spin. Jesse and Jo Ann stayed with the family for about a week before going off somewhere in Texas for rehearsals. Everyone had a great time and Jesse told Billy that he and Jo Ann would stop back in Texarkana again for a day or two in between concert dates and driving back to Los Angeles."

After that trip to Arkansas and Texas, Levingston said, "Jesse was to be on his way back to Southern California to buy his mother a house in Beverly Hills." A March 3, 1960, *Jet* magazine item in Major Robinson's column, "New York Beat," had a slightly different take: "Before singer Jesse Belvin and his wife Jo Ann died after a recent Arkansas auto accident, they were planning to buy a Los Angeles home with the royalties from his *Just Jesse Belvin* album. The money now will put in a trust fund for their children."

"He was going to Dallas when he left my house and said he would be back down in two or three weeks," Billy said. "He was going to come back, but he got killed right before he got to my house. He was seven miles out of Texarkana when he died."

What happened in Little Rock before the accident didn't stay in Little Rock.

The capital of Arkansas had become a battleground in the mid-1950s when nine black students (known today as the Little Rock Nine) registered to attend the previously all-white Little Rock Central High. Integration was to begin when the school year started on September 4, 1957. Numerous segregationist groups threatened to block the black students from entering the school, and Governor Orval Faubus deployed the Arkansas National Guard to support the segregationists. President Dwight Eisenhower ordered the 101st Airborne Division of the US Army to Little Rock to escort the nine students to the school.

Little Rock may also have been home to splintered remains of a Ku Klux Klan contingent that had controlled countywide politics in the early 1920s. The KKK had eight thousand members in Arkansas men at its peak but by the 1950s was barely functioning.

Whether white segregationists requested a separate concert for a white audience is still unclear, but the concert went on as scheduled. After that, the facts get murky again. Rumors began circulating that "disgruntled" whites had slashed the tires of cars belonging to Arthur Prysock and Jackie Wilson. Jesse's car was parked in the same vicinity and it was assumed that either Jesse's tires had been slashed or the brake line had been cut and that one of these was the cause of the accident that took his life.

Doug Saint Carter in his biography of Jackie Wilson, *The Black Elvis*, relies mostly on a biography of Sam Cooke in his recounting of the story: "It was a segregated Friday-night dance: the first audience Negro, the second crowd white. According to newspaper reports at the time, there was to be a white band there, but they never showed up. Wilson played the first half of the gig but refused to go on for the white crowd. An ugly shouting scene followed and [the entertainers] were finally ordered out of town at gunpoint."

Problems can be seen in this account. No white band was named in the ad for the show. No local newspaper accounts have turned up mentioning a white band there. And it would have been very unusual to split a concert into two separate shows, one for whites and another for blacks. As noted, generally audiences were split in terms of seating arrangements. Two shows would have been difficult and costly to organize.

Baby (Justine) Washington, probably the last performer still alive from Little Rock concert, rarely speaks of that terrible time when Jesse died. She had been a lead singer in the Hearts during the 1950s and was launching a solo career. Her biggest hit, "That's How Heartaches Are Made," would come in 1963. Washington was twenty years old and the only woman on the bill that night in Little Rock. She recalled that she came there in a tour bus with other performers but does not remember an altercation or the likes of Ku Klux Klan involvement. But she added, "That doesn't mean something . . . didn't happen."

As Gary Levingston notes, the concert happened in "the bedlam of the civil rights movement, and the KKK was very strong, operating like little gangs. I created my film short *Jesse Belvin: Mr. Easy* about Jesse under the assumption that the KKK slashed the tires and cut the brake lines." Levingston also says that Jesse received death threats before the concert, but direct threats would have been difficult because there would have been no way to contact a performer like Jesse who was on the road. To stay in touch at the time, performers called home, agents, and loved ones from a pay phone or, if it was important, sent a telegram. In addition, no performers reported anything about death threats before the concert. If the Klan, for example, had issued a statement threatening the upcoming show, it would have been sent to the local newspapers, but nothing like that has surfaced in Little Rock libraries.

The story of the slashed tires emerged two weeks after Jesse's death, in his hometown newspaper, the African American *Los Angeles Sentinel*. This would have been big news for the paper since Jesse was a beloved singer who grew up and still lived in Los Angeles. Under the headline "Slashed Tires on Belvin's Auto Probed," on February 18, 1960, the paper reported: "A pressing investigation got underway this week to probe reports that tires on singer Jesse Belvin's car had been willfully slashed hours prior to the fatal accident that claimed the life of the singer, his wife, and three others [actually two others] Feb. 5. Investigators said it has been definitely established that tires on the cars of entertainers Jackie Wilson and Arthur Prysock, who were also en route to Dallas from Little Rock, were slashed before the trio left the city."

A month later, *Jet* picked up the story, repeating details from the *Sentinel* story and adding, "The three cars [of Wilson, Prysock, and Belvin] were parked side-by-side outside a Little Rock dance hall, where the entertainers appeared for a segregated dance. All three left, according to authorities, when [a] white group appeared late for their dance session. Investigators believe that some fans became disgruntled when the entertainers refused to play their session, and slashed the tires."

The story lives on. In 2010, for the Pan-African News Wire, Norman Richmond wrote:

> Shortly after finishing a performance in Little Rock on a bill with Jackie Wilson and Arthur Prysock, the Belvins were killed in a head-on collision in Hope, Arkansas. Jesse and the driver died instantly and Jo Ann succumbed a few days later. In the book, "Dream Boogie: The Triumph of Sam Cooke," Peter Guralnick, talked about how the Belvins died. There had been several death threats on Belvin prior to the concert, and there was speculation that Belvin's car had been tampered with prior to the accident. A black weekly newspaper, the *Norfolk Journal and Guide*, ran a headline, "Did Racism Kill Jesse Belvin?'" Says Guralnick, "It was the same old ugly peckerwood story: the show was booked to play a segregated dance, and when Jackie refused to do a second show for whites, after a 'hot dispute with [the] dance manager,' the *Los Angeles Sentinel* reported, 'Wilson and his group were allegedly ordered out of town at gunpoint. Investigators believed the story went on, 'that . . . disgruntled white dance fans were responsible for slashing Belvin's tires, a conclusion bolstered by the rumor that both Jackie and Prysock also suffered problems as they drove to their next date in Dallas.'"

The Black Elvis gives yet another variant: "Wilson and Prysock had just passed Hope, Arkansas, when they started getting flats. While they'd been arguing in the dance hall, someone had slashed their tires . . . no one ever proved Jesse's tires had been cut, but the accident was a sign of the times. . . . Frazier [Jackie Wilson's chauffeur] provides a possible explanation of why no ever proved the tires had been cut: 'I think one of the policemen cut his tires. He was passing a truck or something and the tire blew out, and that's how he had a head-on collision.'"

What really happened?

According to the concert advertisement, the show was to have started at just before 7:00 p.m. Assuming it was a show of two to three hours, it would have been over by ten, and those performers heading to new gigs, such as

GUESS WHO 63

Jackie Wilson and Jesse Belvin (heading to Fort Worth), would have been in their cars by eleven. If tires had been slashed and this noticed, it would have taken longer to get underway. Jesse was headed south over country roads to Texarkana, Texas. Even today, the drive is over two hours. In 1960, a night journey would have been at least four to five hours even if they didn't stop for food or coffee somewhere along the way. When Kirk was recuperating at Billy Allen's house, he said he had been sleeping in the back seat, with Jo Ann sitting next to Jesse in the front seat and Charles Ford driving.

The accident, a head-on collision between two automobiles, happened outside of Hope, Arkansas, at seven the next morning. Jesse and Ford were killed instantly, as were the two people in the other automobile, Max Gene Nohl and his wife. At that point Jo Ann Belvin was still alive, although she would die from her injuries. Kirk Davis, who had been sleeping in back, survived.

A tepid headline over a single-column story in the *Hope Star*, a local newspaper, simply read, "4 Persons Die in 2-Car Wreck Near Hope Sat." Max Nohl, one of those who died, was a noted deep-sea diver.

> Four persons – including a well-known deep sea diver and a Negro rock 'n' roll singer – were killed Saturday in a fiery two-car crash near here. Two others were critically injured. Dead are Mr. and Mrs. Max Gene Nohl of Milwaukee; the singer, Jesse Belvin, and a companion, Charles Ford, 34, of New York City. Belvin's wife Joann, 25, is hospitalized here and Kirk Davis, another entertainer in the Belvin car, was taken to a Texarkana hospital. The injured remain in critical condition. State Trooper Dwight Pankey said the Cadillac carrying the Negroes was in the wrong lane when it collided with the vehicle carrying the Nohls six miles west of here about 7 a.m. The [Nohls's] car burst into flames. A passing motorist pulled Mrs. Nohl from the car but the flames prevented him from rescuing Mr. Nohl.

The Associated Press picked up the story and its first version ran on the front page of Little Rock's newspaper *Arkansas Democrat* on February 6, 1960. It repeated most of what was carried in the Hope newspaper and contained more than a few errors. Under the dateline "Hope, Ark.":

> Four persons were killed today in a fiery two-car collision near [Hope]. Police said a car containing four Negro entertainers [just two were entertainers] collided with a car occupied by Mr. and Mrs. Max Gene Nohl of Milwaukee, Wisc. The Nohls and two Negroes were killed. The other

two Negroes were reported critically injured. They were hospitalized here [one was hospitalized in Texarkana]. The Nohl car caught fire and burned after the crash. Nohl's body was trapped in the flaming wreckage. One of the dead Negroes was identified as Belvin, singer and recording artist. The other dead Negro was Charles Ford. Injured were Joanne [sic] Belvin and Curt [Kirk] Davis. Police said the Negroes has been in Little Rock and were headed for an engagement in Dallas. The collision was on Highway 67 about three miles [it was six or seven] west of Hope. State Trooper Dwight Pakey [Pankey] said the car occupied by the Negroes was in the wrong lanes [sic] at the time of the accident. Highway traffic was blocked for about 90 minutes.

The *Texarkana Gazette* also picked up the AP story, although, by the time it ran the story on February 7, the wire service had filled out the bare bones. To the Associated Press writer, the celebrity was Max Nohl, and much of the news account filler was about him. The AP noted, "In 1937, wearing a home-made suit of his own design, Nohl descended 420 feet into Lake Michigan for a record fresh water dive at that time." It also reported that in 1958 Nohl had tried unsuccessfully to salvage the Dutch motorship *Prins Willem V*, which had sunk in Lake Michigan in 1954.

As for Jesse, the AP writer, clearly not a rock ''n' roll fan, gave him the last two, short paragraphs that were short on facts: "Belvin, 24, was a popular rhythm and blues singer. His most well-known record, 'Guess Who,' made the top ten listings about two years ago. His latest single disc was 'It Could Have Been Worse.' Belvin recorded several albums for RCA Victor and was considered a promising entertainer because of his versatility." Not his best-known record, "Guess Who" had been on the charts a year earlier, and Jesse still only had one album.

The devilish conspiracy theory that both Jesse Belvin Jr. and Jesse's nephew Gary Levingston believe is that there were confrontations at the concert and that someone nefariously damaged Jesse's car, which was not apparent at the time of departure but caused the accident. There are a lot of holes in this theory. If someone cut the brake line and slit a tire, why did the accident happen so long afterward? Rebecca Miller reported: The show was a concert, not a dance party for two different ethnic groups; the group of performers was not run out of town by segregationists; and, most importantly, no performer from the concert ever reported the alleged events.

The best summation of what happened comes from Etta James, who talked with Jackie Wilson after it all happened, and he explained to her

GUESS WHO

what took place that night. She began, "Jesse's driver, a guy named Charles, had once worked for Ray Charles. Ray let him go because Charles liked to party a little too much. When he should have been napping, he was drinking. After Ray felt the car weaving back and forth on the highway, he fired him. Jesse hired him. Jesse would give anybody a break. Well, after the gig, three carloads of musicians headed straight for Texas."

Notice that there is no mention of a confrontation at the concert or about slashed tires, which would have been memorable and important enough for Jackie to include while recounting the story. Etta continued:

> Jackie's car, driven by his valet, Frazier, was first; Jesse was second. With Charles behind the wheel, Jesse was seated in the middle and his wife, Jo Ann, was riding shotgun. They got up to sixty-five, maybe seventy miles per hour, down a two-lane road. The third car, the one behind Jesse, saw that Charles was straying into the oncoming lane and staying there awhile. Alarmed, they blinked their brights to alert him. That woke him up. He slowed down and then rolled down his window for fresh air. That seemed to help. He resumed his speed, but five minutes later he dozed off again and veered into the wrong lane. He was awoken by the headlights of car coming straight at him. But it was too late. Jackie was a few miles up the road and didn't even know what had happened.

Rebecca Miller says that Jesse Jr. remembered a phone call. He was only four at the time, but the kin with whom he was staying in Los Angeles got a call from Jackie Wilson, and he knew something was wrong. Wilson had reached Dallas, but Jesse and Jo Ann had not arrived. According to Jesse Jr., Jackie said he had car problems, as if someone had messed with the tires, and as a result had gotten to Dallas late. He thought Jesse and Jo Ann should have arrived in Dallas before him and wanted to know if they had called home. Miller surmised that if Jackie had been worried about Jesse and Jo Ann, in that phone call to Los Angeles he would have mentioned any Little Rock fracas or difficulties.

Etta's story continued:

> Musicians in the car behind Jesse's told me of this horrible glow they saw up ahead, this red glare that lit the sky where the two cars collided. Charles was killed instantly. . . . Jesse had his arm around Jo Ann – they were both asleep – but it was so quick that on impact he grabbed her head and shoved it beneath the car radio. The collision was so powerful

that when they opened the door they saw Jesse Belvin, whose head gone through the windshield, was near decapitated. . . . Knowing Charles and Jesse were dead, their main concern was for Jo Ann. But the hospital, run by white doctors, wanted to know who was paying. No one had enough money. Jo Ann was left unattended in a coma with a crushed pelvis, crushed chest, a broken arm. She was left in a coma until they could reach Jackie Wilson in Dallas.

Jackie then drove back to Arkansas to pay the doctors. Perhaps the real controversy should be not regarding how Jesse died but about whether Jo Ann's life would have been saved had she been white.

"Jo Ann lived for four or five days," said Chester Jones.

Billy Allen adds, "I went to the wrecking yard where the car was. It was totaled so bad the front end was pushed back under the windshield. I also went with my uncle and mother to the hospital. Jo Ann at that time was still alive but unconscious."

A week after the accident, RCA Victor Records released its press release, noting, "RCA Victor recording artist Jesse Belvin and his wife, Jo Ann, were fatally injured in an automobile accident at Hope, Arkansas. . . . Belvin[,] considered one of the brightest prospects in the RCA Victor pop record picture[,] died instantly. . . . Belvin's wife waged a week long fight for life, but finally succumbed to injuries suffered in the crash."

Chester said, "I heard about the accident as I was walking to a place called the Gateway Cafe, a truck stop about three or four miles from my house. I had a little transistor radio, and I had it up to my ear listing to a radio station out of Louisiana called KEEM. It was Saturday morning about seven fifteen when an announcer said he was interrupting programming for an important announcement, that singer/songwriter Jesse Belvin was killed in a serious automobile accident in Hope, Arkansas. We were going to do some rabbit hunting when he got back to town. He, me, my brother, and Billy Allen. In fact, my rifle was in the back of Jesse's car. I was in shock. I had just saw them, and now he was dead."

Chester recalled one more thing. "Billy had Kirk's electric guitar and amp, which had been in the trunk of Jesse's car. The guitar was crushed, but the amp survived. Billy still has the amp."

Billy confirmed that story. "I still got Kirk's amplifier. The guitar, a Gretsch, was broken. It was a very pretty guitar with pearl keys, gold and pearl, but the neck was broken. I took the keys off of it and intended to put on my guitar, but someone stole it all from me."

As recounted by Etta, Jackie never mentioned a problem in Little Rock or tires being slashed, which would have been important elements in the story as to how Jesse died. Did Jesse's driver fall asleep and allow the car to drift into oncoming traffic, or was his car "messed with," which subsequently affected its performance hours later? Most evidence points to the former, not the latter, but we'll never know for sure.

Etta went to Jesse's funeral in Los Angeles. It was an open casket, and it took the mortuary "three days to sew Jesse together." According to the musicians in the third car, the impact was so devastating it "separated Jesse's nose from his mouth." Jackie Wilson sang, but he was so broken up he could barely make a sound, said Etta. "We all knew Jesse was the next superstar. He'd just gotten his big break with RCA, just gotten started."

Etta claimed that for almost thirty-five years afterward she often dreamed of Jesse.

PART TWO
GUITAR SLIM

CHAPTER 6

Black Snake Moan

Guitar Slim confusion – A revolution in guitar style and sound – The Texas blues – Blind Lemon Jefferson leads the way – T-Bone Walker is electric – Gatemouth Brown pinch hits

Unfortunately, there has been a little bit of confusion over the first recordings of Guitar Slim. Some discographies begin with the song "Feelin' Sad," with the B-side "Certainly All," on the record label J–B (Jim Bulleit Records). This recording was in 1952. However, Billy Vera, who in addition to being a fine singer and songwriter is also a musicologist, found two Guitar Slim recordings from 1951 on the Imperial label. Then he got confused, writing, "Guitar Slim's first records were made for J. L. Fulbright's Elko label to sell out of his trunk. Imperial purchased [the rights to the songs]."

Elko was another small, independent record company based in Los Angeles. There could be no confusion as to this fact because on its label was the company's address at 823 East Adams Boulevard. Like the bigger Los Angeles record companies such as Imperial Records, founded by Lew Chudd in 1946, tiny Elko also chased up-and-coming rhythm and blues musicians, and both companies made forays east and south to record new artists. Discographer Chris Bentley tracked down all the Elko Recordings, including the obscure and the almost obscure, and could find nothing on the label from Eddie Jones recording as Guitar Slim.

That sent Billy Vera back to the dustbins of history, and he wrote again, "I double checked the Imperial master book, which has it [Guitar Slim's first recording] as an Imperial session in New Orleans on May 16, 1951."

It was very easy to be confused because there was an Elko recording of "My First Date," with "The Rising Sun" on the B-side, by Willie Evans and his Night Owls, with "Sunny Guitar Slim" sitting in. Since neither Willie Evans nor Sunny Guitar Slim have other recording histories, the supposition has always been that they were pseudonyms. Chris Bentley tried sorting it all out by ear. He wrote, "Willie Evans was long thought to be a misprint for Willie Egan and Sunny Guitar Slim was posited as Guitar Slim Green, but having heard the record, I don't think either theory is correct. The disc itself is a grave disappointment with an inexpertly played organ up front overpowering two rather mundane songs."

Here's the problem with that hypothesis. Willie Egan, born in 1933, was a blues pianist, and he did make a record for Elko Records, a song called "It's A Shame," with "Willie's Boogie" on the B-side. This would have been in 1954, although he also claimed that he recorded "Dream House Blues" with "Whipped Cream" on the B-side in 1949, but Chris Bentley could not substantiate that claim and doesn't list the record as part of Elko's catalog. Like other blues singers he did record under other names, such as "Egans" and "Eggins," and for that one record he could have been "Evans" struggling to play an organ instead of the piano. Notably, he seems to have crossed paths with numerous players from Jesse Belvin's orbit, including playing with Johnny Otis, teaming up with Marvin Phillips, and in later years playing a concert gig with Big Jay McNeely.

Confusion continued into the 1980s when Jerry Osborne and Bruce Hamilton published their first record guide for blues, rhythm and blues, and soul singers. The book cautions readers not to confuse Guitar Slim with Norman Green (Guitar Slim Green) or Alec Seward, who recorded at the end of the 1940s as Guitar Slim, Slim Seward, and Georgia Slim.

The Guitar Slim of "The Things I Used to Do," was born Eddie Jones in Greenwood, Mississippi, in 1926. At the same time he began his recording career in 1951, there were two other blues singers with similar names, Guitar Slim Green and Sunnyland Slim, who could have been the Sunny Guitar Slim of "My First Date." Sunnyland Slim was also born in Mississippi, in the small burg of Vance. That's where the associations end, because Sunnyland Slim was considerably older, having been born in1907, and took up the piano, not guitar. When old enough he moved north, first to Memphis and then to Chicago. That leaves Guitar Slim Green.

Not much is known about the background of Guitar Slim Green, who like Guitar Slim (Eddie Jones), was obviously a guitarist. He is reputed to have begun recording in the 1940s, but if he is known at all it's because of some recordings he was doing for Johnny Otis's Dig label. His best-known song is "Stone Down Blues," with Johnny Otis on drums and Shuggie Otis on bass. As one reviewer noted, "certainly, father and son helped push Green away from his comfortable wheelhouse – a wheelhouse that's firmly indebted to T-Bone Walker, whose influence can be heard on Guitar Slim's [Guitar Slim Green's] fluid single-line leads."

Now, depending on who is doing the talking, Guitar Slim (Eddie Jones, the "Guitar Slim" in all mentions going forward) modeled his raucous guitar playing on T-Bone Walker or Clarence "Gatemouth" Brown or both. Aaron "T-Bone Walker" was born in Linden, Texas, and raised in Dallas. Gatemouth, although born in Louisiana, was brought up in Orange, Texas. As Larry Birnbaum noted, "Although he [Guitar Slim] was raised in Mississippi and based his career in New Orleans, Guitar Slim played Texas-style guitar."

Rolling Stone magazine's list of greatest guitar players mentions bluesmen such as T-Bone Walker and more modern musicians such as Jimi Hendrix and Buddy Guy, but it doesn't mention the guitarist that bridged the gap between, Guitar Slim. T-Bone Walker was born in 1910, and fellow bluesman Gatemouth Brown was born in 1924, and they began playing professionally in the 1930s and 1940s. As noted, Guitar Slim was born in 1926, so he was just two years younger than Gatemouth. Guitar Slim's recording career coincided with the onset of the 1950s.

Buddy Guy, who was born in 1936, has spoken often about Guitar Slim as being the first guitarist to really be an influence on him. In a 2004 interview for the Guitar Center, Guy recalled, " At the beginning . . . I saw one of the greatest guitar players I ever saw. He [Guitar Slim] came into Baton Rouge when I was about 16 or 17. He came in playing with this Strat. I looked up and I said, 'what the hell is that?' I didn't even know what it was or that a solid piece of wood [could sound] that loud. I just fell in love. [It was] Guitar Slim, who made that great record, 'Things I Used to Do,' arranged by Ray Charles before Ray made a name for himself."

Buddy Guy has never been shy about talking up Guitar Slim. In another interview, he told the same story but more in-depth. This tale begins at a younger age, when Buddy's father brought home a phonograph, and he heard recordings by B. B. King, Lightnin' Hopkins, and even T-Bone Walker. When he heard a recording of "Things I Used to Do," as Buddy recalled, he basically exclaimed, "what the heck is that?" About that Baton Rouge performance, the more complete story is that Guitar Slim was introduced, but Buddy didn't see him at first, only heard him. Guitar Slim brought a big band with him, which was led by Lloyd Lambert out of New Orleans. One of the big fellows in the band carried out Guitar Slim, slung like a baby over the big man's shoulder. Guitar Slim had on a red suit, his hair was dyed the same color as the suit, and his shoes were white. He was playing while being carried and was still playing when he was dropped to the stage. Said Buddy, "I saw B. B. King once. I saw T-Bone Walker, and I saw Joe Turner. I wanted to sound like B. B. King, but I wanted to act like Guitar Slim."

In the modern era, Guitar Slim invented the image of guitarist as a showman – or shaman, depending on one's point of view.

"No one could outperform Slim," said New Orleans musician Earl King, who knew Slim well. "He was about the performingest man I've ever seen."

"Slim was always causing a sensation," noted Arthur Neville. "He was the cat who would have his valet go out and mix different dyes and paint over his white buck shoes to match the color of his suits. I tried to do the same. We were all matched to the max. Slim was just one of the gunslinger guitarists who turned up the volume on the T-Bone Walker thing. Johnny Guitar Watson came over from Texas – he and I became buddies – and he learned a lot from Slim. We all did."

On the other hand, Birnbaum is in the camp that believes Slim was inspired by the guitar playing of Gatemouth Brown.

Maybe they influenced each other. Robert Palmer, answering the question about the first guitarists to use power chords, distortion, and feedback, in a 1995 *Guitar World* article, wrote that rhythm and blues audiences early in the 1950s were still accustomed to bands featuring honking saxophones as the primary solo instrument and were fronted by blues singers who kept their guitar playing subordinate to the vocals. Slim reversed these priorities and put his guitar playing up front. Palmer wrote about Slim: "He combined early training in gospel singing with a beginning guitar style that led early commentators to dismiss him as an imitator of T-Bone Walker and, especially, the flashier Gatemouth Brown. The blue suits, and hair, the 350-foot guitar cords, and the Jimi Hendrix–like sonic effects soon made it clear that he was an original."

When Slim began to make a name for himself in New Orleans, playing the local clubs, in particular the Dew Drop Inn, a reporter for the Africa American *Louisiana Weekly* described him "as an exact copy of Gatemouth Brown."

On the other hand, Slim was showman, and when onstage he could more easily be confused with T-Bone Walker, who not only pioneered the use of the electric guitar in jump bands but also, as author Charlie Gillett observed, developed a dazzling stage act that was reputed to have inspired Elvis Presley in its use of the guitar as a stage prop. T-Bone did the splits and held the instrument behind his head while he continued to play. Sometimes for sexual provocation he ground the guitar against his body or pointed it suggestively at the audience.

To rephrase Buddy Guy's quote, Guitar Slim may have wanted to sound like Gatemouth Brown, but he really wanted to act like T-Bone Walker, following two exemplars of what was once called southern blues.

BLACK SNAKE MOAN

In the early twentieth century, blues was a particularly rough form of musical expression and was as much an outlier to popular music as the equally primitive hillbilly sound was to what eventually became country music. This all began to change as both blues (called "race music" early in the twentieth century) and hillbilly began settle into more defined styles after World War II, as black and white teenagers started buying more records in these styles and attending live performances. In the mid-1960s, Charles Keil wrote a book called *Urban Blues*, in which he noted, "Many of the early rock-and-roll singers, white and Negro, were influenced also by what might be dubbed the postwar Texas clean-up movement in blues singing." Keil mentioned T-Bone Walker as part of this movement. Keil concluded the modern blues style had been transformed and remolded after the war, and "once again it was Texas and the surrounding states that nurtured the new style." He would add, "While the rock-and-roll specialists were distorting and reshaping this type [of music] to meet teenage demands, Mississippian B. B. King adopted this cleaner Texas or Territory-band style and refined it still further."

In 1966, Keil interviewed B. B. King and asked him which guitarists appealed to him when he first started to learn. King named jazz guitarist Django Reinhardt, bluesman Elmore James, and T-Bone Walker. And when asked who influenced his distinctive sound, he answered, "Blind Lemon Jefferson. . . . I used to listen to him on my aunt's Victrola, and he sang in a style I really liked."

Blind Lemon Jefferson was the man who established the Texas guitar sound, picked up by Gatemouth Brown and more notably T-Bone Walker before Guitar Slim took the baton and carried it into the modern era.

Again, it was Keil who first recognized this link, writing that Blind Lemon Jefferson and T-Bone Walker were the "foremost exponents" of two Texas music "stylings," country and urban blues. Indeed, sometimes the recordings of Blind Lemon Jefferson are referred to as Texas blues, and he is often referred to as Father of the Texas Blues.

The most published picture of Lemon Henry Jefferson (only two are known to exist), born in or near the small outpost of Coutchman, Texas, mostly a ghost town today, shows a robust young man, looking like a sixteen-year-old version of Fats Domino. He's nattily dressed with jacket, white shirt, and tie. A string, not quite a guitar strap, is slung across his right shoulder, and he's strumming right-handed. The only oddity is that he's wearing spectacles, but if you look closely it appears as if his eyes are shut. Lemon, who would become "Blind Lemon," was born blind.

The photo dates back as early as 1928, although he looks much younger than his thirty-plus years. It appeared in an advertisement, probably from

76   CHAPTER 6

the African American *Chicago Defender* newspaper on May 19, 1928. The promotion was put together by a local recording company called Paramount, which used "The Popular Race Record" as its slogan. The company highlighted its new release "Lemon's Worried Blues" and used the picture under a big header, "Worried Blues," then, in smaller print, "by Blind Lemon Jefferson."

Coutchman (its name is sometimes misspelled "Couchman") never boasted more than three hundred people, and, when Lemon was born in 1893, probably less than one hundred people lived there. His parents were sharecroppers. No one really knows where Blind Lemon picked up blues, but speculation is that he heard itinerant musicians who traveled through the area. In any case, he was something of a blues prodigy and with the help of others became an itinerant musician himself, playing in nearby towns of Wortham and Kirvin before making his way to the Dallas area. According to the Texas Historical Society, around 1912 he started performing in the Deep Ellum area of Dallas, although the 1920 census has him living in Freestone County with his half-brother. In later years, T-Bone Walker would guide Blind Lemon around the speakeasies of Deep Ellum. However, during his younger years in Dallas he hooked up with a family friend, a slightly older musician named Huddie William Ledbetter. The famed blues guitarist better known by his picturesque nickname Lead Belly, credited Blind Lemon with teaching him single-string runs on the instrument.

Lead Belly was born in Louisiana in 1888 or 1889, and his father saved enough money sharecropping to buy 68.5 acres of farmland on the Texas shore of Caddo Lake. His industrious father gave him a guitar in 1903, and as a teen Leady Belly began playing in nearby black communities. *Guitar Player* in 1996 quoted him as having said, "There'd be no white man in 20 miles. I got 50 cents a night and I played sukey-jumps when I was 15 years old because I had a horse and could go out and ride."

As Donald Myrus wrote in his book *Ballads, Blues and the Big Beat*, "[Lead Belly] learned songs while playing in saloons and on the streets of innumerable small towns and cities, some as large as Dallas. For a while he accompanied Blind Lemon Jefferson, another exceptional Negro guitar player and singer. . . . At the beginning [of the twentieth century], Jelly Roll Morton played piano in New Orleans . . . at about the same time Leadbelly and Blind Lemon Jefferson were singing the blues in Texas."

Their paths diverged. Starting around 1915 and for the next twenty-five years, Lead Belly was often incarcerated on various charges. He also was spending time in Shreveport working as a musician in the red-light district. Lemon stayed in Texas.

In the 1970s, music writer, singer, and musicologist Robert Palmer tracked down pianist Sammy Price, who knew Lemon from his Texas days, and interviewed him about the seminal blues musician. "Blind Lemon was using the term 'booger rooger' and playing in that boogie-woogie rhythm as far as, oh, 1917–18, when I heard him in Waco," Palmer quotes Price as saying. "A little later, in Dallas, he used to spend every day walking from one end of town to the other, playing and singing on the street and various taverns for tips."

Lemon remained a Texas busker until 1925 when a scout for Paramount discovered him and took him to Chicago to record. It was a perfect match, Lemon was prolific, and Paramount was the premier company in the 1920s recording race music.

Paramount began as a manufacturer, pressing records for other companies, one of which was Black Swan Records. That company hit on hard times, and Paramount bought it out and starting making records targeting the African American market. Besides being an able promoter of talent, the company had a large mail-order operation that reached deep into rural America, and most of its race recordings were arranged under the auspices of the capable J. Mayo "Ink" Williams, an African American talent scout.

Lemon's first recording session was in March 1926 (some sources say 1925), and over the next four years he recorded almost one hundred songs and emerged as the most famous country bluesman, or folk bluesman, in America. A more modern bluesman, John P. Hammond, who recorded Lemon's songs, said of him, "Blind Lemon influenced everybody, because his records in the 1920s were all over the United States. He especially had an impact on a lot of white players – vocally, more than his guitar style. His guitar style was so advanced, unique, amazing, and just hard to do."

Music journalist Jas Obrecht noted, "[Lemon's] guitar became a second voice that complemented rather than repeated the melodies he sang. He often halted rhythm at the end of vocal lines to launch into elaborate solo flourishes. He could play in unusual meters with a great deal of drive and flash, and was adept in many keys."

Birnbaum wrote, "His high, penetrating vocals and dexterous guitar work, alternating rhythmic strumming with intricate single-note runs, virtually defined the country blues." In Palmer's words, "On his records, Jefferson would often start off playing a rocking rhythm, only to stop playing at the end of a vocal line, hammer on the string in imitation of what he'd just sung, and then plunge back in with a snappy, syncopated figure."

Of the many songs Lemon wrote and recorded, two stand out and have withstood the test of time. At one time the two songs, "Black Snake Moan" and "Match Box Blues," were recorded for Okeh Records and appeared on a 78 (a large disc played at a speedy seventy-eight revolutions per minute).

"Black Snake Moan" was inspired by Houston blues singer Victoria Spivey. Born in 1906, she began her career hard, playing saloons and whorehouses, often working with Blind Lemon Jefferson. Also a songwriter, Spivey popularized the metaphor "black snake," referring to a man's appendage, in her song "Black Snake Blues." "What a mean black snake carried me to this gate / Brought me to my mistake, hard for me to take / What mean black snake that's doing me this a-way."

During a session for Paramount in 1926, Lemon recorded a reworking of the Spivey tune, which Lemon called "That Black Snake Moan." The following year, Lemon was in Atlanta recording a bunch of songs for Okeh, and one would be released on the 78 with "Match Box Blues."

Samuel Charters, who wrote the book *The Poetry of the Blues*, spends a lot of ink writing about that song:

> One of the most direct of the erotic blues is Blind Lemon Jefferson's "Black Snake Moan," which uses the common Texas symbolism of the black snake as first recorded by a young girl from outside of Dallas [Houston], Victoria Spivey. *Hey, ain't got no mama now; Hey, ain't got no mama now; She told me late last night, you don't need no mama no how.* As Lemon is singing he is already feeling the frustration of desire. *Um-um black snake crawlin' in my room; Um-um black snake crawlin' in my room; Yes, some pretty mama better get this black snake soon; Uum – what's the matter now; Uum – what's the matter now; Tell me what's the matter, baby? I don't like no black snake no how.* He has gotten a girl to visit him, but she refuses to lie with him. She answers his questioning . . . with her petulant, "I don't like no black snake no how." *Well I wonder where this black snake's gone; I wonder where this black snake's gone; Lord, that black snake, mama, done run my mama home.*

For "Match Box Blues," Lemon once again borrowed from a female blues singer. This time it was Ma Rainey and a line from her 1924 recording of "Lost Wandering Blues": "Standin' here wonderin' will a matchbox hold my clothes." Lemon's new rhyming line: "I ain't got so many matches, but I got so far to go."

The song would be recorded numerous times by both country and blues singers. Then, in 1956, Carl Perkins redid the song in rockabilly style, simply calling it "Matchbox" but retaining almost the same key wording as

Lemon. The song wasn't a hit until the Beatles remade the Carl Perkins version in 1964; it became a top twenty best seller that year, when the Beatles had four number one records and two more in the top ten.

The lyrics from a lesser-known Lemon song also resurfaced in the mid-1950s to become a part of hit record. In July 1927, Paramount released his record "Rising High Water Blues," with "Teddy Bear Blues" on the B-side. The credits note piano accompaniment by George Perkins, and one stanza goes: "I say, fair brown, let me be your teddy bear. Oh, let me be your teddy bear; tie a string around my neck and I'll follow you everywhere." A Philadelphia boy named Kalman Cohen must have heard that recording – and had it stick.

In the mid-1950s, by this time known as Kal Mann, Cohen teamed up with friend Bernie Lowe to write songs for the nascent teenager market. The two proved to be dexterous, with numerous hits from Charlie Gracie's "Butterfly" in 1957 to Bobby Rydell's "Wild One" in 1960 and hits for Chubby Checker and Pat Boone. Part of the reason for their success was an abiding interest in the blues, dating back to their youth. Mann, the lyricist in the team, could recall phrasings from songs he heard as a teenager in the 1930s. Mann and Lowe's most successful tune was one they delivered to Elvis Presley, "(Let Me Be Your) Teddy Bear." Mann's lyrics – a "borrow" from Blind Lemon: "Baby let me be your teddy bear; put a chain around my neck and lead me anywhere; oh let me be your teddy bear." In June 1957 the song hit number one on *Billboard*'s pop chart and settled into the top position for seven weeks. By that time, Blind Lemon Jefferson had been dead almost thirty years.

♪♪♪♪♪

Before David Bartholomew became Imperial's A&R (artists and repertoire) man in New Orleans, responsible for talent scouting and artist development, and before he began recording Fats Domino, and before he became the premier record producer in 1950s New Orleans, he fronted a band at the Club Rocket in New Orleans. At that time, Don Robey, who pretty much controlled African American nightlife in Houston, made Bartholomew an offer to play in Houston at his premier night spot, the Bronze Peacock Dinner Club, known as the Peacock. Soon Bartholomew and his band were playing a five-week gig at the Peacock, sometimes backing the hottest guitar player on the mid-South coastal circuit, T-Bone Walker.

Aaron Thibeaux Walker gained his nickname by people mishearing his middle name. He was born in Linden, Texas, but grew up in Dallas. His mother played guitar, and his stepfather played just about anything with strings and taught Aaron to do the same.

In an interview with Arnold Shaw, T-Bone reminisced, "I was born in Linden, Texas, on May 28, 1910. Waxahatchie is my wife's home. But I was raised in Dallas and my wife was raised in Waxahatchie and moved to Fort Worth. That's where we got married in 1935. My mother took me away from Linden when I was two. When I was a kid, I had a stepfather, and he and his brother played like a mallet and guitars. . . . Blind Lemon was a very good friend to my family, a very good friend to my mother."

For local folks who enjoyed music, the Walker household was a hub. One frequent visitor who came to jam with T-Bone's stepfather was Blind Lemon Jefferson, which is how T-Bone became the young man chosen to guide the singer around Dallas for gigs. It was on-the-job training, and T-Bone too became a busker by the time he entered his teenage years. It wasn't as if there was a dearth of good blues players in the mid-South trying to earn a dime or two. There were many, and T-Bone realized it wasn't enough to just be a good musician, one had to be entertaining as well, so he livened up his street act with showboating and dancing and soon was in demand at local parties and dances. At fifteen, he toured with blues singer Ida Cox, and then at nineteen with Cab Calloway's band. In a sense, he never left the road. He was in the first wave of Texas musicians to migrate Los Angeles, which he did in 1935.

As T-Bone told Arnold Shaw, he ended up Los Angeles because he knew a guy who was moving all his cars to Los Angeles. It would be a free trip if T-Bone could drive one car and tow another, which he did. As T-Bone said, "And when I got there, well, I just stayed."

He became well-known in Los Angeles, including gigs at the Trocadero Club, a popular nightspot on Sunset Strip that allowed integrated audiences. Starting around 1939, he began playing with the Les Hite Orchestra, and that transformed his professional life. According to one writer, while working with Les Hite he "developed his long hornlike guitar style."

"I don't know whether I was the first guitar player to use the electric," T-Bone told Arnold Shaw. "But I was one of the first. The guitar player with Andy Kirk had one. And the guitar player with Les Hite had one. I started playing the electric after I left Les. I think it was 1939."

The statement is confusing because he toured with Les Hite's orchestra in the 1940s, and it was with them that he recorded "T-Bone Blues," which made him a star in that decade – although he didn't play electric guitar on that recording. However, it was about 1939 that he took up the electric. He played the Los Angeles clubs with his electric, assembling his own combo. Not forgetting to entertain, he engaged in unusual stage acrobatics such as splits and playing behind his back. The *Handbook of Texas History* notes: "Walker used a fluid technique that combined country blues tradition with more polished contemporary swing. He was subsequently billed as the 'Daddy of the Blues.'"

Blind Lemon Jefferson used a loose, improvisational style, Palmer wrote, saying, "his single-string work bore fruit in the 1940s in the pioneering electric blues of T-Bone Walker."

On September 12, 1947, T-Bone walked into a recording studio in Hollywood, where he recorded a couple of songs, one of which was "Call It Stormy Monday (But Tuesday Is Just as Bad," which became a blues standard and T-Bone's signature song. He didn't have a great deal of fondness for the song, which was originally intended to be the B-side for the forgotten tune "I Know Your Wig Is Gone."

"Stormy Monday"' is a blues song with a long history," wrote Keil. "T-Bone Walker made it famous, but the lyric goes back to blues prehistory, to work songs and spirituals."

Despite "Stormy Monday" being a huge hit and T-Bone continuing to record and sell well, Birnbaum maintained that T-Bone's influence was far out of proportion to his record sales, not only because of his flamboyant stage antics but because guitarists copied his "jazzy chord progressions and slinky single-note runs, punctuated by slides and bends."

Back in New Orleans, Bartholomew took the concept of "Stormy Monday" and wrote a new tune, "Blue Monday," which would become a big hit for Fats Domino in 1956 but was first recorded by Smiley Lewis in 1953 on the Imperial label. From 1950 through 1954, T-Bone Walker recorded for Imperial. Guitar Slim's recordings for Imperial were in 1951, and Woody Sistrunk, a musicologist specializing in country blues, suggests that Guitar Slim ended up recording for Imperial because of T-Bone Walker. Another take on that, from Billy Vera, was that T-Bone Walker probably didn't know who Guitar Slim was then, because T-Bone was in Los Angeles when the then-unknown Guitar Slim stood in front of the studio microphone. The irony is that T-Bone Walker and Guitar Slim were both recording for Imperial at exactly the same time, but Walker was in a Los Angeles studio, while Guitar Slim was in a less-sophisticated New Orleans recording booth.

Gatemouth Brown took up the guitar because of T-Bone. Although born in Vincent, Louisiana in 1924, his family moved to Orange, Texas, when he was a small boy. His father was a musician who made extra money playing house parties, and he taught Gatemouth to play a slew of stringed instruments, from guitar to fiddle. As Gatemouth got older, he became a regular in his father's band.

After fulfilling his military service during the World War II years, he returned to Texas in 1945 and began playing drums with bands in the San Antonio area. His first big break came because of Don Robey, the king of Houston nightlife for African Americans. Robey was an entertainment entrepreneur with vision and reach. From the later 1940s, he was largely responsible for Texas's contribution to the chitlin' circuit, including the Keyhole Club in San Antonio, where Gatemouth was playing with Bob Ogden's band. Don Albert, Robey's man in San Antonio, introduced Gatemouth to the boss, who took a liking to him and said the next time Gatemouth was in Houston he should visit Robey at the Peacock. Robey gave the young man his business card.

About this time Gatemouth lost his enthusiasm for the drums and switched back to the guitar, a move inspired by seeing a T-Bone Walker concert. Preston Lauterbach, author of a history of the chitlin' circuit, quotes Gatemouth saying: "T-Bone Walker had the people just screaming and hollering, women falling out, knocking down the walls, tearing down chandeliers, and I said, 'God Almighty, what is this guy doing to these people.'"

According to Johnny Otis, women used to throw their undergarments onto the stage when T-Bone played. Two decades later, the same thing would happen when handsome Welsh singer Tom Jones took to the stage.

Gatemouth met T-Bone a few times and practically begged him for guitar-playing tips, Lauterbach says.

This all leads to one of the best known pinch-hit stories since Lou Gehrig stepped up to bat for first baseman Wally Pipp and then continued to play for 2,130 straight games. The tale begins with Gatemouth hitchhiking to Houston, heading for the address on the business card that Robey handed to him. Finally, getting to the Peacock, Gatemouth realized that he didn't even have enough money for admission, but he was able to make contact with Robey, who let him in for free. T-Bone was concluding a long multiweek gig at the Peacock, but on this particular night his ulcers flared up, and he couldn't make it to the stage to even pick up his guitar, which was waiting for him under the spotlight. Robey looked over to Gatemouth and, like Yankee manager Joe McCarthy to Gehrig, said, "You're up."

Gatemouth later recalled: "I picked up his guitar, and for no reason on earth I started in E-neutral, that's the only key I knew, and I invented a tune right on the spot." The song would become known as "Gatemouth Boogie,"

BLACK SNAKE MOAN

and the audience loved it. The only person not happy was T-Bone, who told Gatemouth, "Never pick up my guitar again."

An alternative version of the story has T-Bone the one who suggested Gatemouth as a substitute since he was not feeling well before his show. In that version, Gatemouth, knowing he was going to be taking T-Bone's place, wrote "Gatemouth Boogie" before his show. If we are to believe the Robey version, in which he pushed Gatemouth onto stage as a last resort, Gatemouth made up "Gatemouth Boogie" on the spot.

On "Gatemouth Boogie," Gatemouth sang, "My name is Gatemouth Brown, I just got into town; if you don't like my style, I will not hang around."

(In 1955, Guitar Slim, on his eponymous record "Guitar Slim," sang, "Now they call me Guitar Slim, baby, and I'm come to play in your town; now if you don't like my music, baby, I will not hang around.")

Whatever happened, the result was that Robey immediately signed Gatemouth and installed him as a headliner at the Peacock.

A reporter for the *Houston Informer*, a black newspaper, wrote, "Altho this man did not sing like T-Bone, he has him skinned forty ways when it comes to guitar playing. Gatemouth drew almost as much applause from patrons as T-Bone."

Gatemouth was everything that Robey wanted as a performer and more, working the crowds at the Peacock, especially the women, into a frenzy, so he decided to take Gatemouth on the road, which meant a full stop in New Orleans, where there were many African American clubs (nightclubs were segregated in most of the South at that time). The craziest of the town's juke joints was the Dew Drop Inn, and Gatemouth landed there in mid-July 1947. Although not as well known in New Orleans as in Houston, Robey had enough influence to get Gatemouth some good press in the local black newspapers. Preston Lauterbach was able to dig up some clippings from the time, one of which read, "Talk of New Orleans this week is a slender fellow with varied formal attire and voice that shouts the blues." A second story labeled Gatemouth "a new find and a sensation that has been rockin' Texas."

Sitting in at the Peacock that same summer was another Robey find, Bartholomew, playing a five-week engagement, sometimes backing T-Bone Walker. In the audience one night during Bartholomew's gig at the Peacock was Lew Chudd, who had founded Imperial Records the year before to record Mexican music. Living in Southern California, Chudd thought there was an untapped market for Mexican music, but he'd come to Texas and was scouting the fertile bayou region with blues in mind. In June 1947, Chudd recorded Poison Gardner and his All Stars, and a Texas singer named "Fat Man" Hamilton was involved. "Fat Man" would be a nickname to remember, but the singer eventually disappeared into the chitlin' circuit of juke joints. Singer Billy Vera's mother, who also had been a performer, bumped into Gardner at a club in northern Ohio. She was from Cleveland and began her career singing at local nightspots.

While in Houston, Chudd got around to talking to Bartholomew, who really knew the players in the area. Lew said he would pay Bartholomew to be both an artist and talent scout. The offer sounded enticing, but then Lew left town, and nothing came of it – not for a couple of years.

In music, all newcomers seem to knock off their idols. T-Bone Walker supplanted Blind Lemon Jefferson, and Gatemouth Brown did the same to T-Bone Walker. Guitar Slim climbed over both T-Bone and Gatemouth.

New Orleans guitarist Earl King, who knew Guitar Slim's style so well he could tour as him, liked to tell a Screamin' Jay Hawkins–style story about the old school guitarists and his idol Guitar Slim. Jeff Hannusch quoted King in his book about New Orleans R&B: "Gatemouth Brown, T-Bone Walker, Lowell Fulson and Guitar Slim were all performing one night [in 1954] at the White Eagle in Opelousas, Louisiana. Slim was headlining because 'The Things I Used to Do' was a scorcher. They were all sitting in the dressing room and Guitar Slim walked up to 'em and said, 'Gentleman, we got the greatest guitar players in the country assembled right here. But when I leave here tonight, ain't nobody gonna realize you even been here.' Well, they all laughed, but that's exactly what happened."

Feelin' Sad

CHAPTER 7

Guitar Slim first attracts attention as a dancer – Deciding on New Orleans – Cosimo Matassa opens J&M Recording Service – "Good Rockin' Tonight" rocks – Fats Domino arrives – Meeting Huey Piano Smith – Dropping in at the Dew Drop – Recording in Nashville –"Feelin' Sad" Number One in New Orleans

In 1947, Don Robey signed Gatemouth Brown to a management contract and then quickly trundled him off to Los Angeles, where they signed a two-year deal with Aladdin Records, a company run by brothers Eddie and Leo Mesner. Aladdin initially recorded jazz singers but almost immediately segued into rhythm and blues, although they were uncharacteristically hesitant when it came to Gatemouth. The performer recorded four numbers for the company. First up was "Gatemouth Boogie," which came out in 78 format with "After Sunset" on the B-side. A second 78 had "Guitar in My Hands," with "Without Me Baby" on the B-side. Jerry Osborne and Bruce Hamilton have both as being recorded in 1947, but that doesn't mean they were released to the public at that time.

The Aladdin contract called for two records to be released in 1947 and another two in 1948. If two songs of on a 78 record count a two records, then Aladdin fulfilled the contract. In any case, Aladdin strung out Gatemouth and Robey. In an interview with *Billboard*, Robey exclaimed, "I wanted [Gatemouth] to have a record out because he was playing at my club. But Aladdin waited until the last day of the year before releasing Brown's second record. So I was mad."

Robey was angry enough that he formed his own record company in Houston, Peacock Records, named after his nightclub. The year was 1949, and it put Houston solidly on the map as a Gulf city where one could make a name for oneself in the music industry.

Legendary bluesman Robert Johnson is said to have met the devil and been given musical genius in exchange for his soul, a story connected with his song "Crossroad Blues." Johnson may have actually stood at the crossroads where Highway 61 going north and south and Highway 49 going east and west intersect outside of Clarksdale, Mississippi. Indeed, in "Crossroad Blues," he sings that he went to a crossroad, tried to hitch a ride, and everyone passed him by. But there is also metaphor at work here: "I went to the crossroad, mama, I looked east and west. / I went to the crossroad, baby, I looked east and west. / Lord, I didn't have no sweet woman, ooh well, babe, in my distress."

Robert Johnson was looking for direction.

With the United States in a depression during the 1930s, much of the country's population was on the move, pulling out of Dust Bowl farms heading for greener pastures, more often than not west to California. The South had its own plague, repressive Jim Crow laws that were intended to rob the country's African American population of economic and political opportunity and inflict violence on them. For poor Blacks struggling in the South, important escape hatches from the repression were home-grown parties, fish fries, and black township juke joints, with hooch and hot music supplied by locals. These loose gatherings created a group of musicians who played what might be called country blues. Those talented men and women who had greater ambition looked to move on from the small towns of the South. Starting early in the twentieth century, for those in the Delta region along the great Mississippi, the easiest escape route was north on the Highway 61, not yet fully paved, which led first to Memphis and the bustling nightspots of Beale Street. If even Memphis was too small, one continued north to St. Louis and either headed west to Kansas City or continued on to Chicago.

As noted in earlier chapters, during the 1930s families from the Texas and Oklahoma areas headed west to California for jobs and that included musicians who looked for better opportunities to record, as there wasn't then a stable recording industry in the South. However, some musicians instead headed to the one place in the region where there was opportunity to play to bigger audiences: New Orleans, which was where jazz originated at the end of the 1800s. Louis Armstrong may have left New Orleans for Chicago, but the same wild clubs and nightlife that created opportunity for him were still going strong a half century later. Then, in the post–World War II years, this region from New Orleans to Houston finally established places to record.

This brings us back to Robert Johnson. Like other bluesmen from the South, he played mostly juke joints and busked on street corners – basically anywhere he could make pocket change. He is believed to have only entered

FEELIN' SAD

a recording studio twice, during the mid-1930s, in San Antonio and then in Dallas. Both sessions were with pioneering record producer Don Law, an Englishman who immigrated to Alabama in the 1920s. After starting out as a bookkeeper with Brunswick Records in Dallas, he moved over to A&R and talent scout for American Record Corporation, which took over Brunswick. Although Law is most famous for his country music discoveries, including Bob Wills, Lefty Frizzell and Marty Robbins, in 1936 and 1937 he was the guy who pushed Robert Johnson in front of a microphone, recording almost thirty songs.

So, when he came to the crossroads, Robert Johnson must have taken Highway 61 south, not north. It would have taken him straight to Baton Rouge, Louisiana, where he would have needed to make a second decision as to which direction his life would take. The obvious choice was eastward to New Orleans. Instead, he shifted his guitar and rucksack to a comfortable position on his back and headed west to Texas.

He wasn't the only Mississippi Delta musician to turn south on Highway 61. Eddie Jones (Guitar Slim) was born in Greenwood, Mississippi, on December 10, 1926. His father Sam Jones never lived with his mother. As a child Guitar Slim either never knew his father or learned who he was but avoided the man because he was neither fatherly nor welcoming. Sam Jones lived on Race Track Plantation, according to the Mississippi Blues Commission.

Eddie's mother died when he was five. As a result, he was raised by his grandmother on the L. C. Hays Plantation in Hollandale, Mississippi, a town on Highway 61 about fifty-five miles southwest of Greenwood and eighty miles due south of Clarksdale (up the road on Highway 61). While growing up, Guitar Slim spent time working in the fields, sometimes plowing behind a mule. His first public singing was in church.

In the late 1940s, money was tight across the South, but there was hard work available. One of those jobs meant working all Sunday at a cotton press. A man could work a full day and get paid in cash when the stint was over. A childhood friend of Guitar Slim told an interviewer in the early 2000s that Eddie worked the press all day, got paid in the evening, "balled" all night, and on Monday at about 9:00 a.m. started walking down Highway 61, heading south toward the Gulf.

Eddie Jones was an unusual kid for the Mississippi Delta. In truth, he probably would have been an unusual adolescent anywhere in the United States, since he was quite a dandy. This might have made him the object of derision or scorn for some, but two childhood friends claimed Eddie could always deflect with comedy. There were some boys around town who would come around to "pick on him," but he could always jump back out of danger, hop about or do a little dance. Childhood friend Julius Ballard said of him, "He was real nice, perhaps too nice." That might have been a good thing, though, because many of his contemporaries ended up running afoul of the law or beaten down by Jim Crow repression.

Before he was a musician, Eddie drew attention to himself with clothes and his dancing. In the Delta, many African Americans owned just one pair of shoes or, with good fortune two pairs. Eddie had more. Becoming a young man, Eddie discovered that if he painted his shoes, either black or white, he could get a better look. He owned a going-out-at-night silky shirt with big sleeves, and sometimes he wore a straw hat. And on the weekends he would head off to the juke joints whose owners, bartenders, waitresses, and patrons were all African American. "He could dance with two women better than the average person could dance with one woman. He would jump and come down doing the splits. He could lean back on his heels until his head touched the floor. If he drank enough beer, there weren't enough women for him," said Ballard. The older he got, the greater was Eddie's charisma, and at this point it was all because of his diabolically acrobatic moves on the dance floor.

To be able to party all night, even if just drinking beer at a juke joint, one had to work, and that meant moving around the Delta region to wherever the jobs were. Sometimes this meant bunkhouse jobs, when a lot of workers were needed at one time for an extended period and basic housing had to be supplied.

What happened next in the Guitar Slim story is a little fuzzy. According to Larry Birnbaum, Eddie's exuberant dancing attracted attention at a Hollandale club, and, around 1948, blues guitarist Willie D. Warren hired him to dance with his band, later letting him sing with the group, all the while teaching him to play guitar. When he had spare time, Ballard said, he would hang out on Morgan Street in Hollandale, where there was a pawn shop with used musical instruments, and the owner would allow to Eddie to play at will. According to Birnbaum, Guitar Slim toured with Willie D. through the end of the 1940s.

Louisiana music curator David Kunian offers another version of the story. Kunian says that Willie D. Warren was an Arkansas boy whose family moved to Lake Village, Arkansas, around 1937 when he was about thirteen. He quickly learned guitar and formed his own band, which gigged around the Delta region. Kunian tracked down one of the musicians who played

FEELIN' SAD

with Willie D. in his later Detroit years. In this musician's memory (of hearing Willie D.'s recollection), Willie D. was working in the Lake Village area driving a tractor on a big farm that employed a lot of people. One of the new kids working there was Eddie Jones. The work was hard, but on the weekends everyone would drink, break out the instruments, and kick up a storm of dust. Catching Willie D's attention (and everyone else's) was Eddie, with his remarkable dancing. He was a contortionist, an acrobat, and an incredible entertainer. Willie D. liked the kid and started teaching him guitar chords. Eddie had a real good ear for the music and was able to conquer the guitar "real quick."

Hollandale and Greenwood were a lot closer to Memphis than to New Orleans, and in the late 1940s more Delta musicians headed north. However, Lake Village, Arkansas, was in the southeast corner of the state, about twenty miles from the Louisiana state line. If Eddie did spend some time gigging with Willie D.'s combo in Louisiana, he would have gotten an earful about New Orleans. Sometime after the job in Lake Village ended, Eddie apparently headed back to Hollandale, but he already knew where he would be in the near future. Saying good-bye to friends and family, like Robert Johnson at the crossroads farther north on Highway 61, Eddie began looking for a ride out of town. He too wanted to go south, but not to Texas. He was headed to the Crescent City. The year was 1950, and he was about to have a new persona: Guitar Slim.

From the advent of recorded music early in the twentieth century through the World War II years, the best recording studios were in New York and Los Angeles. In Nashville, the first serious homegrown recording began in 1946 when three engineers from WSM radio launched Castle Recording Studios. By the following year, Castle had moved from the radio station to a bigger space at the old Tulane Hotel. That year, 1947, one of the major record companies in the country, Decca, took advantage of Castle's location in the heart of hillbilly music country to record soon-to-be-famous singers Ernest Tubb and Red Foley. That was also the breakthrough year for another southern entrepreneurial effort, J&M Recording Service in New Orleans.

After World War II, a young man named Cosimo Matassa was looking for a business to start in his hometown of New Orleans. At first he came up with the idea of selling appliances and bought an old grocery store on the corner of North Rampart and Dumaine Street to house his new business. To add income to the slow-selling appliances, Cosimo also began selling records. Despite New Orleans's musical history, in the late 1940s there wasn't a major record store there, and pretty soon records were providing the bulk of Matassa's income, so he shifted gears and created J&M Music Shop. Matassa never locked into one mercantile path. When something new, interesting, and potentially lucrative came along, he jumped. Due to the success of the record business, getting to know local musicians, and having realized that there were no established recording studios in New Orleans, he opened a recording studio at the rear of his store in 1945 or, more likely, 1946.

Matassa told Jeff Hannusch: "It seemed to me that a recording outlet for a city with so much music in it was a good idea. I had attended technical school during the war so I decided to try and open a studio. I bought a brand new Duo-Press disc cutter, set it up in one of the building's back rooms and opened the J&M Recording Service. We cut direct to disc on that machine. That means we recorded the actual master right there in the booth."

Business was slow at first, servicing local school groups and glee clubs. Then a New Jersey record company, Deluxe Records, started coming down to New Orleans scouting for rhythm and blues singers and found nothing but talent and more talent, recording, among others, Dave Bartholomew and Annie Laurie, who sang the first hit version of "Since I Fell for You," which later in the 1960s was an even bigger hit for Lenny Welch. With nowhere else to turn, Deluxe recorded all the singers at J&M Recording Service. They were so pleased with the results that they came back again in 1947 and recorded Roy Brown's "Good Rockin' Tonight," which many musicologists feel was the immediate precursor to rock 'n' roll if not the first of the genre.

"Good Rockin' Tonight" was such a hot record that Syd Nathan of Cincinnati-based King Records bought a majority interest in Deluxe, along with Roy Brown's contract and unreleased masters. This caught the attention of Lew Chubb at Imperial Records in Los Angeles. He had already scouted Texas a couple of years before, but then he was mostly recording country and western singers before rolling into Houston and meeting with Dave Bartholomew. The Deluxe deal revived his interest in the Gulf region. Deluxe may have discovered all that talent in New Orleans, but he knew that he could do better – he knew people there, and he knew people who knew people. The year was 1949. Rick Coleman writes in *Blue Monday: Fats Domino and the Lost Dawn of Rock 'n' Roll*: "Dave Bartholomew was astonished to see a short white man in a suit standing on his steps at 1561 La Freniere Street. . . . Two years after he'd met Bartholomew at the Bronze

Peacock in Houston, Lew Chudd had finally arrived. . . . Bartholomew drove Chudd to the black business district where they met a sandy-haired, middle-aged man from New Jersey, Al Young, at his Bop Shop record store at 302 South Rampart. Young was a musical prospector, who . . . hung out in black nightclubs listening to music and drinking heavily."

Young was the one from whom Deluxe Records learned about the talent in New Orleans. He also distributed Imperial Records. Bartholomew and Young didn't cotton to each other, but each had their special talents. Young had great contacts in New Orleans, especially with the disc jockeys, and he had a knack for promotion – some would say self-promotion. Bartholomew was a musician with vision and skill. He also had his own band, with some very skilled musicians including Earl Palmer on drums, Red Tyler on tenor sax, and Salvador Doucette on piano. Theard Johnson was the original vocalist for the group, but they occasionally used a fellow named Tommy Ridgely who had a higher voice. If they needed a woman singer, Jewel King would step in.

For Imperial's first recording session in New Orleans at J&M Recording, Bartholomew brought in his band. He also arranged and produced those first recordings for Ridgely and King. It was King who had Imperial's first hit record out of New Orleans, a jaunty blues number, "3×7=21," about a young woman who turns twenty-one who wants to go out and have fun. The songwriter was the multitalented Bartholomew. The red label notes the record number, 5055, and around the outside it reads: "Manufactured by Imperial Record Company Inc., 137–39 North Western Avenue, Los Angeles, California."

Chudd didn't really like the "primitive" equipment at J&M Recording and felt the recordings were "muddy," but he had quickly made a hit record there so he asked Bartholomew if he knew anyone else. The city was rife with boogie-woogie piano players, and Bartholomew pulled in John Leon Gross, who performed as Archibald. He updated an old blues number about a gambling dispute that ends in murder, which he called "Stack-A-Lee." Like Jewel King's recording, Archibald's song made the charts. (The song would be a number one hit for Lloyd Price in 1959 as "Stagger Lee.")

In his biography of Fats Domino, Coleman describes Imperial's next find. "Before Chudd left town, he decided to check out a boogie and blues pianist in the Ninth Ward. . . . He called Bartholomew, and together with Young, they traveled down bumpy roads past the Club Desire to a ramshackle club. . . . the Hideaway. . . . They were shocked to see the bar packed with revelers. Antoine 'The Fat Man' Domino was rocking the house."

Bartholomew knew Domino because he occasionally sat in with his band, and he introduced him to Chudd, who loved Domino's jingly piano style, particularly on the rousing "Junker Blues." They decided to record Domino at J&M, but there was problem because "Junker Blues" was a song about drugs. Perhaps Bartholomew remembered Chudd recording "Fat Man" Hamilton, or maybe Domino was by then known as "Fat Man," but in any case Bartholomew turned "Junker Blues" inside out, rewriting it as "The Fat Man." In December 1949, Bartholomew brought his band to J&M to play behind Domino, and they recorded "The Fat Man" and a number of other tunes in a session that lasted close to six hours. The Imperial 78 carried the number 5058, and the songwriters were listed as Bartholomew-Domino.

The song became popular and was number thirty-two on the list of top R&B singles of 1950, according to *Big Al Pavlow's The R&B Book: A Disc-History of Rhythm and Blues*. Jewel King's "3×7=21" was number thirty-four. Among the better-known R&B songs that year were Ivory Joe Hunter's "I Almost Lost My Mind (number six)," Nat King Cole's "Mona Lisa" (number eighteen), Larry Darnell's "For You My Love" (number three), and three versions of "Rag Mop" (numbers twenty-three, twenty-nine, and forty-six).

Antoine Domino became Fats Domino, and his career skyrocketed. Every musician within two hundred miles of New Orleans came to J&M Recording, and the city was afire with some of the best rhythm and blues singers and musicians in the country. No wonder Guitar Slim opted to go south instead of north to Memphis. New Orleans was where it was happening, baby, and he finally arrived in 1950.

When stepping down the streets of New Orleans for the first time, Guitar Slim was still Eddie Jones, a tall, lanky, handsome dude who was very distinguished dresser, stylish to some odd extremes. Some writers say he was given the name Guitar Slim, while others believe he chose it. Regardless, the appellation fit him like the color-coordinated clothes he liked to wear. The name change wasn't accepted immediately. It took about year of making a musical spectacle of himself before his birth name began to slip into history.

In his book *Deep Blues*, Robert Palmer summed up Guitar Slim's arrival this way: "By the time he arrived in New Orleans in the later 1940s [actually 1950] and put together a trio with the future rock and roll star Huey Piano Smith, Jones was singing the way sanctified preachers preached – groaning, screaming, torturing almost every syllable, investing even the most shopworn blues lines with what would later be called 'soul power.' . . . He was also an astonishing guitarist with his own almost frighteningly intense version of T-Bone Walker style and an individual way of wresting screaming high-note sustains from his overworked amplifier."

Guitar Slim's physical relationship with that amplifier was important. As Gaynel Hodge remembers, even by the early 1950s everyone who played electric guitar had just a short cord, maybe five feet long, between the guitar and amplifier, but "Slim got one so long that he could go out into the audience . . . it was so long he could go outside and run."

Indeed, Guitar Slim used the long cord to walk bar tops, traipse into the audience, and sometimes keep walking right out of a club and onto the street while still playing. And he played loud. Earl King claims that Guitar Slim was getting fuzztone distortion before anyone else. Another trick of his: drowning out opening acts by warming up loudly backstage.

Guitar Slim knew how to attract a crowd. Art Neville recalled, "No one was sharper than Guitar Slim. . . . He had come to New Orleans with a guitar cord long enough to let him play out on the street and draw people in like the Pied Piper. Slim was always causing a sensation."

New Orleans singer Gerry Hall, who would eventually join Huey Piano Smith and the Clowns, said she came across Guitar Slim because when he first came to New Orleans he moved into her neighborhood, which had a corner bar that was very popular, especially for young people. After the bar closed on a Saturday night, Hall said, you would hear this whining guitar – even though it might have been daybreak. One morning she woke up and couldn't believe she was hearing a guitar, because the parties had broken up hours before. She put on some clothes to go see what was happening. At a boardinghouse nearby, where Hall's girlfriend lived with her mother, Guitar Slim had taken a room. "I didn't know who he was, but it didn't matter when he came in, whether it was noon or two in the morning, he would play that guitar up, sing, serenade the whole neighborhood."

Since he was not yet known, one New Orleans musician recalled, the hardworking Guitar Slim had a day job toiling at a sausage factory in town. No one ever commented on whether he found a moment for sleeping.

About the same time, Robert Parker, who led the house band at the popular nightspot Club Tiajuana (that's really how the name was spelled), was heading to a local eatery called Sam's for a po' boy sandwich when he saw a crowd gathered out front. There were so many people that they spilled off the sidewalk and onto the street. From a distance, Parker first thought there was a fight, but when he got closer he realized it was a guitarist playing. Sam, the owner of the eatery, allowed Guitar Slim to plug in at the restaurant and let the cord run out a window to reach the street corner, where he was entertaining. He looked like a prospect, so Parker went back to the club and told the owner, Oscar Bolden Jr., about this guitarist who drew a lot of people to street gigs. Bolden then went to talk with Guitar Slim. Parker said, "They got together and Mr. Bolden gave him a room at the back of club [a place to stay]."

The Tiajuana was at one time part of the Gold Leaf Hotel and like some other African American clubs in the South usually had rooms to rent for musicians who came into town. In the South, clubs and accommodations were often part of the same structure, and if a musician was in residence for an extended gig, he or she could make a long-term rental. It wasn't the ritziest club in town, but the Tiajuana had a good enough reputation that guys like Dave Bartholomew would hang out there looking for talent. The accommodations were decent, and the club was a riot of entertainment – what more could an up-and-coming musician ask for?

Willie Norman "Bill" Sinegal, a New Orleans hero for his Mardi Gras song "Second Line," was twenty-two years old when Guitar Slim hit town. The two quickly became friends, and sometimes Sinegal, who played bass guitar, would sit in with Guitar Slim's band. In an interview with Hannusch, he retold a story Guitar Slim had imparted to him about how he had come to New Orleans. It was something about a friend of Guitar Slim having killed a white man and Guitar Slim's having sold a guitar to raise money to help his friend get out of town. When word got out that Guitar Slim had helped the man, his life was in danger, so he bought a ticket to New Orleans. It was hard to say if there was any truth to that tale, but Sinegal did vouch that Guitar Slim had worked in a sausage factory in Arabi, Louisiana, and lived at the Gold Leaf Hotel atop the Club Tiajuana.

Good musicians notice good musicians. Soon after his arrival in New Orleans, Guitar Slim was introduced to a high school student named Huey Smith, who was said to be a fine, bluesy piano player. Guitar Slim immediately recognized oodles of raw talent in the lad and, more importantly, someone who had that pure joy of entertaining. Quickly they joined forces.

Over the long haul, Huey would have something that Guitar Slim didn't have – a rounded career. He would become a session musician, bandleader, singer, and songwriter with a number of chart-making hits. He was so in tune with Guitar Slim's exuberance for performance that he named his best-known group Huey Piano Smith and His Clowns, employing rock 'n' roll's first successful drag queen, the talented Bobby Marchan, who had a number one R&B hit in 1960 with "There's Something on Your Mind." Even Huey's best-known hits were more fun than serious, including "Rockin' Pneumonia and the Boogie Woogie Flu Part 1" (a top ten pop hit for Johnny Rivers in 1972), "Sea Cruise" (a number fourteen record for Frankie Ford in 1959), and, with his own band, "Don't You Just Know It," a top ten hit in 1958.

New Orleans music producer Wade Wright, locally known as "Wacko," started out in the business as a drummer. Four years after "Don't You Just Know It," Huey Smith was in town playing Kate's Club when his drummer got sick. Wacko says:

> My mother was the program manager at a black radio station. One of the disc jockeys asked my mother, "Doesn't your son play the drums? Because Huey needs a drummer real fast." She called, and I went down there. I didn't know it was a black club until I got there. Everyone was black except me. But I went in and asked for Huey. He was sitting at the piano. I said, "I heard you need a drummer." I ended up as the only white guy in the band. I was about eighteen years old, and I played all night until the sun came up the next morning. Huey was slick and had a good band. Robert Parker played saxophone. Saxophonist Red Tyler was there too. Bobby Marchan sang; he was out of his mind, drinking firewater. He was gay, but he chased the skirts. You know if the cops would have come in the joint they would have taken me to jail for crossing the segregation line.

Huey also had one other thing that Guitar Slim didn't have – a long life. Indeed, in the rough world of popular music, he hung around long enough to get ripped off in countless ways. Huey would record the original "Rockin' Pneumonia" for Ace Records in 1957. It was a huge R&B hit and sold a million records but didn't have equal success on the pop charts. Huey had to put Ace Records owner Johnny Vincent's name on the record as cowriter of the song, and Vincent would treat Huey even worse on "Sea Cruise." Huey wrote, arranged and sang on the recording, but Ace replaced the vocal track with one by a young white singer named Frankie Ford, and that was the record that became a hit. Smith eventually quit the business and became a Jehovah's Witness. He died impoverished at the age of eighty-six.

But all that was in the future. In the beginning, it was two talented young musicians on the make. When Guitar Slim arrived in New Orleans, Huey was a student at Walter L. Cohen High School in the city and had his own combo, the Joy Jumpers, which, despite his age, was gigging in local clubs. Guitar Slim was scrounging for a showcase. One veteran piano player remembered seeing him playing for drinks at the Savoy Club. A friend of Huey's told him about this guitar player who sounded like Gatemouth Brown and often came into his father's store. Huey wanted to meet him, so his friend called him when Guitar Slim came by. The two played a few songs together and realized they had compatibility. They started playing as a duo at the Hotel Foster on LaSalle Street.

One day while Huey was in school, another student tapped him on the shoulder and said there was a man outside looking for him. As Huey Piano Smith's biographer John Wirt, tells the story: "Slim's appearance, including orange hair and pant legs of contrasting bright colors, tickled the students. They crowded the school's windows, laughing at the man outside who resembled a clown. But Slim had something serious on his mind. 'Come on, boy,' he yelled to Huey. 'The man at the Tiajuana want us to play on intermission.'"

They did so well that owner Oscar Bolden turned to them when one of the club's featured performers, singer-pianist Spider Bocage (also known as Eddie Bo), left for an extended engagement in Mexico. The duo added a drummer, Willie Nettles, and became the permanent seven-night-a-week replacement.

Wirt interviewed Huey before he died, and Huey explained how they sounded. He would have to adapt to Guitar Slim's habit of not completing all twelve bars, or measures, of a song, which is called "jumping time." Huey told Wirt, "Slim was going to the wrong place, and I went wrong with him. The people didn't feel it because we were wrong together."

About that long cord? "That's what people used to be amazed about," Huey told Wirt. "And he turned that thing up loud, and you heard it all down the block. And he played it behind his head, acting a fool. He was a performer."

"My friend Eddie Jones, who called himself Guitar Slim," B. B. King wrote in his autobiography, "would attach a long cable to his guitar and prowl through the audience, even roam out in the street. He'd duckwalk along the bar and do Olympic-quality gymnastics. He'd also wear crazy-colored clothes and dye his hair and give you a helluva show for your money."

Word about Guitar Slim, Willie Nettles, and Huey Piano Smith appearing at the Club Tiajuana was spilling out through the African American community – if not among all musicians in New Orleans. So it was not unexpected that the manager of the most popular black nightspot in the city came knocking. By the end of the summer, the Slim-Smith-Nettles trio opened at the most famous, craziest, most entertaining club in town, the Dew Drop Café. Or as the promotions once proclaimed: "The South's swankiest night spot." Guitar Slim would soon take residence in one of the apartments above the Dew Drop.

Another enterprising African American businessman, Frank Painia, originally acquired a hotel because he didn't feel there were decent accommodations for blacks when visiting New Orleans. The year was 1939, and he called his new venture the Dew Drop Inn. During the war years, New Orleans boomed, and the entrepreneurial Painia started booking jump-bluesmen and jazz acts to entertain the defense workers and military who washed through town. It was an easy decision to open up a nightclub at the Dew Drop. From the start, it wasn't just any old nightclub; the place was as risqué as it was musical. For two decades, the emcee was a drag queen known as Patsy Vidalia; comedians would open a show there; and shake dancers shook their booty. It seemed nothing was out of bounds for the Dew Drop. Most importantly, it was the place in New Orleans for about forty years where African American entertainers could perform. Besides the shows, there were late-night jam sessions. Painia plucked Larry Darnell out of a revue called Brownskin Models and gave him a job at the front bar, because he was boyishly good-looking, and customers, male and female, would drink up while watching him perform. Darnell had the number three R&B song in 1949, the romantic "For You My Love."

Blues guitarist Little Freddie King played in the house band at the Dew Drop for about four years in the early 1960s. Earl King, Little Richard, the gender-bending Esquerita, and Sugar Boy Crawford and his female vocal group the Sugar Lumps were regulars. When Freddie King was a teenager he worked at a macaroni factory in New Orleans and after work would stop at a little club on Magazine Street where Guitar Slim would play. "We drank together a couple of times, and he and I would talk about music," King recalled. "He was a hard-drinking guy and he loved his women. He chased a lot of women. He was also a good singer and real good guitar player. He played the roots of blues. I even went to see him play twice, and he still was putting on a number one good show.

Guitar Slim's son Rodney Glenn Armstrong, who took the name Guitar Slim Jr., tells a story of hanging out with Earl King at the Dew Drop Inn in the 1960s. "Earl was the one who started calling me Guitar Slim Jr. back when I was learning to play the bass. My brother Barry already taught me how to play the guitar, because my daddy had been dead about a decade. Anyway, Earl brought me by the Dew Drop. They gave me a guitar, and I didn't know how to play the blues. Earl and his band were heavily drinking, and they said to me play, 'The Things I Used to Do.' Earl was so far gone he thought I was my daddy."

Did Guitar Slim inspire him? King said he did. "I loved his songs so well

I used to practice them until they were automatic with me. When he played, I already knew his licks."

The first mention of Guitar Slim in the press came in a September 1950 issue of *Louisiana Weekly*. A review read: "New Orleans's newest gift to the show biz world is Guitar Slim, held over at the Dew Drop. The New Orleans blues sensation has made a terrific impact on blues fans in New Orleans. Acclaimed to be an exact carbon copy of Gatemouth Brown, the singing guitarist includes 'My Time Is Expensive,' 'Gatemouth Boogie' and several other performances by made popular by Brown."

Starting in the late 1940s, Percy Stovall was the premier source for live R&B entertainment throughout the bayou South. Almost every important New Orleans musician worked for Stovall at one time or another, writes Hannusch, who interviewed him before he died. Stovall's recollection was that he came home one evening and found Guitar Slim sitting on his porch. Guitar Slim wanted Stovall to be his booking agent, but Stovall wasn't interested. Guitar Slim's response was "Stove, you can make as much money in one night booking me as you do in a week now." It still took a lot of lobbying on Guitar Slim's part before Stovall came around.

At one point, Stovall worked Guitar Slim in tandem with the singer and guitar player Eddie Lee Langlois, who would eventually call himself Eddie Lang, but for a while was known as Little Eddie as he stood just over five feet in height. When they would play together at the Dew Drop, Slim would put him on his shoulders, and they both played their guitars as Guitar Slim marched into the audience. Sometimes they would stand on tables across the floor from each other and compete in guitar duels

When Guitar Slim was not at the Dew Drop, Stovall would book him regionally or at other clubs in New Orleans, including the Tiajuana. At first Stovall would book Guitar Slim into small towns, where the competition wasn't so intense. Stovall claimed he booked Guitar Slim on the same bill with Fats Domino in Monroe, Louisiana, in a kind of battle of the bands situation. Before the gig, the boastful Guitar Slim is said to have told the established Fats, "I'm gonna run you offa that stage tonight." That night, before a raucous, jammed crowd, Guitar Slim ended his performance by screeching his guitar while walking out the back door of the place and into a waiting car. Everyone was stunned, and management didn't know if they should wait for Guitar Slim to come back or push Fats Domino onto the stage. Guitar Slim didn't come back, and Fats came onstage and said, "Ain't gonna be no battle tonight. You just saw it."

As B. B. King noted, "If you were a guitarist looking for a cutting contest, you wouldn't wanna mess with Slim." Guitar Slim was so good, Stovall booked him for return gigs at places he had already played. And just like that he was back at Club Tiajuana. From the April 28, 1951, issue of *Louisiana Weekly:* "Guitar Slim continues to pack them in as a headliner, where his combo jumps each weekend with Huey Smith Jr. on piano. And Little Willie Nettles on drums. The place is constantly packed with the New Orleans café crowd."

Meanwhile, the competition for Lew Chudd's attention never abated between Al Young and David Bartholomew, whom Billy Vera called "the middleman in New Orleans between the record companies and the artists." Around mid-1951, David and Chudd got into what Vera called a tiff. It began at the end of November when Fats Domino went out on tour backed by Bartholomew and his band. It was a grueling slog, with money squabbles and a blizzard. The only good to come out of it was during a stop in Kansas City, when David got to enjoy one of the city's "Blue Monday" shows, Monday evening club performances on Vine Street. Upon leaving town, Bartholomew jotted down "Blue Monday," thinking it would make a nifty title for a song. Back in New Orleans, Bartholomew went to talk with Al Young at his record store. Bartholomew barely made a dime from the tour (likewise Fats), but there was Young waving a year-end bonus check he'd received, $1,500 from Chudd. As Rick Coleman writes, Chudd had "thoughtlessly forgotten Bartholomew, who had not only produced Imperial's hit records but also went through hell in the two tours with Domino promoting them. The bandleader assumed a racial motive. He took his frustration back to his wife, Pearl. In a fit of anger, Bartholomew determined to quit Imperial."

Vera is a fan of Lew Chudd, calling him a "fair guy," which in Vera's book is high praise. At the time, most record producers were exploitive to their very core. "When I was a consultant for Specialty," he said, "we hired a woman who used to work for Chudd in his royalties department. She was an older woman, and I asked her about Lew. She said he was very fair to the artists. 'His rule to me was if the royalties come in an odd number, make sure the artists get the extra penny.'"

Why Chudd didn't compensate Bartholomew is anyone's guess, but it would prove a problem for Guitar Slim. Record companies had become aware of Guitar Slim's performances and the kinds of crowds he attracted. Imperial came knocking just as Bartholomew, the label's A-team producer and technically the leader of the house band at J&M Recording, was walking out the door. Chudd's decision was to have Al Young produce. It was a mistake.

The first six months of 1951 were not Imperial's best in New Orleans. Even with Big Jay McNeely, Fats Domino, and Smiley Lewis in the studio, there were no hits to be had. According to Huey Piano Smith biographer Wirt, Guitar Slim and Huey Smith auditioned separately for David Bartholomew. Huey was turned down, while Guitar Slim was successful. By the time of Guitar Slim's recording session, though, Bartholomew had walked out and Young was in charge.

In May 1951, with Young as head of Imperial production in New Orleans, a slew of nonstarters came through studio, including talented but never-a-star Ernie Andrews, Ethel Davenport, Monte Easter, and Dan Grissom. By mid-May, it was Guitar Slim's turn. The record credits would read "Eddie 'Guitar Slim' Jones and His Playboys"; the band was just Huey Smith on piano and Willie Nettles on drum. The group recorded four tunes. The first record was "Bad Luck Is On Me," with "New Arrival" on the B-side, and the second was "Standin' at the Station," with "Cryin' in the Morning" on the B-side. Young muscled Guitar Slim to get cowriting credits for all the songs.

As it turned out, Young initially wouldn't see much in the way of royalties from any of the songs. "The session was rather chaotic . . . and the records sounded and sold poorly," writes Hannusch. Vera's take wasn't much kinder. "If you can judge anything by the Guitar Slim records, Young certainly was not a good producer. There was a lack of quality in those sessions for Imperial." In fact, Vera found the Guitar Slim recordings on Imperial so dismaying that he maintains Huey Smith, whom he called "a straight-ahead guy and serious musician," was not in the studio for those recordings. "You can tell it is not him," he said. "The band consisted of really very poor-quality musicians."

The records, if not the history of the songs, disappeared and were forgotten by all except dedicated Guitar Slim fans.

Although Imperial never asked Guitar Slim to record again, the company re-released both records in 1954 after he hit big with "The Things I Used To Do." The original recordings were so obscure that "Standin' at the Station" garnered a review by *Billboard* magazine in its October 9, 1954, issue as if it was a new recording: "The Southern blues chanting style stands out as usual on this Guitar Slim reading. The guy's many fans will want this. Good wax here." For the B-side "New Arrival," the same reviewer took note of Guitar Slim's musicianship: "This is standard blues on which Slim's guitar solos take top honors."

The June 30, 1951, *Louisiana Weekly* reported, "Guitar Slim continues to hold the blues spotlight at the Tiajuana Club at 1205 S. Saratoga, where he is holding forth nightly with his combo. The crowds constantly pack the place especially on Friday, Saturday and Sunday nights."

FEELIN' SAD

Stovall, who was blind, began booking the trio of Guitar Slim, Huey Smith, and Willie Nettles in small towns within a day's drive of New Orleans. They traveled in Stovall's vintage limousine, often with Nettles driving. The equipment was in a trailer the big limo pulled. This tour was a miniature version of the chitlin' circuit that any southern African American musician had to play to make money. Someone like Roy Brown would finish a gig, and then the trio would pull in. Then they would check out, and another bluesman would check in. The population in these locations, generally small communities in the heart of a wider agricultural area, was so starved for entertainment that the shows generally sold out. For the musicians, the money was decent.

By 1952, Stovall was booking the trio, now with Little Eddie Lang, on a wider loop and in bigger southern cities, including Nashville. Lang was sixteen at the time. Wirt writes, "Known as the Boy Wonder, Lang played guitar just like B. B. King. Lang and Guitar Slim made a crowd-thrilling pair. Business started coming, like water from a pitcher. Everybody wanted to see that little boy and the man walking tables, walking the bar." In later years, Little Eddie was one of the original members of Jessie Hill's House Rockers. New Orleans singer Jessie Hill's biggest hit was "Ooh Poo Pah Doo," which rose to number twenty-eight on the pop charts in 1960.

In Nashville, the group played Grady's Supper Club and possibly the Kitty Kat Club . Also while there, Stovall was able to arrange a recording session for Guitar Slim and Eddie Lang with local producer Jim Bulleit.

In 1946, Bulleit and C. V. Hitchcock founded Bullet Records in Nashville. Bulleit was also an early investor in Sun Records in Memphis. The company advertised "hillbilly records from the home of the Grand Ole Opry." The label's biggest hit was "Near You," by orchestra leader Francis Craig. The pop tune stayed atop the record charts for seventeen weeks in 1947. It was the first Nashville-produced record to sell over a million copies and forced major labels such as Decca to open an office in the city so as to stay competitive in the hillbilly market. Bullet was the first to record country singers Chet Atkins, Pee Wee King, and Sheb Wooley. The label also recorded gospel and blues. Cecil Gant recorded with Bullet, and the label also released B. B. King's first commercial single "Miss Martha King."

Bullet Records couldn't find a successful follow-up to "Near You," and two years after its release Jim Bulleit sold out to his partners. He then opened Bullet Enterprises, a holding company for several labels focusing on hillbilly, blues, and gospel, all of which required less production than pop records by orchestra leaders and thus were cheaper to make. In an early ad for "New Bullet Records," Bulleit listed records in a hillbilly series, a gospel series and a blues series ("Sepia").

Probably in late 1951, Bulleit announced plans to form a new label to be called J–B Records. With Nashville getting crowded with record companies, Bulleit scouted for country music talent in Texas, finding the likes of Ray Price, whose first record "Jealous Lies" was on Bullet. In late 1951, at the Blackstone Hotel in Fort Worth, Bulleit recorded a country singer by the name of Johnny Mathis (not the black singer Johnny Mathis of "Chances Are" fame), and he released a Mathis record the following year on the J–B label with fine print reading "Jim Bulleit Record Co.; Nashville, Tenn."

In Nashville, Bulleit issued the Little Eddy recording of "My Baby Left Me," with "Darling You Know I Love You" on the B-side, on his Bullet label, but the Guitar Slim offering of "Feelin' Sad" with the even more gospel sounding "Certainly All" came out on the newer J–B. Jeff Hannusch interviewed David Lastie, who played sax on the record. Lastie recalled, "We was working at the Kitty Kat Club in Nashville, and me, Huey, Little Eddie Lang, and Willie Nettles did the session with Slim. 'Feelin' Sad' was a good little record, it had a church sound to it. We worked pretty good off it."

The song begins with piano notes from Huey and Guitar Slim moaning a wordless dirge, and you wonder just where it's going. Then Guitar Slim sings: "The way I love you, darling it's a sin. You mended my heart you broke once, baby. But now you broken my heart again." A third verse speaks to current events of the day: "I was in Korea in '51 / I had no love and that was no home / I would send you all my money, baby / And all the time you were doing me wrong." The whole thing ends with Guitar Slim asking friends to pray with him. It is a strange song. Palmer called it "unadulterated backcountry gospel with secular lyrics." He was a huge fan, writing, "The song's eight bar verse form and melody line, the piano accompaniment, the discreet horn section, which contributed chords the way an organ might have – almost everything about the record was gospel rather than blues or pop." Bulleit pushed the record, and it became in hit in South.

In the December 6, 1952, issue *Cash Box*, a one-column ad, stretching from the top to the bottom of page 19 was headed "'Jim Bulleit's Back with Three Big Hits on His New J-B Label!" And the first record mentioned is "Feelin' Sad" ("It broke in New Orleans for a national race hit"). Also noted are pop singer Carole Wilson's "Contented" and Bob West's "Weeds of Hate" ("breaking for a big hit in the folk field"). At the bottom it read: "Contact your nearest distributor or call Jim Bulleit, 421 Bway, Nashville, Tenn., Phone 5–3563."

FEELIN' SAD

The next week, "Feelin'; Sad" made it to *Cash Box*'s "Rhythm 'n Blues Reviews," the songs expected to be hits. On December 13, 1952, the breakout song was Little Walter's "Sad Hours," while the sleeper of the week was Dinah Washington's version of the standard "I Cried for You." Neither song would be a big hit. The remaining fourteen selections on the list included records by Charlie Parker ("Tico Tico") and Tito Puente ("El Mambo"). Another "Fat Man" showed up – Fat Man Matthews and his record "Later Baby" was a pick. And a couple of friends were represented: Dave Bartholomew ("Who Drank the Beer While I Was in the Rear") and Larry Darnell ("Christmas Blues").

The review for "Feelin' Sad": "Eddie Jones gives an emotional performance as he renders the slow beat blues expressively. The effect of dramatic arrangement is heightened by the tearful vocal. This waxing will reach the listener." About the B-side, "Certainly All," the review said, "A spirited quick beat bounce, sung with a joyful treatment by the western artist. The happy feeling is aided by a rhythmic handclapping."

That issue of *Cash Box* also looked at the top ten blues records netting "heaviest play" on the radio, focusing on six markets: Harlem, Chicago's South Side, New Orleans, Philadelphia, Savannah, and Memphis. Willie Mabon's "I Don't Know" was number one in Harlem, Chicago, and Memphis. Little Walter's "Juke" was number one in Savannah, the Clovers' "Hey, Miss Fannie" was number one in Philadelphia, and Guitar Slim's "Feelin' Sad" was number one in New Orleans. On January 17, 1953, *Cash Box* looked at five of the same six locations, adding Houston and dropping Savannah. Willie Mabon's "I Don't Know" was now number one in all cities, but "Feelin' Sad" was still doing well in New Orleans, hanging in at number seven.

Vera once asked Jim Bulleit about the record. He responded, "I managed to get a little action going with it in Nashville and New Orleans." David Kunian simply said of the record that it "combined blues and gospel in a way that had never been done before. It attained a modest popularity around the South."

In 1953, Ray Charles covered the song in one of his earliest recordings at Atlantic Records. "I contend that what Ray got from Guitar Slim was the churchy-gospel passion," said Vera. "Before making the change he was a little better than average jump-blues singer. He didn't have that star quality yet."

CHAPTER 8

The Things That I Used To Do

Everyone comes to New Orleans – Sign Guitar Slim before anyone else – "Worst piece of Sh**" – "The Things That I Used To Do" number one – "The Story of My Life" esteemed today – Ray Charles borrows from Guitar Slim

The biggest change in the rhythm and blues market in 1952 came from urban areas where young men were singing group harmony that came to be called doo-wop. Among the doo-wop groups with top R&B songs that year were the Dominoes ("Have Mercy Baby"), the Clovers ("Ting-a-Ling," "Hey Miss Fannie," and "One Mint Julep"), and the Ravens ("Rock Me All Night Long"). Nevertheless, the market was still dominated by traditional R&B singers such as B. B. King with "3 O' Clock Blues," Willie Mabon and His Combo with "I Don't Know," and Ruth Brown with "5–10–15 Hours." New to the scene were young R&B crooners like Johnny Ace with "My Song" and Chuck Willis with "My Story."

And speaking of stories, if one dug a little deeper into the 1952 R&B charts, there was a good one in New Orleans, where Lloyd Price with "Lawdy Miss Clawdy" (number six R&B song of the year), Fats Domino with "Goin' Home" (number fifteen R&B song of the year); and Shirley and Lee with "I'm Gone" (number twenty-three R&B song of year) were all recorded at J&M but came out on different labels: Shirley and Lee on Aladdin, Fats Domino on Imperial, and Lloyd Price on Specialty. This came about because of the amazing talent in New Orleans and the falling out between Lew Chudd and Dave Bartholomew, as noted. The backing band in each recording was led by Dave Bartholomew.

Deluxe Records out of New Jersey was the first outside record company to arrive in New Orleans, and it was quickly followed by Los Angeles–based Imperial Records. Aladdin Records, founded in Los Angeles in 1945 by Eddie and Leo Mesner, was the next to arrive, in 1950. It was Eddie who made the journey to New Orleans looking for talent, and his first stop was to see Cosimo Matassa at his studio. Local girl Shirley Goodman, who was

THINGS THAT I USED TO DO

all of thirteen years old at the time, and a few friends had raised enough money to record a couple of songs at J&M. When Eddie Mesner was in the studio he happened to hear the tape of that recording, and, as Shirley said, "Eddie went crazy over it." More importantly, he went crazy over the girl singer with the high voice, Shirley.

Shirley recalled, "Eddie Mesner asked me if I'd like to make records, and I said, 'Yeah sure.' He wanted to put a boy's voice with mine. He auditioned all the boys who were in the group. He came up with Lee [Leonard Lee] because he had a deep, bluesy voice, and he thought we contrasted. I had known Lee and his family all my life, so things worked out between us." Four years later, Shirley and Lee would have a tremendous hit, "Let the Good Times Roll," which reached number one on the R&B charts and was an early crossover to the pop charts, where it was top twenty hit. After many years in pop music purgatory, Shirley would still later reemerge in the disco era of the 1970s with another hit record, "Shame, Shame, Shame."

Meanwhile, in 1952, falling out with Chudd gave Bartholomew the time and opportunity to work with other musicians and music executives, including Eddie Mesner. He produced the first three Shirley and Lee releases.

Hard on the heels of Eddie Mesner came Art Rupe, founder of Specialty Records in Los Angeles in 1944. Rupe was up to his neck in the West Coast created blinders for him. Doo-wop music was on the rise, especially in Watts, where he usually scouted for talent, but Rupe just didn't see it and so went looking for blues singers elsewhere. Philip Ennis claims that Rupe felt his LA musicians were "getting somewhat glib" and quoted him as saying about Los Angeles blues singers, "I didn't feel the spontaneity that I felt originally. Either I needed a change or they needed one."

Rupe could have gone anywhere, but he was already successful selling records in the South and had few good sales people in place, stretching from Jackson, Mississippi, to New Orleans. So he opted for New Orleans because he knew people there and was already a big fan of Fats Domino. "I was impressed with Fats Domino. I really dug him; liked his sound," Rupe said.

Ennis quotes Rupe: "I went down to find some talent in New Orleans and I made an announcement on a black radio show called *The Okey Dokey Radio Show* that I was looking for talent. I had no way of getting this talent to come to this recording studio, Cosimo Matassa's. It was one little recording studio in the black section, right off the French quarter there, where the black people went to."

In 1952, Bartholomew and his band dominated the recording sessions at Matassa's J&M. Still in the Imperial fold before the tiff with Chubb,

Bartholomew produced "Goin' Home" for Fats Domino, which became a number one R&B hit that year. A local disc jockey noted, "Dave . . . was a maestro when it came to arranging a session. Dave found the talent he needed in Fats. But Fats fooled him too. There was more talent there than what Dave originally thought, and Dave was able to mold it to sell millions of records."

Bartholomew told Jeff Hannusch, "I always felt Fats was a country and western singer because he didn't sing from the bottom. Fats played triplets at the piano; he got it from a guy called Little Willie Littlefield out in California. That was Fats' style; so once he started, he couldn't leave it, 'cause that's what the people wanted to hear."

While Rupe was in New Orleans looking for talent, Cosimo Matassa introduced him to Bartholomew, which was a big deal for the Californian, who realized Bartholomew had produced and played behind Fats Domino. When Rupe asked Bartholomew if there was anyone else around town worth recording, Bartholomew suggested a teenager making a name for himself, Lloyd Price. The backstory is that when Lew Chudd came to New Orleans three years before, he went to The Hideaway to hear Fats Domino. Lloyd Price was on the bill that the same night, but Chudd only had ears for Fats Domino and signed just him, ignoring Price. Although still in high school, Price got a job at radio station WBOK providing jingles, one of which included the phrase "Lawdy, Miss Clawdy." Price expanded the phrase into a full song, and, in March 1952, Price, Rupe, and Bartholomew and his band crowded into J&M Recording to the lay down tracks. Sitting in for the day was Fats Domino, who is tinkling the keys on the distinctive intro to the song, where Lloyd exclaims "Lawdy, lawdy, lawdy, Miss Clawdy." The next lines have the singer ogling Miss Clawdy but asking her not to excite him ("I know it can't be me").

The song was a major R&B hit in 1952, easily outdoing any Fats Domino entry for that year. Lloyd Price would have a long career in the music business.

The authors of *Rock of Ages: The Rolling Stone History of Rock and Roll* summed up the situation this way: "Both ['Goin' Home' and 'Lawdy, Miss Clawdy') were recorded at Cosimo Matassa's studio, because it was virtually the only place in town, and both featured members of Dave Bartholomew's band, because they seemed to have the hit formula. . . . 'Lawdy Miss Clawdy' had a medium-tempo bounce to it that defied you to forget it, and it wasn't long before black teenagers had invented a dance, the stroll, to go along with the song. It was becoming more evident every minute that New Orleans was a gold mine for independent rhythm-and-blues labels."

By most accounts, Rupe landed in New Orleans in 1952, although Hannusch says otherwise. The journey from California wasn't Rupe's first trip to the South, he says. Rather, Rupe had come in 1951 to Jackson, Mississippi, visiting with a young man named Johnny Vincent (John Vincent Imbragulio), who not only worked for Music Sales of New Orleans, an important independent record distributor for the Gulf region, but also owned a record store in Jackson. Rupe needed someone to promote his label throughout the South and hired Vincent, who quickly sold his record store and took over Specialty's New Orleans operations. The 1951 journey is not fully accepted by musicologists. Vera, who wrote a book about Specialty Records, doesn't think Vincent was signed so early. "Art did 'Lawdy Miss Clawdy' in March 1952, his first New Orleans session," Vera said. "Vincent wasn't with Specialty yet."

Vera called Vincent a hustler. New Orleans record producer Carlo Ditta, who knew Vincent in later years, laughingly labeled him a "redneck Italian." His tongue was firmly in cheek, because Ditta also claimed Italians in the South "didn't have [a] hang-up on race." Johnny Vincent got his start by hustling race records, Ditta added. "He was a colorful character and one of the true pioneers of rhythm and blues and American roots music."

Vincent was dedicated. He would pop bennies (speed) and stay up for days to chase down artists, going into places where few white folks would go in the 1950s. One could often find him at the Club Tiajuana or the Dew Drop, and many thought him a drug dealer. At the time in New Orleans, the illegal drug trade was run by the Mafia, and Carlos Marcello was the crime boss of the city. Except for some of the black nightspots, Marcello ran most of the clubs in New Orleans. Again, according to Ditta, "Vincent was dying to get in on all that action, the clubs, the music, alcohol, whores and money."

Supposedly it was Frank Painia, owner of the Dew Drop, who tipped off Vincent to Guitar Slim, but by 1953 Vincent would certainly have known who Guitar Slim was. He had become one of the biggest draws not only in New Orleans but also throughout the chitlin' circuit of the Gulf South. By this time Guitar Slim was residing at the Dew Drop, and Painia took on the duties of managing the singer, including his bookings.

New Orleans wasn't the only town in the South with African American entrepreneurs. Sixty miles west of New Orleans sits the small city of Thibodaux, Louisiana, and in 1932 a local man named Hosea Hill opened a bar there and called it the Sugar Bowl. It was open fourteen hours a day and managed to survive the Depression and World War II because one of the regular features of the place was a crap game. Eventually, Hill brought in musical entertainment, even forming a house band called Hosea Hill's Serenaders. By 1952, Hill was so successful that he bought an apartment building on Lagarde Street in Thibodaux and tore out the ground floor for a bar, café, and dance floor. As he began to bring in name acts, he and Frank Painia, who was in the talent management business, became friends and eventually business partners, booking acts together. When it was obvious to Painia that Guitar Slim's band was no longer holding together, he brought in a group of Hosea Hill's Serenaders, led by Lloyd Lambert, to back up Guitar Slim. Lambert claims it was Painia who introduced Guitar Slim to Johnny Vincent, but Huey Piano Smith always said he was the one who brought Guitar Slim to Victor Augustine's record shop (Doc Augustine's Novelty Shop on Dryades Street) to meet Johnny Vincent. That story jibes more closely with Vincent's recollection: "I went over to Doc's, where Slim used to rehearse at. Huey Smith and Earl King would be in there too. Slim was just a fantastic performer. Nobody could outperform him."

This wasn't a meet-someone-new get-together. The competitive and hustling Vincent was on a mission to sign Guitar Slim to Specialty. He had heard Guitar Slim was supposed to sign with Atlantic Records and was determined to get there first. As he later recalled, "This was one artist I just had to get," and he did.

For a guy who was living life in the largest way possible, with plenty of late-night jams, vast quantities of hooch, and platoons of women at the door, Guitar Slim also found time to write most of his songs. Guitarist Earl King told an interviewer, "Slim's room was something else, man. If you went up there, there'd always be about seven or eight women," and more importantly for Slim, "he'd have songs written with eyebrow pencil on pieces of paper tacked to the wall."

A friend of Guitar Slim, Bill Sinegal, claims "The Things That I Used to Do" was written a couple of years of before it was recorded. "He used to call me to his room and say, 'Sinegal come here and listen to this – nothin' can stop this from become a hit.'"

Earl King recalled that the idea for the tune came to Guitar Slim in his sleep. In a kind of Robert Johnson at the crossroads story, Guitar Slim, in his own telling, said in his dream he was met by the devil and an angel, both of whom held the lyrics to a song. And as in the Johnson tale, Guitar Slim opted to go with the devil, who gave him not musical genius but, close enough, the song "The Things That I Used to Do."

Johnny Vincent and Specialty Records got their man, who had a song to record, so what was left to do was roll over to J&M Recording and lay down tracks. On October 16, 1953, a small crowd of musicians drifted into J&M. This wasn't a Dave Bartholomew band; it was a Lloyd Lambert group. At the session he played bass and had Oscar Moore on drums. There were plenty of horn players, such as Frank Mitchell, Gus Fontenette, Charles Burbank, and Joe Tillman. Guitar Slim plucked his Gibson Gold-Top. One unique addition to the group was a young blind pianist named Ray Charles, who took over arrangement and production during the session.

Ray Charles made it to the recording because Vincent had bailed him out of jail after Charles was arrested for smoking weed outside the Dew Drop. It could have been worse. At the time, Charles was a heroin addict. In return for the bailout, Vincent asked Charles to do him a favor and sit in as pianist for the Guitar Slim recording session. No good deed goes unpunished, as Charles would find out, because recording "The Things We Used to Do" was, to use Ditta's word, "torture."

Ray Charles was born in Georgia as Ray Charles Robinson, raised in Florida, and by the time he was a teenager was already a seasoned musician, moving from one town to another. His first recording contract was with Swing Time Records, but he was still a raw talent and hadn't yet discovered his voice. In his early years he tried to sound like Nat King Cole.

As it had been for Guitar Slim, 1952 proved to be a defining year for Charles. First, Atlantic Records decided to take a chance on the pianist and bought out his contract from Swing Time. Then, by the end of the year, he was in New Orleans, booked into the Pelican Club, where the *Louisiana Weekly* reported he broke attendance records. Charles liked the musicianship he found in New Orleans and decided to stay for a while. As a resident, he couldn't help but hear Guitar Slim's "Feelin' Sad," which was very popular on New Orleans radio stations, and it resonated deeply with him. Charles was particularly impressed by Guitar Slim's combination of the blues and gospel in the same song.

When it was time for Atlantic to make its first Ray Charles record, the company's big guns, Ahmet Ertegun and Jerry Wexler, came to New Orleans from New York. Their first decision was not a good one. They would record at J&M but without Dave Bartholomew's band. Atlantic had used a group called the Gondoliers on a Joe Turner record, "Honey Hush," which became a number one hit, so they thought they would try their luck again and brought in the Gondoliers to back Charles. The recording session was in August 1953, and nothing brilliant came out of it, but there was one song that would prove to be prescient regarding Charles's future success as a singer, a cover of Guitar Slim's "Feelin' Sad."

Hannusch wrote: "When Charles listened to Slim he felt a revelation. Here was a blues artist baring his soul the same way an emotion-charged Baptist preacher would in front of his Sunday congregation. If an undisciplined musician could successfully combine gospel and the blues, why couldn't a skilled and schooled one like Ray Charles?"

Charles would have been happy to be at the recording session with Guitar Slim so if Vincent asked him for that favor, he would have jumped at the chance. As always, however, there is an alternative account of events. Frank Mitchell was also interviewed by Hannusch, and he claimed that Frank Painia had "hooked Slim up" with him and Ray.

In either case, Ray took over the recording session. "Slim ran the songs down," Mitchell added. "Ray came up with the horn charts and arrangements. I wrote them down for the other musicians." Matassa concurred: "Johnny Vincent was there, but he was more or less a cheerleader. Ray became the producer by default. He was real confident in his abilities and showed each musician what they should play. He kept the reins on Slim as best he could, which, believe me, wasn't easy."

How tough was it to record "The Things That I Used to Do"? Depending on who is talking, the session took from one complete night to two days to complete. Charles was so ecstatic when it was all done, he yelled "yeah!" in relief, which can be heard at the end of the recording.

The lyrics form a lament, and the singer declares : "I used to sit and hold your hand, baby / Crying and begging you not to go." The next verse begins: "I would search all night for you, baby / Lord, and my search would always be in vain." (It seems that he knew all along that she was with another man.) In the end, he sings, "I'm going to send you back to your mother, baby" – and he'll return to his family too because he can neither please her nor get along without her.

Vincent mailed off a recording of "The Things That I Used to Do" to Rupe, and the loquacious Rupe's quick response, Ditta said, was "This is the worst piece of shit I ever heard in my life," or something to that effect. Rupe eventually told Vincent that he could release the record but that he would be out on the street if it didn't sell. Vincent wouldn't forget Rupe's threat.

Vincent really dug the record, but he knew he had a tough job ahead, to sell it nationally. There was one key problem, and it was in Cleveland. For all the good Alan Freed was doing there to promote the new music called rock 'n' roll, he didn't always have clean hands. He would eventually admit to having taken bribes from record companies to play their records, a practice that came to be known as payola, and often was referred to as "Alan Greed" behind his back. He tried to get Rupe to switch distributors in Ohio to a company that Freed was starting up with his brother. Rupe didn't want to switch, and Freed got back at him by not playing Specialty Records songs for about two years.

Vincent knew that he had to sell Freed, who could break a song nationally, so he drove to Cleveland to plead his case personally. "He convinced Alan Freed that unless he played this record on his show, he [Vincent] would lose his job," Woody Sistrunk said. "Johnny was a convincing sort and a kind guy. Alan Freed was empathetic and told Johnny, 'I'll play this song tonight.'"

Vincent came back to the studio for Alan Freed's late night show. When the song was played, the switchboard lights lit up. People liked the song.

"It became a huge hit," said Sistrunk. "One of the biggest hits of 1954. As a record collector, traveling all over the country, digging through piles of 78s all over the place, I would find those records everywhere. That was a huge record, people just loved it."

In a *Guitar Player* article in 1984, Earl King talked about Guitar Slim's unique sound. "Slim was getting a fuzztone distortion way before anyone else. Believe or not, Slim never used an amplifier. He always used a PA set, never an amplifier. He was an overtone fanatic, and he had those tiny iron-cone speakers and the sound would run them speakers. . . . Slim always played at peak volume – that's why it was hard to record him."

Lambert, in the same article, explained that Guitar Slim would attain a tinny kind of sound by turning all the bass controls as low as possible and dialing up his treble as high as it would go.

King concluded, "A lot of people didn't take Slim seriously, but I did." Slim gave King the idea to write lyrics from a psychological approach, saying "things people wanted to hear" in a passionate, AME Church preacher kind of style.

Also recorded in that first session for Specialty were "Well, I Done Got Over It," "A Letter to My Girlfriend," and "The Story of My Life."

"The Things I That Used to Do" was released in December 1953 with "A Letter to My Girlfriend" on the B-side, and it was an immediate hit in selected markets. Before the year was out, "The Things That I Used to Do" was the number one record in New Orleans and a top ten record in Newark, New Jersey, which was probably because Guitar Slim had hit the road as hastily as gigs could be arranged – and the Northeast wanted him. A column called "Stars over Harlem" in the December 26, 1953, issue of the *Cash Box* gushed: "WOW! Just gotta use this expression to describe the excitement created when Specialty Records' Guitar Slim and company dropped their latest wax ditty 'The Things That I Used To Do' in the Harlem area. The way the guys and dolls are crowding the uptown retailers for this waxing is really amazing, and Art Rupe would be happy to know that unless something comes from way out of deep left field soon, and mighty soon, this waxing could very easily be the big one for Xmas and the holiday season."

By the third week in January, *Billboard* had the record as fifth-best-selling R&B record nationally and fifth in the list of R&B records played in jukeboxes, which at one time was what streaming is today (except that you could only listen in public places). By mid-March, the song was the number one R&B record in sales and the most-played R&B song on American jukeboxes. It was number one in Atlanta, Charlotte, Detroit, Los Angeles, New Orleans, and St. Louis; number two in New York; and number three in Chicago. *Billboard*'s competition, *Cash Box*, had the song number one on March 20, beating out Roy Hamilton's "You'll Never Walk Alone," Johnny Ace's "Saving My Love for You," Muddy Waters's "I'm Your Hoochie Koochie Man," and Ray Charles's "It Should've Been Me."

Finally, on April 3, *Cash Box* dropped "The Things That I Used to Do" out of the number one slot and replaced it with Roy Hamilton's "You'll Never Walk Alone." In the same issue, the "Stars over Harlem" column noted, "Guitar Slim and gang will be dropping anchor in these parts for a string of one one-nighters long before the ink dries."

By the first week in June – more than six months after it was released – it was still the tenth-best-selling R&B song in America's retail shops and still in the top ten in Atlanta, Chicago. and Los Angeles. This was at the same time as some extraordinary R&B hits, including the Midnighters' "Work with Me Annie," Joe Turner's "Shake Rattle and Roll," the Clovers' "Lovey Dovey," and the Spaniels' "Goodnight, Sweetheart."

Since Rupe was very fair to his musicians and didn't allow the practice of falsely attaching his or anyone else's name to a song, Guitar Slim got full credit and his full share of royalties, which were evidently quickly adding up: on June 5, 1954, *Billboard*'s "Rhythm and Blues Notes" column reported, "Here's an interesting note: Charles Brown, Amos Milburn and Guitar Slim all bought brand-new fishtail Cadillacs this week."

Billy Vera said, "Guitar Slim was often not very smart financially, but he did just happen to luck into an honorable record label owner. Art [Rupe] never put his name on anyone's song. In fact, Lloyd Price told me, 'as long as [Rupe] owned Specialty Records I got a statement and a check every six months like clockwork.'"

THINGS THAT I USED TO DO

In July, Guitar Slim was teamed with the Clovers in a string of one-night dates throughout Texas.

A *Cash Box* poll at the end of 1954 found "The Things That I Used to Do" the fifth-most-popular rhythm and blues record of the year. Number one was the Midnighters' "Work with Me Annie." The website Playback. fm has "The Things That I Used To Do" the number two R&B song of 1954. That year, the only African American performer on the *Billboard*'s list of top thirty pop songs of the year was Nat King Cole. Instead of Johnny Ace, B. B. King, Fats Domino, Ray Charles, Dinah Washington, and Ruth Brown, the pop charts showed the likes of Kitty Kallen, Perry Como, the Four Aces, Archie Bleyer, Jo Stafford, and Eddie Fisher.

Billboard listed "The Things That I Used to Do" as the top R&B song of 1954 and one of the top three R&B records of the entire decade. The song would be on the charts for twenty-one weeks, six at number one, and would sell over a million copies.

It had a lasting effect on up-and-coming singers. Etta James in her autobiography wrote: "Me and my girlfriend would steal costume jewelry from J. J. Newberry's, sell it to the corner candy-store owner, and buy blues records. One of my first was Guitar Slim's 'The Things That I Use to Do.' Well, I'd crank that sucker up and grind against the walls. The big booming sound of Slim's voice, the way he shouted out his message, the bump of the beat – that was my music."

When "The Things That I Used to Do" began to fade from radio playlists and jukeboxes, Specialty released in April 1954 a second Guitar Slim platter from the initial recording session, "The Story of My Life." Over time, that song has gained esteem. In a February 1982 issue of *Guitar Player*, Frank Zappa said of Guitar Slim's solo break in the song, "It is one the best early distorted guitar solos; it really sounds like he's mad at someone." Bill Dahl at Allmusic said the song was one of "several stunning follow-ups" to "The Things That I Used to Do." Indeed, it is the guitar work that has kept this song alive especially for more later musicians such Stevie Ray Vaughan.

Back in 1954, however, the song struggled to gain traction despite a push by Specialty. Two mentions of "The Story of My Life" appeared in the April 24 issue of *Cash Box*. In the column "Rhythm and Blues Ramblings," the New York columnist wrote: "New Guitar Slim etching, 'The Story of My Life,' gonna bring lots of orders to Specialty. Deck is a natural and coming on top of his powerful "The Things That I Used to Do,' it should create a big splash."

In the same issue, the "Stars over Harlem" columnist wrote, "Frank Sinatra's 'Don't Worry 'Bout Me' [is heading] homeward bound faster than a

Willie Mays line drive. This baby is loaded with the nice things expected of The Voice and much more. . . . Ditto: Guitar Slim's 'The Story of My Life.'"

By the next month, of the six cities featured in "The Cash Box Hot" column, the record only charted in the top ten in two cities: at number ten in San Francisco and number three in New Orleans. Then it was gone.

What happened? Partly it was the song, and partly it was rapidly changing tastes in music. "The Story of My Life" is an odd song in that it didn't show progress from Guitar Slim's earlier work. In some regards it was a full retrograde, harking back two years to "Feelin' Sad" in that it too begins with long gospel moan. Then it jumps immediately into the deeply personal, psychological lyrics that Guitar Slim excelled in writing, "If my mother had not died and my father left this child at home," followed a blues guitar break between stanzas. About three-quarters of the way through the song, Guitar Slim launches an extended solo. In truth, it was a somewhat gloomy tune.

The full lyrics tell another Guitar Slim sad story. He claims that if his mother had not died and father left him home, his life wouldn't be so miserable. The story line doesn't get any happier. The last line reports "misery every day." Great blues but not exactly uplifting.

For an indicator of why the song failed, one only has to look at the May 29, 1954, "Hot" column in *Cash Box*, where "The Story of My Life" trailed two songs that were lively, sexy, fun, already very close to rock 'n' roll and very far from country blues: number one "Work with Me Annie" by the Midnighters and number two "Shake Rattle and Roll" by Joe Turner. Also in the top ten in New Orleans at the time was "A Mother's Love" by Guitar Slim acolyte Earl King. It appeared on no other city's chart.

So pre–rock 'n' roll records were replacing the true blues songs of the past, while the rhythmic tunes of the R&B charts were coming to be dominated by the urban sound of doo-wop and the smooth, crooning of handsome young men like Johnny Ace. In the top twenty R&B records for 1954 were rock 'n' roll-ish songs such as "Work with Me Annie," "Shake Rattle and Roll" and even "Dim Dim the Lights" by Bill Haley and His Comets, an all-white group. Then came a huge flock of doo-wop melodies, including the Charms' "Hearts of Stone," the Five Keys' "Ling Ting Tong," the Drifters' "Honey Love," the Chords' "Sh-Boom," the Crows' "Gee," and the Penguins' "Earth Angel," followed by a continuum of pre-1960s soul, from Roy Hamilton's way-over-the-top "You'll Never Walk Alone" to Johnny Ace's restrained "Saving My Love for You."

To complicate things, by July Imperial Records tried to cash in Guitar Slim's success by rereleasing songs from its own 1951 recording sessions.

These were not quality recordings, and thematically both were downers, which was not going to enhance Guitar Slim's popularity on radio stations – and particularly not on jukeboxes, where kids would pump coins to listen to dance tunes. Teenagers wanted to feel good, not get depressed. Nevertheless, *Cash Box* got suckered into reviewing the tunes as if they were brand-new.

In its July 10 "Rhythm 'n Blues Reviews" column, one the three highlighted records was Guitar Slim's "Cryin' in the Morning," with "Woman Troubles" on the B-side. The reviewer wrote, "Guitar Slim has woman troubles on both decks [both sides of the disc]. Slim, in the fast moving 'Cryin' in the Morning,' woke up one morning and found his woman had left him. He sings of his own virtues. Slim handles the material in a style calculated to win spins and sales. The flip [side], 'Woman Troubles,' is a slow blues. Poor Guitar Slim finds all his luck running bad. His wife has quit him and all his woman are putting him down. In addition to monetary and friend woes. Slim sings his sad tale with feelings. Two good platters."

Also in the reviews column that week were records by Gatemouth Brown ("Okie Doke Stomp"/"Depression Blues") and New Orleans singer Leonard Lee ("Tryin' to Fool Me"/"When the Sun Goes Down") without Shirley Goodman. Neither of those records caught on.

Specialty kept trying without success to find a fortunate follow-up to "The Things That I Used to Do." In August, "Later for You Baby," with "Trouble Don't Last" on the B-side, was released to seeming quietude. The record must have gotten airplay in New Orleans because a local songwriter name Bobby Charles (Robert Charles Guidry) rewrote the tune using a popular hipster phrase, "see you later, alligator" (a common refrain was "after a while, crocodile"). At a concert in Abbeville, Louisiana, Charles, the lone white boy in attendance, approached the headliner, Fats Domino, with the song. Fats just laughed at the song title, "See You Later Alligator," and passed it back to the young man, who decided to record it himself. Much to Bobby Charles's surprise, it began to get airplay. Bill Haley heard it and rushed his band into the studio to record a streamlined version of the song, which became a top ten record in 1956.

For musicians in New Orleans during the early 1950s, there was no such thing as six degrees of separation. For the song crowd, it was always more like two degrees of separation or just one long rhythmic and incestuous dance line. One of the last big record companies to scout talent in Louisiana was Chess Records, which was founded in Chicago in 1950. Although behind the curve due to a late start in business, the Chess brothers, Leonard, Phil, and Marshall, who founded the company, picked up well-known singer and New Orleans hometown hero Paul Gayten to be producer and take on A&R duties. He recorded Bobby Charles and Clarence "Frogman" Henry.

Henry was another Louisiana bayou prodigy. Born in Algiers in 1937, he wrote the song "Ain't Got No Home" in 1956 after singing at the Joy Lounge, which was a hot nightspot in Gretna, across the river from New Orleans. The weirdly attractive tune was sung by Henry in three voices: those of a man, a woman, and a frog, hence the nickname "Frogman." Gayten heard Henry sing it live and brought Henry into J&M Recording. Henry recalled, "I was nineteen years old and wrote 'Ain't Got No Home.' Paul got in touch with Leonard Chess and recommended Chess record me. I recorded it at Cosimo's studio, home to a lot of hits. Paul Gayten produced the record."

The song reached number three on the R&B charts and crossed over to the pop charts where it was a top twenty hit. Of course, Henry was sent out on the road to support the song, sometimes teamed up with Fats Domino. In Washington, DC, both performers were staying at a hotel for African Americans, a business owned by a New Orleans investor, when who should come by but Guitar Slim. "I really wanted to talk with him, but he was so sleepy we didn't have much in the way of a conversation," said Henry. "He wasn't performing in DC that I know of. He came by to hang out with Fats."

Henry never crossed paths with Guitar Slim again. Neither cursed by narcissism or alcoholism nor blessed with genius, he had a long life and decent career, with two more top twenty hits, "You Always Hurt the One You Love" and his biggest record, "But I Do," which rose to number four on the *Billboard* pop charts in 1961. In 2020, I interviewed him for this book.

Before 1954 came to a close, Specialty pushed out one more Guitar Slim record, "Sufferin' Mind," with "Twenty-Five Lies" on the B-side. "Sufferin' Mind" is one of Guitar Slim's most accessible records, moving as close as he had yet gotten to pop. His usual guitar solo was replaced by a smooth saxophone break. Lyrically, it was still as somber as prior Guitar Slim songs. Here the recurring theme is mental suffering. Why is the singer suffering? It's over a cheating woman, as usual. The song nears its end with a weird, cryptic line beseeching, "Forgive me for what I do." What that is, we don't know.

Billboard magazine caught up with the song in a review on November 13, 1954, treating "Twenty-Five Lies" as the A-side and writing: "An up-tempo ditty about a guy with a lying gal. Very effective warbling by Guitar

Slim." As for the "Sufferin' Mind," the other side, the reviewer noted: "A sincere Southern blues vocal on a moody weeper. Slim fans will want."

The next week, Art Rupe slipped a fast one into the *Cash Box* column "Rhythm and Blues Ramblings." The Los Angeles section of the column reported, "Guitar Slim's latest entry on the Specialty label titled "Sufferin' Mind" has been selling big here in LA and prexy Art Rupe reports that sales all along the East Coast have been very gratifying too."

Nice try but a bit of an exaggeration. The market was rapidly moving away from Guitar Slim. In the November 13 *Billboard* was a review of a new record from Chess, the Moonglows singing "Sincerely," now a doo-wop classic – or a pop classic (the McGuire Sisters' 1959 cover), depending on one's taste. Above, in "This Week's Best Buys" (according to sales reports in key markets, releases recommended for extra profits), one of the two recommendations was another soon-to-be doo-wop classic, "Earth Angel" by the Penguins. Doo-wop was taking over except for certain geniuses who learned from Guitar Slim.

In her book *Nowhere to Run: The Story of Soul Music,* author Gerri Hirshey wrote of Ray Charles, "Ray's music has been getting freer, more emotional and less mannerly ever since he began working with bluesman Guitar Slim, an uninhibited shouter." About the time "Sufferin' Mind" was released, Charles slipped into an Atlanta recording studio and recorded his first crossover hit record, the classic "I Got a Woman," with its Guitar Slim fusion of what Hirshey called "churchy piano, a strong band and a vocal that bounced between the bedroom and the blessed."

Ray Charles was very much taken with Slim's "perfervid, impassioned, preach-blues style," and it was only toward the end of 1954, after "The Things That I Used to Do" had become a hit, that Ray recorded his first overtly gospel-based single, "I Got a Woman."

C
H
A
P
T
E
R

9

If I Had My Life to Live Over

Creation of Ace Records – Keeping to the road – To Atlantic Records – Recording on the ATCO label – The "best" drinker – Death in New York; funeral in Louisiana – Guitar Slim Jr. gets a Grammy nomination

In February 1955, *Billboard* magazine sported a small square ad at the bottom of a page. Its headline read "A Moneymaker!," and just below was the song title "Stand by Me," by Guitar Slim. (This was not the same "Stand by Me" as sung by Ben E. King in 1961.) In bubble script were the words "Specialty Records," and a mailing address was included: 8504 Sunset Blvd, Hollywood 46, Cal.

But Specialty got one-upped. In the same first column, at the top of the page, Aladdin Records of Beverly Hills, in a bigger ad, promoted "Two Big Ones! Watch the charts. Real humdinger." One of the records was the quickly forgotten "Please Let Me Know," by the Five Pearls. But the second record, Gene and Eunice singing "Ko Ko Mo," would indeed become a big hit on the R&B charts. It was also covered by a slew of white, middle-of-the-road singers such as Perry Como and the Crew Cuts, whose versions both made the top ten in the pop charts in 1955.

Gene and Eunice were Gene Forrest (Forrest Samuel Wilson Jr.) and Eunice Levy (Eunice Hazel Russ). Whatever they were serving up in the itty-bitty community of Texarkana, Texas, they should have been exporting it to the world. Eunice was born there one year before Jesse Belvin and six years after Peppermint Harris and lived there at the same time, meaning they all grew up together. Gene was also born one year before Belvin in the same city as Belvin, San Antonio, so maybe the creative waters flowed there first.

Guitar Slim's "Stand by Me" got little respect from *Billboard* magazine. In its January 29, 1955, issue, the reviewer for the "Review of New R&B Records" column saw it as the B-side of "Our Only Child." The review for "Stand by Me" read: "Slim sells the rocker with a lot of spirit and the ork [orchestra] backs him with a beat. It could get some coins. The flip side is more in his groove." And the "flip side" review noted: "Slim turns in a

IF I HAD MY LIFE TO LIVE OVER

sock [knock someone's socks off] performance here of an intriguing piece of material in which he lectures his wife about running around and leaving their only child alone. Item is off the beaten path, but the chanter's performance and guitar could help it go." It didn't.

Of all the songs reviewed that week, the only one to click with the public was Etta James and the Peaches' recording of "The Wallflower," which was an answer song to the Midnighters' "Work with Me Annie" and is sometimes known as "Roll with Me Henry." It was a monster, topping the R&B charts for four weeks and coming in at number nine in the list if *Billboard*'s top R&B songs of 1955. "Work with Me Annie" was about sex, so the song got cleaned up for "Roll with Me Henry" and then got whitewashed even more, turned to "Dance with Me, Henry," a version that became a bigger hit for Georgia Gibbs.

Of the three songs in the spotlight that week, the most intriguing song for the reviewer was a spiritual, "Sinner, Sin No More," by the Dixie Humming Birds. It was produced by Don Robey's Houston label. Peacock had grown up.

In 1955, it was back to Texas for Guitar Slim in what was looking like the last real gunslinger showdown in the blues world. Bill Simon, a *Billboard* magazine columnist who wrote "Rhythm-Blues Notes" took notice. On April 23, 1955, he wrote: "Texas currently is shaping up as one of the hottest territories for rhythm and blues record acts. The packaging of Lowell Fulson (Chess) and Choker Campbell's band (Atlantic) is paying off on one-nighters through the Lone Star State, and Ray Charles (Atlantic) heads that way in May. An interesting package is set to hit the same trails in July, coupling Guitar Slim (Specialty) and T-Bone Walker (Atlantic). This should reach an all-time high in blues guitar battles."

While Guitar Slim was on the road and getting ready to dethrone spectacular blues-shredder T-Bone Walker, who was probably his mentor in spirit, the New Orleans scene he knew from one year before was in the midst of a massive change. Johnny Vincent, the man who had gotten Guitar Slim to record "The Things That I Used to Do" was out at Specialty. In New Orleans, there were always two interpretations to anything that happened in the music industry. The same was true for Vincent. Did he plan his exit or was he pushed? The answer is probably a little of both.

According to Huey Piano Smith, Vincent was plotting to form his own label while still working at Specialty. He still hadn't forgotten Rupe's threatening to fire him if Guitar Slim's record didn't succeed. Smith told John Wirt: "Johnny was putting half of Specialty's stuff in his briefcase." After he formed Ace Records in 1955, Vincent produced all those songs he clipped from Specialty. Said Smith. "He put it out on Ace after Specialty paid for it."

The other interpretation is that Vincent got canned for financial reasons, a budget cutback. Vincent claimed it was because Rupe had agreed to pay him royalties for Guitar Slim's big hit but never did, which was a doubtful claim, since as Rupe didn't play that game. The firing could have been because Rupe suspected Vincent wasn't being a forthright employee, thought that Vincent was not a very good producer, or found someone who could replace him.

In any of those cases, the result was that Vincent immediately created Ace Records. In Vincent's telling of his story, he said, "I went into New Orleans and ran into Eddie Bo, Al Collins, and Bobby Marchan. I asked Cosimo about recording them, and he said, 'Okay.' So we went right in.'" Hmm, how fortuitous, just bumping into so much talent who wanted to record.

In the end, it wasn't any of those singers that who make it for Ace Records. It was Guitar Slim's friends, Huey Piano Smith and Earl King, who saved the label. Again, Vincent's story: "While I was in New Orleans, I went to see Earl King and Huey Smith, and I told 'em, 'Look, I haven't got much money, but if you guys want to make a record, I know a lady in Jackson [where Ace Records was based] who has a studio and will let us use it cheap."

Among the songs recorded in that session was "Those Lonely, Lonely Nights," by Earl King. It was his first hit record on the R&B charts. Smith didn't score right away. It wasn't until 1957.when Huey Piano Smith and His Clowns (with Bobby Marchan) recorded "Rockin' Pneumonia and the Boogie Woogie Flu," which was the first Ace Records single to reach *Billboard*'s R&B and pop charts. The record sold over one million copies, which was good in many ways for Vincent, including having his name listed as the cowriter so he could collect individual royalties – essentially stealing from Smith.

Rupe might not have been so quick to let go of Vincent if he didn't already have someone better in-house and waiting in the wings. That guy was Robert "Bumps" Blackwell.

Around 1948, Ray Charles lived in Seattle where he played in a jazz band with Quincy Jones and a local boy named Robert Blackwell. By the 1950s everyone dispersed in different directions, with different careers. Blackwell ended up in Los Angeles because he wanted to attend UCLA and learn composition. Looking for work, he visited Specialty Records, where Art Rupe hired him immediately. Rupe was still searching for blues singers

IF I HAD MY LIFE TO LIVE OVER

he could sell to white teenagers, and Blackwell, who was African American and played with up-and-coming Ray Charles, looked like the guy who fit the bill. In fact, Rupe asked Blackwell to find another Ray Charles, a person who could transform gospel into rock 'n' roll.

Blackwell told music historian Ed Ward: "One day a reel of tape, wrapped in a piece of paper looking as though someone had eaten off it, came across my desk . . . the voice was unmistakably star material. I can't tell you how I knew, but I knew. The songs were not out-and-out gospel, but I could tell by the tone of his voice and those churchy turns that he was a gospel singer who could sing the blues."

A couple of problems arose. Firstly, Rupe wasn't as sure as Blackwell about the singer, Little Richard Penniman, and had to be convinced, and, secondly, Don Robey had already signed him to Peacock. Blackwell didn't need convincing, and that latter situation took care of itself sine none of Little Richard's recordings for Peacock were successful.

Sight unseen, Specialty signed Little Richard and decided to record him in New Orleans at J&M Recording, using most of the regular musicians who backed Fats Domino. Blackwell finally met Little Richard, and it was a shock. Blackwell recalled, "There's this cat in this loud shirt, with hair waved up six inches above his head. He was talking wild." He may have looked like crazy, man, crazy, but when he got into the studio, he was tame. The first session was the blahs, and the second day felt about the same. They decided to take a break and headed to the Dew Drop Inn for lunch. Little Richard knew immediately this was his kind of place, full of gay and straight men. He made his way to the piano, banged on the keys, and screamed, "A-wop-bop-a-loo-mop, a good goddam – Tutti-Frutti, good booty!" – and Blackwell's world turned. The raunchy lyrics, which originally referred to gay sex, had to be cleaned up for popular listening.

In a 1970 interview, Little Richard remembered it this way: "We met in New Orleans, and I cut some blues songs. During a break in the session, someone heard me playing 'Tutti Frutti' on the piano and asked about the song. We ended up recording it, and it sold 200,000 copies in a week and a half." In January 1956, "Tutti Frutti" rose to number seventeen on the pop charts.

In 1956, the year of Elvis Presley's "Heartbreak Hotel," Carl Perkins's "Blue Suede Shoes," and Chuck Berry's "Roll Over Beethoven," Little Richard's "Tutti Frutti" was the wildest and weirdest of the new music called rock 'n' roll that was blowing away teenagers from one end of the country to the other.

Three days after the recording session with Little Richard, Blackwell attended a Fats Domino concert at the Pentagon Ballroom in New Orleans. Afterward he wrote Rupe, "It was the first all-white rock 'n' roll concert – so 'blues' had definitely gone 'white' here also.'"

In New York, for one of the local radio stations catering to teenagers, its list of the top forty songs of 1956 was almost entirely the new music, rock 'n' roll, R&B, and doo-wop. Middle-of-the-road white singers and bandleaders were almost entirely pushed to the sidelines. Only Dean Martin with "Memories are Made of This," Morris Stoloff with the instrumental "Moonglow," and Gogi Grant with "The Wayward Wind" were left from the old world.

Specialty Records had a new star, and it was time for some of the older players, who were still dedicated to country blues styling, to pick up and move on, including Guitar Slim.

He was a performer, so Guitar Slim kept to the road more than he hung out in a studio. Except for some of the big city venues such as the Apollo, where an occasional white face would appear, Guitar Slim wasn't seeing the changes happening around him. In 1955, as far as he knew, he was still king of the road. There was some changes going on with him too, but it wasn't in regard to his records.

Frank Painia of the Dew Drop and Hosea Hill of the Sugar Bowl in Thibodaux worked together booking the same acts in each of their venues and eventually became business partners and artist managers, booking bayou singers on the chitlin' circuit. At some point early on in their relationship, Frank asked Hosea to take over the management of Guitar Slim, which worked out well with for singer because he moved from New Orleans to Thibodaux and often played at the Sugar Bowl when he was in town. According to Thurston Hill, Hosea's son, "Slim went around the country for three years behind 'The Things I Used to Do,' and every date was booked out of Thibodaux."

When Guitar Slim Jr. (Rodney Glenn Armstrong) was about five years old, he and his mother often traveled with his father and band. He was so young then, his memory of that time is spotty, but he does remember the cars stopping at small places to pick up baloney sandwiches and other sundries. "It was always me, my mother, my daddy, and a car load of people," Slim Jr. recalled. "One time I was in the car, and this woman kept pinching me. They all smoked, and I remember smoke was everywhere. At Hosea Hill's place they used to leave me in the room. One time, my daddy sent me downstairs for spaghetti and meatballs, and when I came back up, the band had set up on the stage. When no one was looking, I banged on the drum and then ran."

Another change was Guitar Slim's instrument. Guitar Slim bought the first Les Paul guitar in New Orleans, recalled Earl King. "Slim was playing one of those big hollow boxes like T-Bone had. But when the solid boxes came out, he got one right away." What Guitar Slim liked about the solid body was that it gave him a little more room on a stage. Stages sometimes tiny. Relying on Lloyd Lambert's memory, Robert Palmer in 1995 reported that Guitar Slim also immediately realized that with a solid-body guitar he could more easily control the feedback and sustain it. He would also turn the bass on his guitar and the P. A. to the lowest setting, while cranking up the treble to ten.

In some pictures of Guitar Slim in action, it appears he also played a Fender Telecaster.

While he played a wicked guitar, Guitar Slim apparently couldn't master basic driving skills. Lambert, who often traveled with him as a band member, didn't think much of his driving. When Painia first booked Guitar Slim through the South, he bought him a brand-new Oldsmobile Delta 88, which was a popular car for aspirational African American musicians in the South. In the legend of Guitar Slim, he got drunk one night and ran the Olds into a parked bulldozer, wrecking the car and nearly wrecking himself. Painia, who had worked so hard to put together the tour, decided to send Earl King on the road masquerading as Guitar Slim.

In Jeff Hannusch's 1984 *Guitar Player* story about Guitar Slim, Earl related, "When I got back to town, the first person I saw was Guitar Slim. He was walking down LaSalle Street with a hospital gown on, a guitar under one arm and an amp under the other, yelling, 'Earl King, I heard you been out there imitatin' me. If you wreck my name I'm gonna sue. I'm gonna kill you.'"

The problem with these tales is that they seem too perfect. Conceding that the events of this oft-repeated story might have actually happened, the question is when? The *Guitar Player* story says that Painia, with Guitar Slim's record at number one in the country, booked a full itinerary for Slim throughout the South. The record was number one in the country around mid-March. Again with Earl King as his source, Hannusch reported that after King masqueraded for Guitar Slim, Slim was back on his feet and ready to hit the road for a tour of the northern theater circuit to support the record. Some reports say that as soon as the record began to take off, Guitar Slim was booked in the North. Was there a southern tour before there was a northern tour? If one goes by the mid-March date for the masquerade, there was just a narrow window for the smashup of the Oldsmobile to have happened because, if *Billboard* is correct, Guitar Slim bought himself a Cadillac before or in April 1954.

About a year later, in the March 24, 1955, *Jet* magazine, columnist Dan Burley wrote about nouveau riche African Americans behaving ostentatiously and caught Guitar Slim in his net. He titled the column "Debunking Pretensions," and described "the air-conditioned splendor in which blues shouter Guitar Slim rode alone in his robin's egg–blue Fleetwood Cadillac on Chicago Boulevard, while just ahead of him – in his band's station wagon – his musicians squirmed, sweated and cussed trying to be comfortable amid a pile of instruments, trunks and other luggage."

When Guitar Slim drove by his home for the first time in that Cadillac, Slim Jr., who was only about six years old, saw the car pull up, got scared, and ran out the back door.

While 1955 was a disappointing year for Guitar Slim, it was a good one for Specialty, which recorded Little Richard and was getting ready to make him a star. The label didn't fully give up on Guitar Slim and would release one of his records in 1955 and then a final one in January 1956. His 1955 recording of "Quicksand" is interesting in that the beat is less deep blues and more what would by the following year be deemed roll 'n' roll, including a saxophone solo that competes with and almost drowns out Guitar Slim's playing. The record was hot, but it hit a cold market and did no better than anything else he issued in 1955.

When "Quicksand" came out, the October 15, 1955, *Billboard* covered it in its "Reviews of New R&B Records." The reviewer wrote: "Against the rough, 'Southern' backing of his band, Guitar Slim shouts out characteristic blues with vitality and his usual satisfying grasp of this idiom. The band is especially good." As for the B-side "Think It Over," the same reviewer was harsh: "Guitar Slim puts considerable feeling and effort into this material, but it doesn't quite make it."

Guitar Slim was in good company that week. Among the others failing to climb out of the discard pit were Earl King singing "Sittin' and Wonderin,'" which was also what he was doing waiting for a better public reaction to the song, and Jesse Belvin with "Love, Love of My Life," which found no love. The single tune that week to grab the golden ring was the Robins' light-hearted classic "Smokey Joe's Café." That was really saying something because among the big names and soon-to-be-famous acts that introduced unsuccessful records that week were Etta James, Little Walter,

Rosco Gordon, Ray Charles, Chuck Berry, Howlin' Wolf, Charles Brown, and the Ravens. Others in the same boat were acts such as Ernie England, the Moroccos, and the Gay Notes, rarely to be heard from again.

Nesuhi and Ahmet Ertegun, sons of Turkey's first ambassador to the United States, were big fans of American jazz and rhythm and blues, amassing a huge collection of 78 records. After the death of their father, they decided to stay in the United States and started a recording company, which they called Atlantic. It was incorporated in 1947, and Herb Abramson was hired to run the company. Starting in 1949, with Stick McGhee's "Drinkin' Wine, Spo-Dee-O-Dee," the company began producing a long, long string of R&B and eventually rock 'n' roll and soul hit records. Early success stories for Atlantic included Ruth Brown, the Clovers, and Big Joe Turner.

As noted, the company signed Ray Charles in 1952. Fast-forward four years, and Atlantic, Ray Charles, Guitar Slim, and the music industry were all going through changes. After the success of "I Got a Woman," it was all success for Charles, the exact opposite of what was going on with Guitar Slim. At Atlantic, Herb Abramson was drafted into the army, and, in his stead, Jerry Wexler became president of Atlantic. Nesuhi Ertegun didn't have a big part in Atlantic until 1955 when he joined the company as head of A&R and took over its jazz division. Abramson's stint in the military was over in 1955, but then there were new bodies in management.

The March 17, 1956, issue of *Billboard* carried a story about the growth of the record business. From 1954 to 1955, the sales of 45s ("singles") were up 38.4 percent, but the big shocker was the "unprecedented increase" in the sales of twelve-inch LPs, up 127.9 percent in 1955 compared to the same period the year before.

Toward the bottom of the same page was a smaller story. The headline read "Guitar Slim Signs with Atlantic." This built on a press release from Atlantic about the signing of Guitar Slim and the re-signing of other current Atlantic acts. According to the book *First Pressings: The History of Rhythm and Blues, Special 1950 Volume*, a February1952 issue of *Billboard*, a headline read: "Atlantic Renews Pacts on McPhatter, Clovers; Signs Guitar Slim." Basically, the story didn't change although the headlines were different. "Atlantic Records has renewed pacts with several of its top artists and his signed a new talent. Latter is Guitar Slim, formerly of Specialty." Both articles went on to say that the company had re-signed Clyde McPhatter and the Clovers, "both consistent performers in the best-selling ranks." At that moment, both acts were at the top of their game, with McPhatter on the charts with "Seven Days" and the Clovers with "Devil or Angel."

This doesn't mean Atlantic was not excited about taking on Guitar Slim. In March, Wexler and Ahmet Ertegun flew to New Orleans to cut the first records with their newly signed star. For his part, Guitar Slim had been on the road with a bluesy mix of performers, Joel Turnero, Roy Gaines, Margie Day, and Lloyd Lambert. The one nod to doo-wop on the tour was the Turbans, who'd had a big hit with "When You Dance" the year before. The Atlantic signing would temporarily change Guitar Slim's status. In the fall, he would be headlining at a popular R&B venue in Florida, Ernie Busker's Palms Club of Hallandale Beach. Starting that summer, Busker's Palms Club would host some big names on the chitlin' circuit. including a number of Atlantic acts. Bo Diddley in June would be followed by Joe Turner, the Cadillacs, Ruth Brown, Little Walter, Ray Charles, and finally Guitar Slim on September 24.

The biggest change for Guitar Slim during his tenure at Atlantic came a couple of months after he joined the label. With Abramson back from the service, the question was what to do with him. Wexler had been so successful that it was obvious Abramson wouldn't be taking back his old position. Probably due to competitiveness, Wexler and Abramson were never going to be best friends. However, Abramson also chafed at working with Nesuhi Ertegun, who was having good success with the company's jazz division. The solution was to start a new label called Atco, with Abramson in charge of A&R and sales. Abramson told the press he planned to focus on rhythm & blues, rock 'n' roll, and pop, and he quickly recorded a platoon of performers, with few successes. He did score with the Coasters, though. He also was first to record Bobby Darin, but the singer didn't become a star until after Ahmet Ertegun took over his recordings.

Also ending up on the Atco label was Guitar Slim, which mostly left him on the road. In the summer of 1956, Atco unleashed a slew of mediocre records by such forgotten performers as the Castelles, Frankie Marshall and His Band, Pauline Rogers, the Tibbs Brothers, and the Royal Jokers. In between were Guitar Slim's "Down through the Years," with "Oh Yeah" on the B-side; the Coasters' "One Kiss Led to Another," with "Brazil" on the B-side; and, in a nod to doo-wop, a Philadelphia group called the Sensations, which in 1962 would have a number four pop hit with "Let Me In" on the Argo label (not Atco).

The June 16, 1956, "Review of New R&B Records" in *Billboard* spotlighted the new Guitar Slim record, "Down through the Years": "A powerful blues, with Guitar Slim's shouting registering solidly. Slim's performance is loaded with church sound and emotion. Watch it." The B-side, it said,

IF I HAD MY LIFE TO LIVE OVER

was "a piece of uncommon material which will add plus value to any deejay show. Side has a smart backing, and relaxed feeling."

The record was released at the same time as two songs that would become tremendous hits, "Rip It Up," by Little Richard, and "My Prayer," by the Platters. Dominating the R&B charts at that moment were ghosts of Guitar Slim's past and compatriots from Atlantic, Fats Domino with "I'm in Love Again," Ray Charles with "Hallelujah, I Love Her So," and Clyde McPhatter with "Treasure of Love."

Guitar Slim's output at Atco was meager. In his three years at Atco, he would release a total of four singles. One of those was in 1957, and to Atco's credit it gave the song a big promotion in the trade magazines, placing a nearly full-page ad featuring a black-and-white photo of a relaxed and handsome Guitar Slim. It read: "Guitar Slim's Great Big Hit from the South – Spreading Like Wildfire!" If only! The songs were "If I Should Lose You" as the A-side and "It Hurts to Love Someone" as the B-side. As could be expected, Guitar Slim was already on the road when the record came out. In July, he was at the Eldorado Ballroom, a chitlin' circuit club in Houston. An advertisement in the *Houston Informer* spotlighted Guitar Slim and Lloyd Lambert and Orchestra. Coming in behind him were Jimmie Reed, Etta James, and Clifton Chenier, to be followed by Charles Brown.

It would be another six months before Atco released another Guitar Slim record, and the company went in big one more time, partly because the label had thought it would try something different, recording him in New York instead of New Orleans. To musical tastemakers, the company wrote, "By recording him in our ultra-modern hi-fi studios, we were able to inject a crazy, new sound that makes his disks more exciting than ever."

The promoted record was "I Won't Mind at All," with "Hello, How Ya' Been, Goodbye." The advertisement for the trade publications was almost a half of page. The idea was to approximate a feature story, with the headline reading "Portrait of a Philosopher." The copy below explained, "No we're not kidding. Guitar Slim is a philosopher. His songs are exclusively concerned with the earthy turns of life. And because of their quality they never fade away, as you travel across the country and keep tuned in on the radio, it is a fantastic how many of hits of the past are continually aired." The copy also boasted of Guitar Slim's "twanging blues guitar and raspy, but unforgettable blues voice."

Although his voice had dropped at least an octave since his early records, its harshness is much more apparent on his last record, "When There's No Way Out" from July 1958. On the B-side was Guitar Slim's life summation song, "If I Had My Life to Live Over," and his voice here was shot. It was like a bicycle with flat tire. Guitar Slim could keep pedaling to the end of the line, but it would take a mighty effort. The tune sounds very much like something Fats Domino would have played back in the day when they both hung out on the streets of New Orleans. Guitar Slim says he would do it all over again, but lawdy, Miss Clawdy, that would be so very hard to do.

Lawrence Cotton, who played in Guitar Slim's band through most of the mid-1950s, said, "He didn't take care of himself. He drank so much that he had the DTs."

The ever-loyal Lloyd Lambert told Hannusch, "I wouldn't say he was a pretty good drinker. He was the best! Slim just wouldn't take care of himself. A different woman every night."

Others too talked about his drinking. In 1944, Lavelle White (Lillia Lavell White), who recorded as Miss La-Vell and Miss LaVell, moved to Houston from Louisiana at the age of fifteen and immediately started performing in the city's blues clubs. By the mid-1950s, she was touring with Guitar Slim through small Texas towns. "He put on a great show, doing flips and things. He used to leave the bandstand and go into the crowd. And he dressed weird; he wore red all the time including his shoes and his hair." White recalled. "He did drink a lot – that was his thing and I often thought maybe it was the alcohol that made him put on a better show."

Considering that kind of touring life, it's little wonder that most biographies of Guitar Slim report that he drank himself to death. In a general sense that's true, because, after a lifetime of mistreating his body, he paid the price. However, it is not exactly accurate.

To find out what really happened, we turn to two of his oldest friends, Earl King and Lloyd Lambert. Here's their combined story. As early as 1958 the excessive drinking had worn Guitar Slim down, and he came off the road, recuperating somewhat. Part of that was also physical since he "got ruptured" from riding his guitar onstage. He went on a last binge and then just quit drinking. King recalled bumping into Guitar Slim at the Dew Drop before his last tour and Slim saying, "Earl, all this liquor I been drinkin,' all the wrong things I been thinkin,' you know my body's been slowly sinkin.'" He could have been writing another song.

He just couldn't stay off the road. In the dead of winter, February 1959, he headed north for a tour in the Northeast. In Rochester, New York, Guitar Slim came up to Lambert and said he was too tired, that he couldn't go on. Lambert covered for him, letting him come out for a couple of songs. Guitar Slim did come out, managed to get through only part of a song, and then

IF I HAD MY LIFE TO LIVE OVER

had to leave the stage. The next venue was the following night in Newark. He finished that gig but collapsed right afterward. The band drove him up to the Cecil Hotel in Harlem, where they were going to stay the night. Lambert paid a valet to take Slim to a doctor while he checked in. When Lambert got to the desk there was a call waiting for him. The valet was calling to tell him Guitar Slim had died.

Lambert told Hannusch, "It wasn't the liquor the killed him. The doctor said it was bronchial pneumonia. Today they could have saved him, but all that drinking and hard living brought his resistance down."

Guitar Slim was thirty-two years old at the time of his death.

Hosea Hill paid to have Guitar Slim's body shipped back to Thibodaux, Louisiana, for an open-casket the funeral at Mount Zion Baptist Church there. Slim Jr. can still recall looking down at his father, who appeared to have a smile on his face. "I was seven years old and wanted to scream and howl, but I never did. My mama was doing the crying for both of us," Slim Jr. says. "I heard the preacher say, 'Yeah, he don't have no family here,' and then this old lady who I never saw before said, 'Yes, he do. He has two children [four, actually], and one of them is here now. So they brought me to the pulpit, and the whole church started clapping."

Thurston Hill, Hosea's son, told one of those myth-making stories that embellished the Guitar Slim aura. "In the front pews of the church were five or six women and a bunch of kids. They were all fussing. The women claimed Slim was their husband and the daddy of their children. Hosea called all those women to the back of the church and said, 'ladies, the undertaker hasn't been paid yet, and he needs some money from Slim's wife or he can't bury him. At that point it got real quiet, and none of them claimed Slim as their husband."

It was another story too good to be true, but, as they say in the movies, when the myth becomes the fact, print the myth. And there is one more story. It is said that Guitar Slim is buried with his Gold Top guitar. There's no proof of it, but if true it would be a super mojo.

The story of Guitar Slim's wife and children is still a bit murky. He was either married once or twice before he left Mississippi for New Orleans. With a wife called Daisy (surname Bowdre) he had two daughters, Annie Lee and Sarah May. Daisy died in 1952. In his early days in New Orleans, he had a steady girlfriend named Albertine, who was married to someone else, a preacher named James Armstrong. Guitar Slim and Albertine had two children, Rodney (Slim Jr.) and Barry.

"Albertine's mother was black, but her father was white," said Carlo

Ditta. "Her father's family name was Rodino. She has been in a band, either as a singer or dancer. Although she had children with her husband, she hooked up with Guitar Slim around 1952 and they were together for at least three years. After the affair was over, she went back to James Armstrong."

Slim Jr. maintains that Guitar Slim and Albertine never broke up. "My mama loved my daddy so much, that's all I ever heard all my life, over and over, was how wonderful he treated her, how good he was. That's all she talked about since I was a baby. She would tell me, 'oh, you move like your daddy' or 'you talk like your daddy.' She would talk about him all the time, like the party they had and when everyone went home my daddy told her she was one of the best women in the world. She said he never cursed at her and never said anything bad to her."

Albertine claimed she and Guitar Slim met at the Tiajuana Club, where he was playing. Albertine went with a friend, and Guitar Slim singled her out as they were about to leave, saying, "if you stay awhile, I'll play some songs for you." To which Slim Jr. adds, "and then I popped out."

The memories Slim Jr. has of his father are all soft and warm like a cat. "He was good to me," he said. "I used to suck my thumb, and one time he put his thumb in front of my face and said, 'Always remember thumb.' It worked."

Albertine and Guitar Slim's children were musically inclined but suffered through mental health problems and addiction over the years. "Barry was very talented and used to play in Rodney's bands. He was the lyricist. I have a music video of Barry whispering to his brother because he couldn't read from the notebook," said Ditta. "I bailed Barry out of jail; he had been locked up in Jackson, Louisiana, in the same place of incarceration where Buddy Bolden died. He was caught stealing cigarettes and wouldn't take his Thorazine."

Slim Jr. has had substance abuse problems. Ditta produced his album "Story of My Life," which was nominated for a Grammy Award for Best Traditional Blues Album in 1989. He lost to Willie Dixon.

"Back in the mid-1970s, I was walking down Orleans Avenue and there was a black nightclub called Dorothy's Medallion that I passed," Ditta recalled. "There was a sign in the window that read 'Snake Dancer Tonight,' and Guitar Slim Jr. and I went back that night, and the place was packed. Guitar Slim Jr. got onstage. He was young, strong, and launched into his father's 'The Things I Used to Do' before slipping into Stevie Wonder's 'Signed, Sealed, Delivered, I'm Yours.' He knocked the fuck out of both of

IF I HAD MY LIFE TO LIVE OVER

them. I talked to him about making a record, but he said he wanted a million dollars. A decade later, I paid his rent and his car insurance and got him into the studio."

The trade papers carried the story of Guitar Slim's death; it just wasn't headline news. One short news item carried the headline "Guitar Slim Goes Home." It noted, "Guitar Slim, one of the last of the down home blues singers and guitarists, passed away last week."

In the February 21, 1959, *Cash Box*, toward the bottom of page 48, under the headline "Guitar Slim Dies," it reported: "Guitar Slim, Atco Recording artist, died in New York on February 7. His age was 32. Burial took place at Thibodeaux, Louisiana, his home, on February 12."

Then the story slipped into its own bit of mythmaking. "He had no musical training; he simply saw a guitar in a pawn shop window one day and taught himself how to play. . . . Guitar Slim was a singer in the 'down home' Southern tradition. He made his first record for Imperial in 1952. In the following year, he was signed by Specialty: his first record for them, 'Things I Used to Do' was a big hit. Another hit made by him for Specialty was 'The Story of My Life.' Slim came to Atco in 1956. Again his first record was a hit, "Down Through the Years.' . . . In the tradition of blues singers, Guitar Slim wrote most of his own material."

Robert Palmer, who interviewed Earl King in the mid-1990s, wrote about Guitar Slim's and Earl King's influence on the 1960's high priest of "sonic guitar," Jimi Hendrix. Palmer concluded, "Not only did Hendrix build a certain aspect of his style on King's screaming high-note melisma, he recorded his own version of Guitar Slim's "The Things I Used to Do" and Earl King's "Come On," explicitly laying bare the roots of his art as they extend back through King to Guitar Slim to the likes of Gatemouth Brown to the father of electric blues, T-Bone Walker." Palmer didn't mention Blind Lemon Jefferson.

If Guitar Slim had hung on for another five years, he would probably be remembered more than he is today. When British Invasion musicians revived interest in traditional blues, guys like Muddy Waters, Howlin' Wolf, and even T-Bone Walker enjoyed career renaissances. Nevertheless, when opportunity arose, Guitar Slim nailed it. Afterward, no matter how fast he ran, he continually slipped one step, two steps, and then three steps behind the march of time.

As his song said, "Hello, How Ya' Been, Goodbye."

PART THREE

JOHNNY ACE

C
H
A
P
T
E
R

10

I Wonder

Cecil Gant and the soft blues revolution – The Sepia Sinatras – Texas/ Gulf Coast music pipeline goes straight to Los Angeles – Memphis remains the place for blues musicians coming up from the Delta – B. B. King finds a job and a hit record

For a number one record, it has to be one of the worst recordings ever. The Second World War was still going strong, and most of the big bands, with that gloriously large, all-encompassing sound, were on hiatus, but recordings were still being made. Radio stations were playing newcomers like that skinny New Jersey kid Frank Sinatra, musicians too old for service were looking for work, and sophisticated recording studios were empty. So you have to wonder about the song "I Wonder" by a private in the U. S. Army named Cecil Gant.

The keyboard was as tinkly as a toy piano, the sound quality too echoey, and the voice unsophisticated, though bluesy. Listening to the song, one gets the feeling that Private Gant walked into a second-rate nightclub, sat down at the piano, and started noodling, words coming as fast as he could think of them. Drinking glasses clinking and someone hacking with a smoker's cough should be heard in the background, but there is no background. The song is just Gant and his piano.

Billboard magazine was mostly dismissive of the recording. In its January 6, 1945, issue, a reviewer lamented its "poor" quality, adding that the recording "sounded more like something picked up with a machine hidden under a table in a smoky back room."

What was the attraction?

Perhaps it was the inherent uncertainty of the singer, a feeling reinforced by the gnawing wounds wrapped in words. "I wonder, my little darling, where can you be again tonight; while the moon is shining bright; I wonder." For GIs overseas or about to be shipped to unknown destinations around the globe, cut off from loved ones, the song encapsulated every insecure feeling that stung them.

According to Arnold Shaw, who wrote extensively about Gant, *Billboard* took an interest in what the magazine called "the wonder race ballad 'I Wonder.'" In Shaw's words, *Billboard* "stressed that 'the song itself' rather than the 'sepia lad's delivery'" made the record a success.

Why the word "sepia?" In the mid-1940s *Billboard* was having trouble figuring out how to label the burgeoning African American record market. (The term "African American" wasn't yet used in the mid-twentieth century). To chart this sector *Billboard* was using the label "Harlem Hit Parade." Mostly this chart was based on Harlem record sales because the number of stations playing black music, even if just for an hour or two at night, was so small it wasn't worth tracking. In 1945, "Harlem Hit Parade" was replaced by "*Billboard*'s Most-Played Juke Box Race Records," so this whole segment of American music market was suddenly referred to as "race records." Despite the fact that this term managed to hang around until the end of the decade, when it was replaced by "rhythm and blues," not everyone was comfortable with it. The word "race" in this context was inherently a segregating demarcation, as if to say this music was by and for African Americans and had nothing to do with the pop music on the hit parade, which was sung by white singers. It should be noted that black performers such as Louis Jordan, Nat King Cole, and the Mills Brothers were regularly on the pop charts during the late1940s.

Instead of using the term "race records" some folks, including Nashville's Jim Bulleit, opted to use the word "sepia" in reference to African American musicians and the music they made, and then the term "black" became a racial defining word in the late twentieth century.

Amiri Baraka, as LeRoi Jones in his 1963 book *Blues People*, wrote: "Cecil Gant, a young Negro war veteran, startled the recording industry and, in a sense, revitalized it, by making some recordings as a boogie piano player and semi-shouting blues singer that sold a great many copies. The companies set about immediately to resuscitate their race fields, only to find that a great many Negroes resented this kind of label being put on their music."

Yet "sepia" didn't work well either because it referred to a specific hue, reddish-brown, as if blacks living in this country were now partly American Indians. The filching of the word probably came from old photographs where the tint was that shade of reddish-brown.

Cecil Gant, promoted on the label of "I Wonder" as "the G. I. Sing-Sation," was born in Nashville in 1915, so he was in his twenties when World War II broke out. In 1944, Gant was in Los Angeles attending a boisterous war bond rally. At a break in the ceremonies Gant approached the bandstand and asked if he could play the piano. Permission granted, the performance went over so well that the army allowed him to perform at other war bond rallies in the city. As Ed Ward tells it, Cliff McDonald, a long-time record man, caught Gant and persuaded him to record the song he had performed. This was literally a garage-band recording, because McDonald's "studio" was in his garage, which apparently was why the recording sounded so tinny. A local company, Gilt Edge Records, distributed the record. It became a huge hit, number one on the "Harlem Hit Parade" and crossing over onto the pop charts. The song was so popular it even made it to the hillbilly stations. Nonetheless, as Ward wrote, "'I Wonder' remained a 'sepia' ballad sung by a 'sepia artist': it did not make the big Saturday night, coast-to-coast *Your Hit Parade* [the nationwide radio show featuring the most popular songs of the week]."

"I Wonder" was important for three reasons. First, a small, independent producer cut a record that became a national bestseller, which gave impetus for all the young entrepreneurs, especially in Los Angeles, to consider becoming record people themselves. Secondly, a young, African American singer crossed over to the popular charts, a phenomenon that would become increasingly popular as the 1940s closed out and the 1950s began. Finally, in regard to the personalities featured in this book, in particular Johnny Ace, Cecil Gant proved there was a tender side to the blues that would attract white teenagers. As Shaw pointed out, Gant's blues-inflected style became a basic strain of R&B that found later exponents in Johnny Ace, among others.

This was an important stream, explains Al Bell, songwriter, producer and co-owner of Memphis-based Stax Records. "These guys like Johnny Ace were very important. Those smooth crooning voices were not the blues' blues and were not hot blues. Their influence came later with the advent of soul music. If you go back and look at artists who succeeded in Detroit or New York, you would be surprised to find many of them came from places like Memphis. They were influenced by the likes of Johnny Ace, because of the way he sang. Johnny was a crooner."

By the end of the 1940s, the blues as a genre of music was breaking into different self-defined sectors. The old acoustic blues had evolved into country blues. The proponents of this style were mostly musicians from the Mississippi Delta who either moved north to and through Memphis or south to the New Orleans–Houston nexus.

On the more cosmopolitan side of the music scene, the pop chart success in the 1930s and 1940s of the Mills Brothers and the Ink Spots, two vocal harmony groups, affected the blues scene as well. A couple of urban groups began placing the harmony approach atop a blues or gospel riff. In the late 1940s, the first to catch on were the Orioles, formed in Baltimore, and the Ravens, formed in New York. In 1948, the Orioles' "It's Too Soon to Know" not only zoomed to number one on the R&B charts but also crossed over the pop charts. This type of urban-blues sound became the core of doo-wop, which dominated R&B in the 1950s. Finally, a third stream of blues singers, the "blues crooners," began to evolve after the success of Cecil Gant.

Bob Rolontz, the "Rhythm and Blues Notes" columnist for *Billboard*, was one of the first to write about the divergent streams of the old blues genre, in an October 16, 1954, column. With foresight he observed: "In case anyone is wondering what is happening in the R&B field these days, it is interesting to note how many different kinds of records are able to make it today – if the material is strong and the singer, or group, comes through with a good performance. Southern blues singers like Fats Domino, Joe Turner, Muddy Waters, Little Walter and Howlin' Wolf are selling; femme singers such as Dinah Washington, Ruth Brown, Faye Adams and Shirley Gunter are also on the best-selling lists. Roy Hamilton and Johnny Ace, ballad singers extraordinary, are always right on top, and Hamilton makes it with standard material. (Roy Hamilton made his name soulfully singing pop songs such as "Never Walk Alone" and "Ebb Tide.")

Although from Nashville, Gant scored his success in Los Angeles, which wasn't unusual. When the parents of Jesse Belvin and many of his friends moved from Texas and Oklahoma to Southern California they were accompanied by another set African Americans – musicians, mostly from the same region.

With the war on and the aviation industry moving more and more manufacturing to Southern California, the pace of African American migration picked up as better jobs were becoming available. And if there were no jobs on the assembly line, Texans and Oklahomans knew a thing or two about working in the oil fields, which were as close by as Long Beach, California.

Somebody had to entertain this group when the hard work was done. T-Bone Walker from Linden, Texas, moved Los Angeles in the mid-1930s when he was twenty-five. By the 1940s, he was probably the most influential bluesman working in Los Angeles. At that time another group of Texas and Oklahoma bluesmen also migrated west, creating what music historian Paul Oliver called a "West Coast blues fusion which layered pop balladry over country blues, boogie-woogie and jazz." Ward called these singers "exponents of the murmuring, gentle vibrato ballad style." They were, he said, the black equivalents of the baritone crooners – in short, they were the "Sepia Sinatras." In the end, the most successful of these singers was Johnny Ace, but a host of other talents got there first or at least about the same time as Ace.

Foremost in this group was Charles Brown, a Texas City, Texas, native who came west to work in the shipyards before settling in Los Angeles in 1943. He was twenty-one at the time.

With all these Texas and Gulf region African Americans moving to California, which didn't have the same rigid segregation of the Deep South (where a nightclub either had to service the black population or the white population, never both), a new generation of Los Angeles nightspots began to emerge that were completely open to anyone of a certain age, regardless of color. These new clubs needed talent, especially those who could play a less raucous form of the blues, which mixed well with some of the well-heeled and Hollywood set that wanted to sit, drink, schmooze, and be entertained. In the mid-1940s, the royalty of the Los Angeles jazz clubs was the Nat King Cole Trio. When they moved on due to the recording success of Nat King Cole, the new kings were Johnny Moore's Three Blazers, with Charles Brown taking the lead. The group's earliest major hit was "Drifting Blues," which rose to number two on the race records chart in 1946. That's also Charles Brown's sultry voice on the Three Blazers' best-known record, "Merry Christmas, Baby." He was considered a major influence on the next generation of blues crooners, including guys like Ivory Joe Hunter, Percy Mayfield, and Johnny Ace.

Probably the most successful in terms of big hits was Ivory Joe Hunter. Another Texan, Hunter was born in Kirbyville in 1914. By 1930, he was featured on a radio station in Beaumont and then six years later was playing the Uptown Club in Houston. In 1942, at the age of twenty-eight, he too made his way to California but north to the San Francisco Bay Area. He formed his own record company, Ivory Records in Oakland, and in early recordings often used Johnny Moore's Three Blazers as his house band. He took a liking to the sound of the lead singer, Brown. After a steady stream of R&B hits, Hunter signed with MGM Records in 1949. By this time he was moving away from straight blues to more pop-oriented ballads, including a huge hit record, the bluesy ballad "I Almost Lost My Mind." By the next year, he was old-school as the R&B world was moving to doo-wop, and his consistency on record charts seriously waned. After the success of Johnny Ace, the blues ballad was back in force, and Hunter enjoyed his biggest hit ever in 1956, "Since I Met You Baby," which was number one on the R&B

charts in addition to becoming his first record to make the pop charts. The song rose all the way to number twelve.

The emergence of Gant, Brown, and Hunter was a part of an evolution that had been going on since the mid-1940s. Nelson George laid it out in *The Death of Rhythm and Blues*: "In 1943 and 1944, large black orchestras led by instrumentalists showed strength, while Nat King Cole, a singer with a crooning big-band vocal style, debuted. Change was evident from 1945 to 1947. The orchestras disappeared, replaced by rough, gravelly voices . . . then by bluesmen with followings among the newly arrived big-city blacks, and finally by smooth, blues-influenced crooners like Private Cecil Grant, Charles Brown and Ivory Joe Hunter."

While Percy Mayfield is not as known as Brown and Hunter because he leaned closer to R&B inflections than pop styling, he falls into the same career cycle, albeit with slightly less success. (His son Curtis Mayfield would be a successful singer and songwriter in the 1960s.) Mayfield was younger than Brown and Hunter, born in 1920 in Minden, Louisiana. Either as a late teenager or when he was twenty, he began performing in Texas and then felt confident enough at the age of twenty-two to take his skills to Los Angeles. It took him a while to catch on, but Art Rupe found him in 1950 and signed him to Specialty Records. It was a good marriage because later that year Specialty unleashed Mayfield's biggest record, "Please Send Me Someone to Love," which became a number one hit on the R&B charts.

Charlie Gillett wrote: "While Gant and Hunter were sometimes oriented toward the white market, Percy Mayfield almost never was, and he sang blues songs, mostly written by himself, in a soft ballad style." As for "Please Send Me Someone to Love," Gillett added that it was one of the most influential songs of the time. "Happening to coincide with the Korean War, the record sold well over a much longer period than was the normal lifetime for a hit – but sold primarily in the rhythm and blues market. Johnny Ace, Jesse Belvin and Ray Charles (with Swingtime, 1949 to 1953) all dealt with simpler, more openly sentimental themes than this, and were among the last of the singers who directed a ballad style at the black audience."

Born on Oklahoma's Choctaw Reservation one year after Percy Mayfield in 1921, Lowell Fulson began playing with local bands around Ada, Oklahoma, in 1938 and then two years later toured Oklahoma and West Texas with Alger "Texas" Alexander. He got drafted and was stationed in the Bay Area. After his release from service, he came back to California and began recording around 1946. For a while he fronted a band that included a very young Ray Charles and tenor saxman Stanley Turrentine.

In 1948, Fulson recorded his own composition "3 O'Clock Blues,' which became his first record to score on the R&B charts. The song would become even more famous three years later when it became a smash hit for B. B. King. It was King's first hit record and went all the way to number one on the R&B charts. In 1949, Fulson had another good run with his record "Come Back, Baby," but once again another singer's later version of the song is better known. In 1954, Ray Charles redid the song as "Come Back," the B-side of "I've Got a Woman," and it was so good it was a top five R&B hit. Fulson also wrote the record "Tramp" for Otis Redding and Carla Thomas in 1967.

As a singer, Fulson is best remembered for his 1950 hit "Every Day I Have the Blues," which was a reworking of the songwriting of someone else, Memphis Slim. (The label for the Swing Time recording by Lowell Fulson lists "Chatman" as songwriter.) Larry Birnbaum tapped Fulson's "Reconsider Baby" (recorded by Elvis Presley in 1960) as his "classic." Birnbaum called it "a distinctive Fulson composition that anticipates the soul blues of Bobby Bland and Little Milton."

One more name needs mentioning: Amos Milburn. Although he was not a blues crooner, he's included here because he ended up on the same career path as the smooth-singing vocalists who also came from Texas. Milburn was born in Houston in 1927 and as teenager fronted a sixteen-piece band playing at the Keyhole Club in San Antonio. In 1946, Ann Cullum (or McCullum), a talent scout for Aladdin Records, arranged to bring Lightnin' Hopkins to Los Angeles for a recording session. Lowell Fulson's old buddy Texas Alexander, who had just gotten out of jail, wanted to accompany Hopkins to Los Angeles, but Cullum wasn't too happy about this development. The "suave" Amos Milburn came along instead, and while in Los Angeles he signed with Aladdin Records. In 1949, a number of Milburn's songs hit the R&B charts, including "Roomin' House Boogie," written by another Texan who came to California, Jessie Mae Robinson. In 1949, Milburn was the number one R&B artist in terms of record sales and jukebox plays.

Unlike many of his contemporaries, from Cecil Gant to Johnny Ace, Milburn was not overly fond of, or dependent on, booze. Yet he is best known for his alcohol-themed songs, from "Thinking and Drinking" and "Bad, Bad Whiskey" to his classic "One Scotch, One Bourbon, One Beer." Milburn's greatest lament begins an order to a bartender: "One scotch, one bourbon, and one beer." It turns out that a woman has started him on his spree. She left in the morning, saying she wouldn't stay. "She's been out all night, and it's the break of day."

In 1945, five independent R&B recording companies (Modern, Philco-Aladdin, Bronze, Four Star, and Super Disc) were founded, all based in Los Angeles. The next year three more started up: Jim Bulleit's Bullet label in Nashville, Mercury in Chicago, and another in Los Angeles, Art Rupe's Specialty. Nelson George, who sees trends where others just hear songs, suggests that this concentration of R&B record labels was why so many southern musicians came west in the 1940s. George wrote, "GIs just back from Asia stayed on and Southern blacks, particularly those from Texas, Oklahoma and Louisiana, found in sunny California a climate, both atmospherically and socially, more temperate than existed back home." It turned out that the migrating musicians found a ready-made audience. In total about a half million African Americans moved to Southern California during the war years.

Although Los Angeles became a rhythm and blues hot spot, label owners realized they would need to mine the source, the Mississippi Delta and Gulf area from which so many musicians hailed. Houston, New Orleans, and Memphis were three key cities. In 1890, the population in Memphis was just under 65,000 people. Ten years later it was over 100,000, and by 1930 the population had grown to 250,000. It was a booming city with a substantial and expanding Black population. Blacks started coming to Memphis in the late 1800s and early 1900s in part because of the lack of employment in the Mississippi Delta and the availability of jobs in a growing city.

A. C. Wharton, who was mayor of Memphis from 2009 to 2015, explains, "Memphis was the first jumping-off station for unemployed African Americans from the Delta. What was happening was the mechanization of the big farms – a cotton-picking machine could harvest four or five rows a time. Mechanization was hitting the whole Delta at one time, so it wasn't as if you could walk down the road and find another job as a sharecropper."

Much of that Delta cotton that could now be harvested more efficiently made its way to Memphis, where it was processed, baled, and sent out to the world, work that was done by African Americans. Wharton adds, "Former sharecroppers with no education could find work in Memphis because the hard work of processing and baling also required no education."

Being a southern town, Memphis was segregated, and the main avenue for the African American section of the city was Beale Street, which became the center of commerce for black Memphis, with its own banks, dentists, doctors, and shopping. It was also the place for entertainment. "By its mere vantage point at the head of the Mississippi Delta basin, Memphis inherited the spontaneous musical expression of newly freed slaves who made their way north. . . . The essence of their songs became a part of the local fabric but was transformed in texture by a new black urbanity," observed Phyl Garland in her book *The Sound of Soul*.

Early in the twentieth century, Beale Street was already known for its music spots. W. C. Handy, one of the first great musicians and songwriters of the twentieth century, came to Memphis to perform at the Beale Street clubs. In 1909, he was able to get published a song he wrote called "Memphis Blues," which has come down in history as the first blues song ever published. Five years later he released "St. Louis Blues," and, to dot the "I," in 1916 he wrote "Beale Street Blues."

The street became famous, and along with the hardworking African Americans migrating from the Delta came a host of blues musicians. As Al Bell explains, they knew that not only African Americans were coming to Beale Street to hear local singers and bands. White folks were starting to come as well, which meant there was more money flowing, and some of those nickels and dimes could end up in their pockets.

John Marshall Alexander Jr. was born in Memphis in 1929. His father was a preacher, and John Jr. changed his name to Johnny Ace when he began singing the blues on Beale Street so as not to embarrass his family. He was one of nine children and like many sons of preachers was obliged to learn to play piano and sing in his father's church. Life in Memphis was a little too constricting, and as soon as he could he enlisted in the navy, perhaps hoping to see the world. But World War II was over, the Korean War hadn't started, he was stationed in Virginia, and that was it in regard to seeing the world. Along the way he got married, and by the later 1940s he was back in Memphis.

Beale Street was still the most important avenue in town for Memphis's African American population, but some of energy had begun to ebb. According to *Beale Black and Blue: Life and Music on Black America's Main Street*, "By the late 1940s, Beale . . . had become tamer. Some of the clubs had closed, and those still open were relying more and more on jukeboxes instead of piano players and blues singers. For most musicians . . . times were harder than in the hard times of the 1930s."

The growing penetration of jukeboxes in honky-tonks not only reduced the live-play hours of musicians but also slowly began altering the nature of the music heard in these clubs and eateries. The harder blues, still popular in Memphis, began to give way to blues without the roots-of-America edginess. In 1948, the top R&B songs in the country included the softer sounds of Ivory Joe Hunter's "Pretty Mama Blues," Nat King Cole's "Nature Boy,"

Dinah Washington's "Am I Asking Too Much," and "More Than You Know," by Johnny Moore's Three Blazers. Also appearing near the top of R&B charts that year were the pre-doo-wop sounds of the Orioles' "It's Too Soon to Know" and the Ravens' "Send for Me If You Need Me" and "Write Me a Letter." That was also the year of Lowell's Fulson's "3 O'Clock Blues."

Listening in was a Mississippi Delta guitar player named Riley B. King, who came to Memphis that year to make a name for himself as a radio musician. Born in 1925, he was four years older than Johnny Ace, and like Ace he started his career singing in a church choir, except the minister there played neither organ nor piano but instead guitar. Legend has it that blues singer Bukka White gave King his first guitar, which might be true because the first time King came to Memphis in 1946, he stayed with Bukka for about ten months before returning to the Delta.

A couple of decades later, when Delta blues singer Linzie Butler came to Memphis, he too began his career in the care of Bukka White. "I started by jamming with Bukka and Furry Lewis, Piano Red, Mose Vinson, and Ma Rainey II," he recalled. "For a while I was playing with Lee Baker and Furry Lewis at Peanut's Pub on Cleveland and Union. Memphis was turning out the blues, baby, whether it was at a party, on a roof, or in a backyard. People still came to Memphis for the blues."

He adds, "These old blues guys came to Memphis in the 1940s because they were trying to make it. Memphis was on the road to Chicago. If you got to Chicago you really made it, but it was a different blues, with more swing. Chicago blues had a little bump to it. That's because the blues changed gradually as you went from state to state. By the time these blues guys got to Memphis, if it was the end of the 1940s . . . that guitar started going electric."

Musicians didn't come to Memphis and automatically have it made. There was a lot of scraping to get by. Lillie Mae Glover, who performed as Ma Rainey II, was born in 1909 and had been on the road as singer since she was thirteen. In the later 1940s, she befriended B. B. King. Interviewed in the early 1980s, she told a story of meeting King at Hamburger Heaven in Memphis after a gig that earned him fifteen cents. He was thinking of quitting the music business, but she told him, "No you can't quit. I think I'm quitting the racket, 'cause I been at it so long, but you keep on, 'cause you're going places."

King and Johnny Ace met in 1949. The older King had become by this time a well-known performer in Memphis, and Ace, just out of the service and eager to find his path, was not necessarily looking for a mentor but found one anyway.

The backdrop to all of this was a radical decision in 1948 by John Pepper and Burt Ferguson, the two white owners of WDIA, a local radio station, to program for the African American population of Memphis, thus becoming the nation's "first all-black radio station." As it turned out, this change benefited some of Memphis's local personalities such as King, who started a brief career at WDIA singing live during a fifteen-minute segment on Saturdays, 5:00 p.m. until 5:15 p.m. By mid-April 1949 he was given a regular, daily fifteen-minute show, which included King singing a jingle for the sponsor, Peptikon health tonic. He eventually got his own show where he was billed as the Beale Street Blues Boy, which eventually got shortened to Blues Boy and finally to B. B., a name that never went away.

In 1949, WDIA deejays had a lot of options in regard to the blues, because what was proving popular in record sales and on jukeboxes was a scattering of the genre. It was as if anything remotely bluesy could be a hit record. Success was unpredictable, which can be seen in the listing of the Top R&B songs for the year.

Louis Jordan and His Tympany Five had the number one R&B record of 1949 with "Saturday Night Fish Fry (Parts 1 & 2)." Jordan had been scoring hit records since the war years and represented the light-hearted vein (sometimes referred to as "hokum") that was always popular in the blues. By 1949, Jordan was still at the top of his game but old school. Number two that year was Charles Brown (no longer with Johnny Moore's Three Blazers) with "Trouble Blues" and then a real outlier, Larry Darnell singing "For You My Love," a cross between crooning and traditional blues. Darnell, twenty-one that year, was already a veteran of show biz, having performed as a dancer in the Brownskin Models, a popular chitlin' circuit troupe. He settled down in New Orleans for a while and got a steady gig at the Dew Drop Inn. "For You My Love" was so popular that it was number one on the R&B charts for eight weeks.

Amos Milburn's "Roomin' House Boogie," more of a traditional jump blues tune with a hot sax intro, was at number four, while the Orioles pushed in at number five with "Tell Me So," a pre-doo-wop weeper with a slow gospel feel. Finally, at number six was a song that presaged the coming of rock 'n' roll, Wynonie Harris's "All She Wants to Do Is Rock," in which he exclaims, "All she wants to do is rock, rock 'n' roll all night long."

In 1949, two singers found themselves on the same label, but their careers would soon go in opposite directions. One of the singers, B. B. King, esteemed by younger Memphis musicians who were striving to make a name for themselves, was in reality also an up-and-comer. That year, he would step into a studio for the first time, recording for Jim Bulleit's Nashville label a straight-up blues number, "Miss Martha King," with "Got the Blues" on the B-side. Soon afterward, King went on the road playing the chitlin' circuit, mostly raunchy roadhouses in small towns like Birdsong, Arkansas. His band consisted of pianist Johnny Ace, saxman Richard Sanders, and guitarist Robert Junior Lockwood.

Already on the Bullet label since 1946 was Cecil Gant, but 1949 would be his last year with Jim Bulleit. He would move on to 4 Star Records in Hollywood. Writer Nick Tosches interviewed Bulleit in 1977 and asking him about Gant. Bulleit said first that he had "never recorded a thing [by Gant] that didn't sell and make money. It was just uncanny." Secondly, though, in regard to Gant's career, which could be summed as a very slow spiral in the wrong direction, Bulleit said: "He drank too much. He would say, 'I want to do a session' when he ran out of money. We would get a bass-player and a guitarist and get him a piano, and I'd sit in the in the control room, and he'd tinkle around on it, and then he'd say, 'I'm ready,' and tap that bottle; and if we didn't get it the first time, we didn't get it, 'cause he couldn't remember what he did."

Two years later, at the age of thirty-seven, Gant was gone. The cause of death was listed as pneumonia, but in some regards he drank himself to death. Does this sound familiar?

My Song

CHAPTER 11

B. B. King tries Amateur Night at the Palace Theater – The Beale Streeters conquer Memphis – David James Mattis creates Duke Records – Johnny Ace records "My Song" – Don Robey buys Duke Records– "My Song" number one nationally

Although there had been buildings at 324 Beale Street, Memphis, since the 1870s, the structure known as the Palace Theater dates from 1919. It was built by Lorenzo and Angelo Pacini but quickly became the entertainment showcase for African Americans. All the major black entertainers played the Palace, going back to Bessie Smith and Ma Rainey in the 1920s.

Starting in the 1920s, the theater introduced Amateur Night, which was more than just a competition; it was also a way for local and itinerant musicians to make a few bucks. The audience could be ruthless – physically driving disliked performers off by throwing things at them. On the other hand, the winning prize was five dollars, and money also went to the second- and third-place finishers. In the 1930s, during the heart of the Depression, a dollar could feed a person for day. Eventually all participants would get a dollar after a performance.

In the heyday of Amateur Night, the 1940s and 1950s, it was hosted by Nat D. Williams, who eventually became the first featured black deejay in the country (at WDIA) and then Rufus Thomas, who would also later work at WDIA before becoming a well-known singer. The biggest hit for Thomas, a funny, loquacious gentleman, was "Walking the Dog."

Thomas often talked about his tenure at the Palace. He told Robert Palmer, "The bigger and better clubs in Memphis had a big band and a floor show. They had people like Duke Ellington and Count Basie coming through . . . the blues with harmonica and guitar and so on, that was the juke joints . . . a person like me might want to go out and dig some blues occasionally. People from the best of families did that from time to time. It was just a part of living."

When he first came back to Memphis, B. B. King, like most unheralded blues musicians from the Delta, was always looking to make an extra dollar just for living expenses. King entered the amateur contest practically every week, singing mostly ballads and novelty numbers. That dollar meant something. As King wrote in his autobiography, *Blues All around Me*, "On Beale Street you could get a whole meal for 20 cents."

Thomas, in another interview, recalled: "Amateur nights on Beale, that's where B. B. King got started right on Beale . . . everybody that come up would get a dollar. And B. B. was happy to come up and get that dollar. Now he knew that I knew that he needed it, and I would put him on anytime he come down there to the Palace Theater. He would play his old raggedy guitar and sing the blues good, and he was a good entertainer even at that time."

It was no stretch for Thomas to make sure King got a place on Amateur Night because King was good and sure to attract to the Palace a few more bodies.

Though King was a frequent Amateur Night participant, and it wasn't a given that he would win. By 1949 the young Turks of Memphis were competing, outstanding musicians like Rosco Gordon, Bobby "Blue" Bland, and Johnny Ace. In fact, King claimed that he never once won the contest.

When not at the Palace, King would take his guitar down to Handy Park and play for tips. The park, which was constructed in the 1930s, was like an open-air meeting hall for the black community. Preachers and bluesmen competed there for the ears and spare cash of onlookers. It was also where old blues musicians could still be found, although King's interest was less with the old guys and more with the younger crowd. At Handy Park and the Palace Theater he began to hang out with a small group of talented musicians, including Bland, Ace, Gordon, and harmonica player Herman "Little Junior" Parker. Also joining the group at times were drummer Earl Forest and saxophonist Adolph "Billy" Duncan.

"There was a caring feeling on Beale Street," King observed. "Musicians would talk to each other, exchange ideas and listen long and hard to each other. I learned so much just hanging 'round the park. . . . I got started a little before Bobby "Blue" Bland, but when he came 'round Beale Street, I loved having him sit in with the little bands of mine."

When King was allowed to form a band at WDIA for his on-air performances, he tended to use his friends, drummers Earl Forest and Solomon Hardy and pianists Johnny Ace and Ford Nelson. The WDIA group was his first back-up band.

According to Forest, Ace first joined Billy Duncan's band in Memphis after he was released from the army around 1949, and he (Forest) and Ace spent lots of time in the studio at Main and Winchester Streets in downtown Memphis.

By the end of 1949, Ace and his loose group of musical friends became so well known in Memphis that they were given the name Beale Street Blues Boys, and the leader at that time was Duncan. These young men knew how to play and how to party. Eventually, Memphis club regulars began calling the group "the Beale Streeters" because of "their taste for the high life of Memphis's main thoroughfare," according to Palmer. King often sat in with the Beale Streeters, or when headlining a gig he would have Forest, Duncan, and Johnny Ace back him up.

The Beale Streeters became the premier band of Memphis throughout 1950 and 1951, with Bobby "Blue" Bland taking the lead on singing duties. However, things were changing quickly in Memphis.

Unlike Nashville, the big music city down the road, Memphis was still without a stable and organized recording industry by the end of the 1940s. Then, at the very start of the next decade, Sam Phillips opened the Memphis Recording Service, which attracted a number of local bluesman. The official opening day was February 3, 1950, and just over one year later Phillips cut his first major hit. Ike Turner and his Kings of Rhythm came into Phillips's studio to record a song called "Rocket 88," with lead singer Jackie Brentson. However, due to confusion over the name of the group, the song was released as being by Jackie Brentson and his Delta Cats. It has often been called the seminal rock 'n' roll record.

While Ike Turner rued the day he was disassociated from "Rocket 88" and lost out, he benefited extraordinarily when those in the business came to recognize his talent. Phillips used him as an in-house producer, and, more importantly, the Bihari brothers, who founded Modern Records in California, hired him as their A&R man in Memphis. One of the first people he brought to Modern was Bobby "Blue" Bland.

Another big change for the Beale Streeters was the success of B. B. King. His first shot at recording didn't result in any success, but Turner took notice and recommended the Bihari brothers sign him. They did, and King recorded in 1950 under the Modern Records subsidiary RPM Records. King at this point effectively moved on from the Beale Streeters.

Also moving on was Rosco Gordon, but in the opposite direction, north. Born in Memphis in 1928, he migrated to Chicago in the mid-1940s and then came back to Memphis the same year as Johnny Ace returned from the service. He, Ace, King, and the others all came together in 1949.

Gordon's win as an amateur at the Palace came in 1950, and afterward Rufus Thomas invited him to play on his radio show. By the next year, he was scouted by Turner, who brought him to the Bihari brothers. They signed him to RPM, and, in 1951, with his first recording, he had a hit, "Saddle the Cow," a bit of piano-based, bluesy hokum. It was the same year B. B. King, also on RPM, had his first big hit, "3 O'Clock Blues." The song was recorded at Memphis's YMCA on Lauderdale and Vance, and it required just two takes. The band backing King consisted of Earl Forest on drums, Richard Sanders and Billy Duncan on sax, and Johnny Ace on piano.

All the Beale Streeters were moving on, except for Johnny Ace. The problem wasn't his talent but his demeanor. He just didn't put himself out there like the other guys. When the Beale Streeters played gigs, the lead singing was always by others. As Preston Lauterbach wrote, "Of this bunch, the shy pianist John Alexander Jr. [Johnny Ace] seemed the least hungry for stardom. B. B., Rosco, or Bobby Bland handled the vocal chores at their shows, and John seemed happy behind the piano and out of the spotlight."

Ace did eventually show some career initiative. After King hit with "3 O'Clock Blues" and began life outside of Memphis, Ace took over King's old band and put it under his name. King said of Ace, "Johnny had looks, guts, determination, and talent. But, don't ever dare ask Johnny to do something dangerous 'cause the boy would up and do it."

In 1951, Bobby Bland recorded four numbers for Modern at Sam Phillips's recording studio, with Johnny Ace accompanying him on the piano. Nick Tosches wrote that these sessions happened in January 1952, although it appears the first release was early in 1952 so the recording session might have been near the end of 1951. In 1952, Bland was drafted, and after midyear he was in the military service.

By 1951, the old Beale Streeters had broken up, but the name of the group was so famous in Memphis that WDIA had a Saturday afternoon show called "Beale Street Blues Boys." One of the few original Beale Streeters on the show was Johnny Ace. With the success of King, by 1951 the show was rebilled as featuring "Bee Bee King's original band." With King, Gordon, and Bland gone, Earl Forest pushed Ace to take over the singing chores.

One other important change happened in the Memphis music scene in 1951. WDIA hired David James Mattis to be the production manager and program director. Mattis (also known as David James) was from Forest City, Arkansas, where he had been an announcer sometimes working with black entertainers such as Howlin' Wolf, who would appear live on the station during fifteen-minute segments. He also ran his own program as the Boogie Man, playing records by African American artists.

Settled into his new job, the hardworking Mattis decided to set up his own label, Duke Records, at WDIA studios in 1952.

MY SONG   151

Prior to Duke, a local producer named Don Kern operated Tan Town records out of WDIA to record gospel groups, but that effort didn't last very long. Mattis in 1952 was following on the heels of Sam Phillips, who had opened Memphis Recording Studios two years before. In 1952, like Mattis, Phillips created his own label, Sun Records. At the time, Mattis had an approach to the industry that was different from that of Phillips. The latter was mostly leasing big names to larger record companies, which favored musicians already established. Phillips tended to favor veteran artists like Rufus Thomas. Mattis, on the other hand, used the WDIA recording studios to capture raw talent coming in off the street. Phillips would take note.

Duke was such a small operation that Mattis bought a drafting set and designed his own purple and gold record label, basically the front end of a Cadillac: the two headlights and V design.

Al Bell already knew Mattis even before Bell started working at WDIA's competitor, WLOK. "I always had a good relationship with him," Bell said. "We would run into each other from time to time or take a meeting together. He was very creative and knew authentic black music. He took that station WDIA and turned it into a monster; it was a powerful station in Memphis, and he did it through programming and the announcers he hired. Eventually Memphis's black population surpassed the white population, and Mattis went after all segments of the urban populace – and I'll be darned if he didn't get them all."

Mattis, because of the station's association with B. B. King, also had an abiding interest in recording the old Beale Streeters. One of the first Duke Records recordings was of Rosco Gordon in 1952. Coming straight in after Gordon was to be Bobby "Blue" Bland for a quick recording session before he headed into the army.

In May 1952, John Alexander Jr. showed up at WDIA's studio to back up Bland's first Duke recording session. By all accounts, Mattis was a no-nonsense kind of guy, and, when Bland came into the studio unprepared, he scrapped the session. Meanwhile, Alexander had come in early and was well prepared. To get warmed up, he teased out a unique, piano-based crawl of the Ruth Brown recording "So Long," which had been the B-side to her big hit "Mama, He Treats Your Daughter Mean." Mattis immediately took a liking to the tune, and as Lauterbach notes, "Mattis tweaked the lyrics on the spot and recorded John Alexander Jr.'s impromptu debut single. John's name sounded too dull, and, in an inspired fifteen minutes, John Alexander Jr. became Johnny Ace and 'So Long' became 'My Song.'"

A slightly different version of this story comes from Nick Tosches, who wrote in 1984: "James Mattis started Duke Records with the idea of capitalizing on the local talent not already signed to RPM or other companies to whom Sam Phillips was selling his records. Johnny signed with Duke in the spring of 1952. It was understood from the beginning that Johnny's actual surname would not be used, so that his father, the Reverend, might be saved from any shame."

In either case, Johnny Ace with the Beale Streeters were the accredited singers on the record. Mattis, under the names "James," took songwriting credit (completely ignoring the existence of "So Long"). Since the A-side was a slow romance, the B-side, "Follow the Rule," was much more emphatic, as was the practice of the day. This was a Johnny Ace tune, and Mattis gave the young man full songwriting credit.

In "My Song," Johnny Ace croons about his woman leaving him, and hours seeming like years, and his heart beating low and slow. He wonders where she has gone and wants her to please come back to him. If only she were to come back, they would be together for eternity. Again, as with "I Wonder," the recording was made in what was essentially a makeshift studio, and today it sounds like it was taped in a cavern. Lauterbach wasn't much impressed with the whole enterprise, writing, "It's about what you'd expect from a mop-up group: choppy, out-of-tune piano and sodden saxophone. Johnny Ace's vocals are monotonous, but sincere and distinctive."

Importantly, it was a departure from a typical blues song that had repetition, circular logic (the last verse often repeating the first) carried by a strong beat. The lyrics to "My Song" tell a story in two lengthy stanzas that are similar but not the same, and Ace delivers it all in a pleading and pained voice. It is also worth noting that Johnny Ace was young and handsome, and teenage girls just wanted to sweep him up and hold him.

"I knew Johnny Ace," affirmed blues singer Lavelle White, and the memory was a gauzy patch of rainbow colors. "I knew them all – Johnny Ace, Gatemouth Brown, Bobby "Blue" Bland, and Junior Parker – but that Johnny Ace, he was gorgeous, he really was. Sharp dresser. Everybody loved him because he was respectful to everybody. He had that silky voice."

Did he ever flirt with Lavelle? Wistfully, she said, "No, he was always busy, always on good behavior. He was a beautiful person."

No, Ace didn't stretch his vocal range on "My Song." Instead, he carefully and tonally hewed to the saxophone in the background, but where in the song it was important to accentuate he amped it enough so listeners could feel the ache in his heart. Released in June 1952, this record was a tour de force. And everyone knew it. Down in Houston, Don Robey understood the song's potency before anyone else, but he would make sure everyone else in the country heard about the record.

MY SONG

Robey, through his artist booking subsidiary, Buffalo Booking Agency, and his influence over the chitlin' circuit in the Texas and the Gulf Coast, had good contacts in Memphis, in particular a guy named Andrew "Sunbeam" Mitchell, who opened the Mitchell Hotel at Beale and Howard Streets. Again, this was a time of segregation, so the Mitchell Hotel catered to African Americans, and it became known as the "Leading Colored Hotel of Memphis." The hotel was located on the third floor of the old Battier's Drug Building, with the second floor occupied by the Domino Club, which later changed names to the Club Handy, a major stop on the chitlin' circuit. He also took over the bookings for the Hippodrome, a venue with seating for over five thousand that had been a roller skating rink but by the later 1940s became the premier stop in Memphis for R&B singers.

At one time, a group of the Beale Streeters – Earl Forest, Johnny Ace, and B. B. King – was living at the Mitchell Hotel. According to Forest, he, Ace, and King all wore the same size suit at that time and often borrowed clothes from each other.

B. B. King remembered Mitchell well: "Sunbeam owned Mitchell's Hotel on the third floor, and there was a lounge, later called the Domino Club, on the second floor[,] where he had jam sessions during the week and name bands on weekends. . . . I call Sunbeam a saint 'cause he'd give you room and board for free if you had a halfway decent story or could play halfway decent blues. Sunbeam loved music and cared for the folks who made it."

Robey had knew Sunbeam – they were already doing work together. It was Sunbeam, skipping past business and ethical legalities, who kept Robey abreast of what was happening in Memphis, including Mattis's Duke Records venture and the talented crop of musicians he was signing. The Peacock label had been formed to record Gatemouth Brown, but its real strength at the start was gospel music. Its roster was powerful, including the Five Blind Boys of Mississippi, the Bells of Joy, and the Dixie Hummingbirds. While Robey did well with gospel, he knew the real money was in secular music so he also signed acts like Willie Mae "Big Mama" Thornton.

Robey understood the problems of being an independent record producer. The one thing an independent could do was record talent, everything after that, including distribution and promotion, took money and connections, which is why most independents licensed their music to bigger companies. Being a record producer was a "cool" business, but owners struggled to keep their heads above water. Robey quickly understood that Duke Records could use his help, but there was a key problem. Robey was black, and Mattis was white, and in the Jim Crow South any hint of a black company moving in on a white company would have raised concerns. So he sent his white sales manager, Irving Marcus, to Memphis to talk about a partnership.

In 1950, after Robey formed Peacock Records, he needed someone to create a national distribution channel. That person was Marcus, who had spent many years with King Records helping to build up that organization. The official Peacock line on the merger with Duke was that it was all happenstance: Marcus was on a trip through Memphis and had run across the Duke label, which was up for sale. That probably was not true, since the Duke label was so new. Mattis was still getting it under way, so a sale would have been far from his mind. Nevertheless, the official story continued in the same vein, that on the strength of "My Song," sung by Johnny Ace, which both Robey and Marcus recognized as having terrific potential, a deal was consummated.

The offer seemed like a good idea to Mattis, who had probably worked with Robey sometime in the prior years. Across town at Sun Records, even Sam Phillips realized it was tough to make a dollar as an independent producer recording black musicians playing the blues, which was one reason he dreamed of finding a white boy who could sing R&B.

"Mattis didn't have capital," says Texas music historian Roger Wood. "He had talent, and he wanted to push it. Robey had capital and connections. He could take these artists, dress them up in tuxedos, and get their picture in the paper. He had connections with DJs. Mattis had a background in radio, but he couldn't get artists booked all over the region; Robey could. In 1952, Robey was clicking on all cylinders."

Lauterbach wrote: "Robey's muscle and Memphis talent seemed to Mattis a powerful combination. The merger appealed to Mattis's sense of racial justice as well – a Southern musical conglomerate of a black entrepreneur and a white bleeding heart would be momentous. Mattis agreed to the partnership, the particulars of which remain unknown, and in August 1952 Robey announced the merger of Mattis's Duke Records and his Peacock Records."

The August 2, 1952, *Billboard* reported the marriage of the companies under the headline "Peacock Adds Duke to Fold." The story began: "Peacock Records has taken over the Memphis-based R&B diskery, Duke Records. The new Duke firm is headed by Don Robey and Irving Marcus of Peacock, and David Mattis of Tri-State Recording. Peacock will continue to issue wax under the Duke label as well as its own R&B and spiritual platters. Duke Records, though a fairly recent addition to the R&B platter firms, has some well-known artists in its line-up, including Rosco Gordon and Johnny Ace."

MY SONG 155

Early in Peacock's history, Robey recorded a seminal gospel hit, "Our Father," by the Five Blind Boys of Mississippi, but it wasn't until 1952 that "he made the most fortuitous business deal of his life," Robert Palmer assesses. "[He did this] by buying the Memphis-based Duke label – recorded masters, artist's contracts and all. Among the artists who came to Robey with Duke were Johnny Ace, Rosco Gordon, and Bobby "Blue" Bland, and, in 1954, Herman "Little Junior" Parker joined an expanding Duke roster. Ace, the sloe-voiced balladeer, dominated the national charts from 1952."

The Duke-Peacock merger started off like a boulder rolling downhill, picking up speed along the way. All the things that Mattis couldn't do in regard to promotion and putting Ace into the market, Robey immediately set out to do. It wasn't that Mattis was unskilled or didn't believe in his singers, but his main job was running a radio station. Robey not only understood what was needed to create a best-selling record but also already had the existing network in place. One week after the ink dried on the legal documents, *Billboard* in its August 9, 1952, issue listed "My Song" on its "Best Selling Retail Rhythm and Blues Records" list for the first time. It was ninth on the list of best-selling R&B songs in the country behind the likes of Lloyd Price's "Lawdy Miss Clawdy," the Dominoes' "Have Mercy Baby," and the Clovers' "One Mint Julep."

Ace wasn't the only Duke recording star getting a boost. In the same issue, the "Rhythm and Blues Notes" column dropped this item: Rosco Gordon would team up with the very-hot Clovers on a tour through California, Washington, and Oregon starting at the end of the month.

Also in that issue of *Billboard*, Robey took the bottom right-hand corner of a page to promote two of his acts, Johnny Ace and Marie Adams, who were promoted at the National Association of Music Merchants, which had its big convention in New York. The ad was headlined "Sensational, Two Show Stoppers" and promoted Marie Adams's new song "He's My Man" (a note proclaiming 22,000 sold at the NAMM Convention) and Johnny Ace's "My Song" (a note boasted that it was the hit of the NAMM Convention, with 43,000 sold.

There was no let-up from Robey. In the *Billboard* magazine that was published after the NAMM convention, on August 16, 1952, "My Song" had moved up two notches to number seven on the "Best Selling Retail Rhythm and Blues Records" chart. In addition, the "Rhythm and Blues Notes" column had this item: "Key R&B manufacturers were in New York this week to attend the music trade show . . . among those attending were: Lou Chudd of Imperial Records, Art Rupe of Specialty, Don Robey,

Irving Marcus and David Mattis of Peacock and Duke, [and] Les Bihari of Modern."

The official Peacock story is that the master of "My Song" was brought to New York for the NAMM convention and that even before the record was released Robey had made it a national hit. In a room at the New Yorker Hotel, where the convention was taking place, Robey said it went down this way: Three or four men sat on a bed, two easy chairs were also occupied, and there was complete silence as a portable phonograph played a simple, somewhat familiar tune, "My Song," by a complete unknown, Johnny Ace. Those Peacock distributors bought big, and the record became the most talked about tune at the show – and then there was an immediate rush by almost every record company in the business to record a cover version of the song.

Cash Box on the same date, August 16, 1952, in its gossip column "Round the Wax Circle," reported from New York: "There was much bidding by publishers around town this week for a tune called 'My Song.' It's recorded by Johnny Ace on the Duke label, which was recently bought by Peacock, and it looks like the hottest thing to hit the R&B market in months. Several pop versions are in the planning stage."

The next week, "My Song" had moved up more two notches to number five on the list of best-selling R&B records, its progress slowed by the Clovers' next big hit, "Ting-a-Ling," which leapfrogged over it. In that week's issue of *Cash Box*, in its "Rhythm and Blues Record Reviews," which covered new songs, there were two singles of interest. First, Johnny Ace's old friend B. B. King unleashed "You Know I Love You," with "You Didn't Want Me" on the B-side. And there was a review of Johnny Moore's Three Blazers with their version of "My Song." The comment: "Fine cover on the new ballad now moving up via the Johnny Ace waxing on the Duke label."

On the same page, the "Rhythm and Blues Notes" column read: "Johnny Ace's waxing of 'My Song' now riding high on the *Billboard* R&B charts, has caused a flock of cover waxings of the hit tune. Okeh has cut the song with thrush Hedda Brooks, Mercury with juke-box 'Queen' Dinah Washington and Peacock with Marie Adams. This is the first R&B ditty that has spurred this many versions in a long time."

Cover versions of hit records were not unusual. At the start of the 1950s, there were so many covers of hit records that one could easily hypothesize a lack of creativity in pop markets. Take a look at three popular songs from 1950: "Rag Mop" had eight versions released same year, including R&B and C&W (country and western) cuts; "Mona Lisa" had seven versions, including R&B and C&W; and "Goodnight Irene" had seven versions,

MY SONG 157

including R&B and C&W. Another song, "Tennessee Waltz," had ten versions released in 1950 and 1951, including R&B and C&W.

Cash Box finally got to review two of the new "My Song" covers in the September 6, 1952, column "Jazz 'n Blues Reviews." The assessment for Dinah Washington's version read: "Dinah Washington throws her hat into the ring with her stylized reading of the exciting slow blues and comes through with a version that is bound to please her legion of fans. Orking [orchestration] is strong and the potent arrangement spots them to advantage."

The lead review in this column was for the lesser-known Marie Adams, and it read: "Johnny Ace started a race to cover this slow beat blues when his release turned into an instantaneous hit, and the diskerie [record company], in an attempt to corner the market, waxed its number one gal singer on the item. Marie Adams lives up to expectations as she smashes through a top flight deck that we think could establish her in the pop field. Marie gives a colorful, passionate reading with Cherokee Conyers and orchestra providing a soft backdrop in the mod of the piece."

In regard to popularity, the quick cover versions of "My Song" were a strong indicator of a recording phenomenon. What hurt, however, was the appearance of a Peacock recording of a Duke Record. Since every new version was an attempt to cannibalize sales of the original, this did not please Johnny Ace. If nothing else, this was a signal as to how Robey treated his musicians, as pawns on a chess board.

Like T-Bone Walker, Marie Adams (Ollie Marie Givens) was from Linden, Texas, and got her start playing clubs in Houston, where Robey discovered her. She had just come off a hit, "I'm Gonna Play the Honky Tonks," so the justification for her recording "My Song" would have been nothing more than elevating her at the expense of Johnny Ace. In any case, It didn't work. Johnny Ace and "Your Song" was taking the market like a hurricane coming off the Gulf. Adams only had that one big hit, but as a Peacock recording act she often toured with Gatemouth Brown, B. B. King, and even Johnny Ace. Then, after Ace died, she recorded a tribute song called "In Memory (A Tribute to Johnny Ace)."

Despite the Marie Adams diversion, Robey cranked up his chitlin' circuit network for a Johnny Ace tour, but this one was different. The record was so popular right away that Robey slotted Ace for the better venues, including Memphis's Hippodrome, where on August 23, 1952, he appeared as a headliner for the first time. Opening for him was his friend Bobby "Blue" Bland, who now was also recording for Duke and trying to get some action before he headed into the army.

All the radio stations that played R&B got on board. As Lauterbach wrote, "Black-formatted radio had quickly become the concert promoter's most powerful tool, doing what newspaper ads and window placards never could do. . . . Dick "Cane" Cole at WLOK was a long time Sunbeam [Mitchell] foot soldier, and Dewey Philips at WHBQ could be relied on to spin a hot new local disc." As for David Mattis, well, he owned a piece of Duke-Peacock and wasn't shy about playing the record.

The concert was massive, and "My Song" sprang to number one on *Billboard*'s R&B best-seller chart on September 27, 1952, and, probably equally important, it was number three on the chart for "Most Played Juke Box Rhythm and Blues Records." On a troubling note, *Billboard*'s "Rhythm and Blues Notes" had a small item about Percy Mayfield, who had been seriously injured in auto accident en route to Los Angeles. It took Percy two years to recover and left him with facial disfigurement, but he still could write great songs such as "Hit the Road Jack" for Ray Charles.

Six weeks later, "My Song" was still the best-selling R&B song and the number two play on jukeboxes nationally. "My Song" prevented B. B. King from having another number one hit with "You Know I Love You," and Little Walter's "Juke" stopped "My Song" from being number one on jukeboxes. That week, *Billboard*'s new record reviews covered Charles Brown's "Rollin' Like a Peddle in the Sand" and Rosco Gordon's "Dream Baby."

At the start of December, "My Song" was still a top ten record in Chicago, New Orleans, and Atlanta. The "Cash Box Rhythm and Blues Ramblings" column on December 6, 1952, noted, "Johnny Ace proved to be the sleeper of the year when he shot out of no place into national prominence and hit the country with the force of an atomic explosion. For a time 'My Song' was Number One in practically every city across the board."

According to *Billboard*, "My Song" was fifth on the list of best-selling R&B songs for 1952, coming in ahead B. B. King's "3 O'Clock Blues" (number nine) and "You Know I Love You" (number twelve) and Rosco Gordon's "No More Doggin'" (number eleven) and "Booted" (number fourteen). Not bad for a bunch of guys who two years before were just slappin' fives on Beale Street and playing late nights at the juke joints for coins and beer.

The Clock

Don't mess with Don Robey – "Cross My Heart" follows 'My Song"
– A old song reemerges – "The Clock" strikes one

I n 1948, the Supreme Court, in a case known as *United States v. Paramount Pictures Inc.*, decided that film studios could not own their own theaters. The ruling basically said that the existing distribution scheme of film studios was in violation of US antitrust law, which prohibited certain exclusive deals. This was a major change in what was a significant part of the entertainment industry. It was a long and winding road of hearings, appeals, and cross appeals before the high court declared the major studios guilty of monopolistic practices in restraint of trade – bloc booking, discriminatory pricing and exhibition agreements, et cetera. The "Big Five" movie companies were ordered to divest themselves of their theater holdings, which were in actuality the main source of their income and power.

Probably because there was no Big Five in the musical world and because independent companies proliferated from the 1940s through the 1960s, no one thought to apply the same jurisprudence likewise to this entertainment industry, and that was a good thing for entrepreneurs such as Don Robey. Coincidental to the founding of Peacock Records in 1949, he owned important entertainment venues such as the Bronze Peacock Club, had his own management company and booking agency (Buffalo Booking Agency), and had control over much of the Texas and Gulf Coast chitlin' circuit on which African American performers toured. Al Bell remembered that Robey and B. B. Beamon in Atlanta controlled much of the chitlin' circuit, while others say Robey and Howard Lewis in Dallas split up all of Texas. Ruth Brown remembered: "The Weinbergs, father and son . . . they controlled Virginia, clear through North Carolina all the way to Louisiana. From there we'd pick up in Georgia and subcontracted again to one of the two famous black promoters in Atlanta, Henry Winn or B. B. Beamon. In Texas, the black kingpins were Don Robey and Howard Lewis, both [actually only Lewis] worked out of Dallas."

Once a performer entered Robey's world, it wasn't much different from being a sharecropper. In theory you were an independent worker, but in reality everything you did for financial gain and all your income were dependent on one person. Writer Ed Ward called Duke-Peacock Records a "plantation" because contracts could be a lifetime thing, unlike at Atlantic Records, for example.

In you were an artist signed by Robey, he would put you under contract to one of his labels, record you in his studio or one he contracted with, control distribution of your records, place you in one of his venues, and finally have his booking agency create a tour, usually on the southern chitlin' circuit – from Georgia westward to Texas – that he controlled or at least greatly influenced. He also would create the backup band for the tours, made up of musicians he contracted. Finally, he would put his name (or his pseudonym, Deadric Malone), on your record as co-songwriter so he could collect royalties.

Just to make sure everyone understood who was in control, he carried a gun wherever he went. As a 2015 *Houston Press* article on Robey noted, "As a one-stop operation, Robey got a piece of everything and used strongarm intimidation to make negotiations go his way."

Just the like the monopolistic motion picture companies, Robey created a whole lot of great entertainment. And big, wonderful careers were established for many African American performers who otherwise might have been left hustling for nickels and dimes in rough-hewn juke joints and barn dances for the rest of their musical lives.

Roger Wood, who interviewed a number of old Houston blues singers, said many of them had high regard for Robey, who not only made their career but treated them fairly. Some musicians such as Big Mama Thornton he nurtured through slow times until he finally found a band and hit record for her.

Roy Head, a white singer, was one of the last big stars for Robey. Signed to Backbeat, one of Robey's secondary labels (along with Song Bird and Sure Shot), he had a number two hit record, "Treat Her Right," in 1965. It would have shot all the way to number one but was blocked by a record called "Yesterday," by the Beatles.

Head has fond memories of Robey. "He was real distinguished, always wore a suit and big-rimmed glasses. He didn't beat around the bush. He was a businessman and a gentleman, gave me a new Cadillac and $1,000 every year. I remember thinking at the time, 'I'm in the business now.'"

Still, one had to be careful where one sat in the boss's presence. In his office he had a gold spittoon on the floor near the end of his desk, and he would turn and spit. Said Head, "He never missed that damn thing; I was always amazed about that."

On the other hand, Robey put his name on Head's record as cowriter to grab a share of songwriter royalties with BMI. He used his nickname. "I got my mechanicals [payment for production and performance]; I didn't let him steal that," said Head. "He used to pay all the black songwriters from the north side of Houston $50 for their songs. That's where he got most of his songs. Then he would put his name on those records."

There are two narratives about Robey, Wood explained. First, there are those who say that if Robey hadn't come along they would have not have had success or played the Apollo, that Robey made their career, and that they were treated fairly. Then there are those who say he would always get his cut – and then some. Texas Johnny Brown fell into the latter category. He wrote a song called "Two Steps from the Blues," which was a big hit for Bobby "Blue" Bland. Robey put his pseudonym on the record. Wood asked Brown about that, and Brown said that he seen his friends get ripped off because they were just selling their songs to Robey. He had held out and felt good that he'd at least gotten half the songwriting credit.

Head's signing with Robey is another story. Head had put together a band called the Traits toward the end of the 1950s. It was locally successful and recorded in a San Antonio studio. A subsequent record got some play on radio stations across the state. The band found a sponsor (a funeral home) and played in "every town in Texas," according to Head. The Traits were playing in a dive southwest of Houston, possibly in Hallettsville, when Houston record producer Charlie Booth walked in. Head asked his guitar player if he knew "Ooh Poo Pah Doo" by Jessie Hill. The guitar player said "sure" but then launched a completely different opening riff, and Head started making up lyrics. It worked. Booth introduced Head to Huey Meaux, another Houston record producer, and they recorded "Treat Her Right" in just one take. Meaux immediately approached Robey about licensing the record. Robey said yes indeed, but neither of the two trusted the other. When they met to discuss the contract, Robey took his gun out and placed it on the table. Meaux not only knew all about Robey, he also tried to emulate him. He took out his own gun, and he too placed it on the table. They understood each other well.

"Robey was one helluva a businessman," said Milton Hopkins, a guitarist who backed up a number of Duke acts including Johnny Ace. "If you didn't know what you were doing, you didn't want to play around with him."

Milton, like other musicians Robey dealt with, was of two minds about him. On the one hand he was discovered by Robey, and on the other hand that didn't mean much. "I was sitting on my porch when this big car pulled up," Milton recalled. "I couldn't imagine who it could be. The window rolls down, and it's Don Robey. He needed a guitarist, and someone told him about this guy sitting on a porch playing. That was me."

That was the positive. Hopkins also noted, "I never made any money with him. The acts [headliners] got paid out pretty good, but it was a shame how he treated the rest of us. There wasn't any money made by the sidemen."

A decade before there was a Motown, Don Deadric Robey became the first great African American music mogul. He was born in Houston in 1903 to a white mother and black father. According to historian Wood, his father may have been a medical person but in any case was influential in the black community early in the twentieth century. Less is known about his mother, but she might have been Jewish – that was a constant rumor in Houston. "Older musicians would say to me, 'you know he was Jewish,'" said Wood, but that might have been because he had Jewish associates or due to the ethnic stereotype that Jews made money. Wood, who looked into Robey's history, says he could find no information to support that claim, although Houston had a sizeable Jewish population in the early twentieth century and the first synagogue in Texas was in Houston's Third Ward, which even then had a large African American population.

For a brief time in the late 1930s, Robey ran a nightclub in Los Angeles, where he picked up the skills to open the Bronze Peacock Dinner Club when he returned to Houston in the 1940s. He also dabbled in other businesses, such a taxicab company, before settling in with the music world. This was still the Jim Crow South, and for an African American to succeed there had to be a certain amount of give and take, mostly give, with the white power structure. Somehow Robey was able to walk that fine line between success and complete accommodation because there are no records yet unearthed of him running into serious trouble with Houston police or the broader city government. There was always the backdrop of some cracker coming after him because he was African American with money, which might be one reason he carried a gun. As Al Bell noted, "back in those days a lot people carried a gun because you never knew when you might need it. I always carried a switchblade knife with me – just in case."

One thing Robey knew was how to take care of key people. If you were a star on his roster, he took care of you. If you were a DJ who was open to payola, you got money too. John Jackson, who wrote an Alan Freed biography, claimed Freed and Robey knew each very well. One of Jackson's sources for his book said that Robey came to New York from Texas carrying with

THE CLOCK

163

him a huge diamond ring. "'Hey man,' Robey told Freed, 'you just made me 400,000 bucks. Don't tell me you can't take this gift from me!'"

Rumors also persist that he was a gambler or ran a gambling operation in Houston. He was the black mafia, said Head. "You either respected Don Robey when you went to see him or you didn't go see him."

It was a lesson Little Richard learned the hard way. He tried to out-swagger Robey, who beat him so bad he suffered a hernia that wouldn't get repaired for years. Little Richard said: "He jumped on me, knocked me down, and kicked me in the stomach . . . right there in the office he beat me up. Knocked me out in one round. Wasn't any second or third round – he just come around that desk and I was down."

Lavelle White was another singer to sign with Duke. A native of Jackson, Mississippi, she moved to Houston when she was fifteen and already married. She immediately separated from an abusive husband and started singing in Houston nightclubs. Her big break came when she met blues guitarist Johnny Copeland, who introduced her to Don Robey. She signed with Duke-Peacock records in 1958.

"He was nice within reason," she recalled, "but in business he did a lot of bad stuff. That guy was tricky, and he tricked a lot of us out of money. He was like a money launderer. He had a bad temper, but he never yelled at me. I never got that close to him."

In his Big Mama Thornton bio, Michael Sporke interviewed a musician who knew Robey. "I talked with him once," the musicians said. "He wanted to record me but I didn't like his attitude. So I wouldn't record with him. He would come in with his briefcase full of money and that was supposed to impress you. And then he would sign you up. Then never paid you."

The same specious actions held true in his other business practices. When Stax Records of Memphis was enjoying success during the 1960s, Al Bell went to Texas to meet with Robey, whom he considered a friend in the business. Over the years they had met often. This time it was a business trip because Stax was interested in buying Duke-Peacock. Accompanying Bell were his key financial people, who were allowed to go through Robey's books. Bell and Robey came up with a potential number where a deal could be swung and then everyone broke for lunch. Well, not everyone. When Bell and his financial people came back to Robey's offices and looked through the books once more, all the numbers had been changed.

David Mattis didn't know who he was dealing with when he formed a partnership with Robey. He would learn very quickly. And so would Johnny Ace.

For a number of months in the fall of 1952 one of the artists Johnny Ace managed to overshadow was another new singer in the same slow-blues vein, Chuck Willis, who released a song titled "My Story." There was some confusion in the market, as Ace and Willis sang in similar styles: cool, flat, and with a plaintive quality that appealed to teenage record buyers. "My Story" went to number two on R&B charts in October, never quite catching "My Song."

The year 1953 was born in optimism, and "My Song," which was released in August 1952, was still one of the top ten songs being played on America's jukeboxes and still a best seller in such major markets such as New York, Los Angeles, and Washington, DC (Willis's and King's records were also still charting at the start of 1953.)

One of the benefits to Robey of having "My Song" become so successful is it that made an impression on the music industry, especially the trade publications such as *Billboard* and *Cashbox*, which were where insiders turned when trying to figure out the market. Now the trade publications would pay attention to anything Duke-Peacock would release, and the label kicked off the New Year with a new Johnny Ace record, "Cross My Heart," with "Angel" on the B-side. The listed songwriters for "Angel" were Johnny Ace and David Mattis, but it's unknown whether Mattis just attached his name to a Johnny Ace composition or actually made a contribution. Mattis would get his comeuppance on the A-side song "Cross My Heart," for which he had to share songwriting credits with Robey, who made no contribution to the creation of the song.

Whether or not *Billboard* needed a reminder about the new Johnny Ace record, Robey advertised big. In the first 1953 issue of *Billboard* was a half-page ad that consisted of Robey's usual two promotions in one. The left side promoted Duke Records and was all about Johnny Ace. The headline read: "Another Terrific Hit." Then came "Both Sides for Johnny Ace," with details at the bottom saying that distributors had purchased fifty-four thousand copies and that "My Song" rated among top sellers of year. The Duke Records logo included the address: 4104 Lyons Avenue, Houston, Texas. The right half of the add focused on Peacock recording artists Lloyd "Fatman" Smith, Paul Monday, and Bells of Joy. The Peacock logo at the bottom had the same address and phone numbers as for Duke Records. Duke Records of Memphis no longer existed. This was now a Robey label.

In the next week's issue, on January 10, 1953, *Billboard* ran a full page of new record reviews for all its categories, Popular, Country & Western, Rhythm & Blues, Latin American, and Spiritual. The five reviews for

R&B were all known performers – Wynonie Harris, Johnny Otis, Big Jay McNeely, Jay McShann and Lucky Millinder – but none of these new songs would become hits. A key feature in this column was "New Records to Watch," and the R&B choices were Lloyd Price's "Tell Me Pretty Baby," Percy Mayfield's "The River's Invitation," and Johnny Ace's "Cross My Heart."

The next week in the *Billboard* each of the three would get a review. For "Cross My Heart": "Johnny Ace's first waxing since the smash hit 'My Song' is another powerful slicing. The warbler turns in a sincere and moving rendition of a pretty, slow-tempo ballad, over an attractive ork arrangement. Side [A] is potent and should be a real coin-grabber for the young warbler." As for the B-side, "Angel," the review read: "Another strong side by Ace, tho not quite as potent as the flip. It's also a slow ballad and the warbler hands in his usual meaningful vocal. Backing is smooth. This side too should rate spins and plays."

And it was off to the races. By the next week "Cross My Heart" was a top ten record in New York, Los Angeles, Cincinnati, Philadelphia, St. Louis, Charlotte, and Detroit. One of the records it competed with in every market was Jesse and Marvin's "Dream Girl."

By the following week, "Cross My Heart" was on *Billboard*'s best-selling R&B list at number five in the country, and it was number ten on the magazine's chart for most R&B jukebox plays. "Dream Girl" that week was number ten and number two, respectively.

On the tour circuit, Johnny Ace's competition was coming from every direction, including from his own record company. Ace had formed his own band and was expected to go on a Robey tour of one-nighters. Meanwhile, Robey put Marie Adams together with Arthur Prysock for a chitlin' circuit run of similar one-nighters. B. B. King, now working with Buffalo Booking, was also hitting the road, with the Bill Harvey orchestra, on a trek of one-nighters through the South. *Billboard*'s "Rhythm and Blues Notes" column on January 31, 1953, reported that King had inked a three-year pact with the Bihari brothers and was touring Texas.

From outside Duke-Peacock, Jesse Belvin, working with agent Ben Waller of Los Angeles, was touring Texas as well as New Mexico and Arizona. He bumped up against Gatemouth Brown who was also doing one-nighters in the Southwest.

There was a fault line here. Robey was relying on his tried-and-true chitlin' circuit, which if given a letter grade were B-stops at best. Almost all the A-stops were in the big cities of the Northeast and Midwest. While

Buffalo Booking was doing a great job keeping everyone busy in Texas and elsewhere throughout the South, at the same time a successful doo-wop group like the Clovers was playing the Earle Theater in Philadelphia and the Howard Theatre in Washington, DC, and then going to New York to cut some new records.

"Cross My Heart" did very well, becoming a top fifty R&B record for the year 1953. It just wasn't the phenomenon that "My Song" was. Perhaps it was the weakness of the touring schedule – lack of visibility in the Northeast – or a bit of burnout. In February, with "Cross My Heart" as the fifth best-selling R&B record in the country and the fifth-most played song on America's jukeboxes, it oddly got no recognition from Robey, who placed a half-page ad thanking disc jockeys but not mentioning the song. Once again, it was a kind of two-in-one promotion. This time Peacock Records was promoted on the left, with mentions of Marie Adams, Gatemouth Brown, Jimmy McCracklin, Willie Mae Thornton, and Sonny Parker, plus a handful of gospel singers. The right side promoted Duke Records, highlighting songs by Bobby "Blue" Bland ("Lovin' Blue"), Rosco Gordon ("Too Many Women"), Earl Forest ("Whoopin' and Hollerin'"), and Johnny Ace's ("My Song" – but not "Cross My Heart").

The Duke acquisition was going great guns. All the listed Duke performers were ex-Beale Streeters. The least heralded was drummer Earl Forest, who was a close friend of Johnny Ace, and in 1953 that caused Robey serious consternation.

Backtracking a year, in January 1952 a number of the Beale Streeters crowded into a recording studio for RPM records. Ostensibly everyone was there for a B. B. King recording session, but the Bihari brothers realized they had so much talent in the room that pretty much everyone got a shot at the main mic. One of the first cuts was B. B. King's "Gotta Find My Baby," which would end up as the B-side on the "Some Day Some Where" single. It was backed by Johnny Ace and Earl Forest. Junior Parker recorded "Bad Women Bad Whiskey" with Ike Turner on the piano. Johnny Ace's debut recording "Mid Night Hours Journey" was backed by B. B. King and Earl Forest. Then Forest sang "I Cried," backed by Johnny Ace. Bobby Bland got a few songs in, including "Love Me Baby," with Johnny Ace, Earl Forest, Junior Parker, and Matt Murphy on guitar.

Forest had been a session musician for Modern Records since Bobby "Blue" Bland started recording for the Biharis in 1951. In the January 1952 recording session, he got in a few songs under his own name. Then when Mattis signed all the old Beale Streeters, both Forest and Bland started recording for Duke. In April 1953, he would have his biggest hit, "Whoopin' and Hollerin,'" which went to number seven on the R&B charts. The Biharis couldn't help but notice the success of both Johnny Ace and Earl Forest and dug into their vault to find the recordings from January 1952. To capitalize on the singers' successes, they combined Johnny Ace's "Mid Night Hours Journey" with Earl Forest's "Trouble and Me" and put it out as a single on Modern's subsidiary Flair Records.

"Mid Night Hours Journey" was a Johnny Ace composition, but he received no credit for it. Joe Bihari brothers took credit under a pseudonym, Josea, a common practice at Modern. When the record was released, *Billboard* took notice under its review column and commented, "This doesn't sound like the Johnny Ace now on Duke Records, but it may have been made a while ago. Under any circumstances it is an effective performance and it should pull spinning and loot on the basis of the name if for no other reason."

But it didn't succeed, and the record didn't make Robey happy. There's no proof, but Robey had enough pull to make sure the record wasn't greeted with hosannas by DJs. The record disappeared without a trace, which was another small grievance held by Johnny Ace.

Perhaps the biggest reason "Mid Night Hours Journey" didn't make a dent was because Duke-Peacock introduced a new Johnny Ace record, "The Clock," that would prove to be another spectacle. The songwriter was David Mattis, who managed to keep Don Robey's name off the record as cowriter. As part owner of Duke-Peacock, he had that right.

The first mention was of the record was in June 20, 1953, when the *Cash Box* " Rhythm 'n Blues Reviews" column highlighted two songs as the next to be hits. One was Dinah Washington's "Never Never," with "My Lean Baby" on the B-side. The other was "The Clock," with "Aces Wild" on the B-side. The column noted: "Johnny Ace, unknown to the trade one short year ago, streaked across the hot charts with a Number One sensation 'My Song,' followed about six months later with another big hit, 'Cross My Heart,' and keeps his record one hundred percent with his third and what looks like a certain click, 'The Clock.'" The song was said to be a slow and sentimental, "hauntingly" sung, and, as with the other Johnny Ace records, simple, melodic, and hummable. It straight-up Johnny Ace – and ear candy for America's teens.

"A devilishly handsome youngster from the Beale Streeters group, Ace sang in a mellow, expressive tenor that caused mass heartthrob everywhere," Ed Ward would write in the 1980s.

In 1953, Al Bell was thirteen years old and growing up in Arkansas, one of his favorite songs on the radio was "The Clock. "I only knew of one Johnny Ace song at the time," remembered Bell. "I fell in love with it and still love it today. It was 'The Clock.' That was just me, but it was different for my classmates. Oh, my God, was Johnny Ace popular with teenagers, especially the females."

It wasn't just girls. A. C. Wharton grew up in Lebanon, Tennessee, before coming to Memphis. He was just nine years old in 1953. "We didn't get much blues music, because Lebanon was in country-western music territory, and my dad listened to country," Wharton recalls. "We were allowed to listen to a little bit of the blues on WLAC, which played the blues at night. I remember listening to Johnny Ace because my mother just loved him and his music. It cast a pall over my household when we heard Johnny Ace died."

English teachers would have objected to the lyrics of "The Clock" since the opening lines use a double negative ("The face of the clock on the wall . . . doesn't tell me nothing at all"), but teenage girls wouldn't have cared. They would have felt the singer's pain, especially in the one repeated line: "The clock and I are so lonely in this room." The slow beat would barely register on a heart monitor.

Billboard in its June 27, 1953, issue listed "The Clock" in its "This Week's Best Buys" column, based on "early sales reports from important markets, which indicated these new records were making solid sales progress." The column observed, "Fast start for this one. Already on the charts in New Orleans with strong reports from New York, Philadelphia, Detroit and Southern areas."

Robey greased the record's progress with ads in the trades. The one in *Billboard* read: "Acclaimed! Third Smash Hit! The Clock Strikes Again for Johnny Ace." *Cash Box* placed the song in its "Award o' the Week' review, with the headline "There's No Stoppin' This One."

Cash Box gossip column "Rhythm 'n Blues Ramblings" on July 4, 1953, boasted two Johnny Ace notifications. First, out of Los Angeles, it reported, "New Johnny Ace etching [record] received this week by the boys [DJs] has already started to make some noise." The lead item that week out of New York was also about the hot singer. It began: "Looks like the recent flood of Grade A released by the rhythm and blues [record producers] will shake up the usual summer slump and give business a real shot in the arm. Peacock [Duke] is really hot with the new Johnny Ace 'The Clock' [and] Earl Forest's 'Last Night's Dream' . . . [while an] Atlantic Records new quartet . . . includes The Clovers latest, 'Good Lovin.'"

THE CLOCK

This "Good Lovin'" was not the same song as the Young Rascals number one hit of 1966. Still, in its day it was a number two record on the R&B charts, and the Clovers were one of the most successful doo-wop groups of the early 1950s. Between 1951 and 1955 the group boasted nineteen top ten records on the R&B charts, including three number one songs. And when it appeared their days in the spotlight were over, they came back in 1959 with a fun crossover hit, "Love Potion No. 9."

As good as "Good Lovin,'" did, and it charted very well, the record didn't stand a chance against "The Clock," which by July 18, 1953, was the number one best-selling R&B record, according to *Billboard*. It was still number one on August 1, also becoming the number one most-played R&B record on America's jukeboxes. It was number one in Charlotte, Chicago, Cincinnati, Los Angeles, and New Orleans and number two in Atlanta and Detroit. The song stayed in the number one position nationally for five straight weeks.

It wasn't until September that the song began to fade as a host of strong new records hit the market, including "Shake a Hand" by Faye Adams, "Crying in the Chapel" by the Orioles, and "Good Lovin'" by the Clovers. At the end of the 1953, "Crying in the Chapel" would be the number one song of the year, followed by "Shake a Hand." Johnny Ace's "The Clock" would be number five and "Good Lovin" number fifteen.

The summer of 1953 was also when time ran out for David Mattis. As Roger Wood commented, Robey was able to "squeeze" Mattis out the business. It wasn't too difficult for a man like Robey as he handled distribution and collection for Duke-Peacock. The problem for Mattis was that Robey collected but didn't distribute. Mattis had been wondering since the start of the year where his money was and accusing Robey of swindling him. They went back and forth in negotiation for about six months, with Mattis finally realizing that he was being strung along. He took a train to Houston and showed up unannounced at Robey's office. In Mattis's words, "That's when the .45 came out." In the end, Mattis sold all the Duke artists' contracts for a total of $10,000 (just under $100,000 in 2020 dollars) and received half of the $17,000 profit (about $163,000 today) from Duke Records. Mattis told interviewers in later years, considering the popularity of "The Clock," a song he wrote, the settlement was a "joke." "I knew damned well that we had collected over $200,000 (almost $2 million in 2020 dollars), but I just wanted out."

In October 1953, *Cash Box* posted a photo of Johnny Ace receiving a gold clock from the Music Operators of America (MOA). In the picture were also Irving Marcus, Don Robey, and five representatives of MOA. The clock, the caption read, was presented on behalf of the nation's jukebox operators, honoring Johnny for three hit tunes ("My Song," "Cross My Heart," and "The Clock") that each sold over a million records.

Wood concluded, "Mattis ended up with a $10,000 settlement, which was a lot more money than he was going to find anywhere else. When he got his money he wasn't in a position to feel ripped off."

Lauterbach had a different conclusion about the nasty business: "Robey was in total control of Johnny Ace."

Saving My Love for You

CHAPTER 13

Teenagers save for "Saving My Love for You" – Big Mama takes on the "Hound Dog" – Evelyn Johnson's tough tours – Too much, too soon for Johnny Ace – "Please Forgive Me" faces tough competition – "Never Let Me Go" a top ten disappointment?

In July 1953, *Cash Box* magazine published a poll of R&B disc jockeys. Among the questions it asked: "What male vocalists do you estimate you programmed the most?" Johnny Ace came in second behind Chess Records singer Willie Mabon, who had a number one hit in 1952 with "I Don't Know" and then repeated that success with "I'm Mad" in 1953. A second question was "What female vocalists do you estimate you programmed most?" The popular Ruth Brown was number one, while another Peacock recording star, Willie Mae Thornton, was number two. Probably the most important question asked was "What records do you estimate you programmed most?" Number one was Willie Mae Thornton's "Hound Dog."

Known as Big Mama Thornton, Binnie Willie Mae Thornton was born in Ariton, Alabama, in 1926. As a teenager she joined a troupe called the Hot Harlem Revue, which played the chitlin' circuit throughout the South. In 1948, while the tour was in Texas, she left the group and decided to stay in Houston, which, as noted, boasted many clubs patronized, entertained, and owned by African Americans. Together with New Orleans, Houston formed a nexus of rhythm and blues talent on the Gulf Coast. By 1950, she made her first recordings for E&W, a tiny local label, and was performing at the Eldorado Ballroom, the major entertainment venue in the black Third Ward. That's where Don Robey saw her, and he then signed her away from the Eldorado to play at his club the Bronze Peacock.

She was a big lady, often dressed like a man, and didn't take a lot of guff from people, which is probably why Robey liked her and went out of his way to nurture her career. After two years of having Thornton under contract at Peacock, Robey saw his chance to get his protégé wider exposure. It was early in1952, when Johnny Otis came to town with his big Rhythm

& Blues Caravan. The two met, and Robey talked Otis into auditioning some of his Houston talent for his show. Otis liked his two women stars, Thornton and Marie Adams. Otis was a shrewd businessman as well as a commanding presence in just about all aspects of the industry. He was a musician, songwriter, producer, band leader, and probably could cook a mean stew on a hotel room burner. The deal they worked out was fair to each of them. Otis would take Thornton and Adams on tour with his revue, record them when the tour returned to Los Angeles, and then give the finished masters to Robey. Thornton benefited the most from the deal. First, she was such an exciting performer she quickly became a highlight of the revue, and her stage reputation began to build. In December 1952, she made her first appearance at the Apollo, playing with the Johnny Otis Orchestra, and then came back to Houston to play at the Bronze Peacock for the holiday season.

Importantly, Otis kept his side of the deal and on August 13, 1952, brought Thornton into a recording studio. He also invited two young, white songwriters to the session. Their names were Jerry Leiber and Mike Stoller, and they would go on to become one of the biggest songwriting teams of the 1950s and early 1960s, writing "Jailhouse Rock," "Kansas City," "Stand by Me," and "Love Potion No. 9," among many others. In 1952, they were just two young men on the make and given an opportunity to write a song for Thornton, which they did. It was called "Hound Dog," and it was a growler of a tune. As with most successes in the music business at the time, there has been a little controversy over the song. Johnny Otis, who was producing the session and even played drums on the recording, didn't like some of the original wording and then helped the young men work through the production. Early releases of the song listed Leiber, Stoller, and Otis as the songwriters. Otis always maintained the credits were deserving, but Leiber and Stoller said no and eventually sued. Otis's name was eventually dropped from the credits after the lawsuit.

"Hound Dog" carried the scent of lawsuits, and attorneys followed their noses. Rufus Thomas recorded "Bear Cat" on Sun Records as an answer song to "Hound Dog." It rose to number three on the R&B charts, making it Sun's first national hit. The crosstown camaraderie between Sun and the Mattis-less Duke ended right there because Robey sued Sun for copyright infringement, and he won. Things would get worse between the two. Little Junior Parker signed with Sun in 1953 and was very successful with "Feelin' Good," which reached number five on R&B charts, and "Mystery Train," which would become an early Elvis Presley recording. Then, in a flash,

SAVING MY LOVE FOR YOU

Parker ended up on Duke-Peacock. Phillips felt that Robey stole his singer, and that became a contentious lawsuit between the two.

Phillips was a real pioneer in Memphis music, recording many great R&B singers – everyone from Howlin' Wolf and B. B. King to Bobby Blue Bland – but Robey was determined to squeeze him out of the black Memphis talent pool. So when a young white teenager named Elvis Presley walked into Phillips's recording studio it was as if the gods were throwing him a lifeline. Sun Records pivoted, and so would the music world.

In the United States, the music industry sometimes moves forward by looking backward. In 1956, Elvis Presley would boast a number one hit with his recording of the Big Mama Thornton hallmark "Hound Dog."

Thornton's original version of the song wasn't released until 1953, and it was a huge hit, sitting atop the R&B charts for seven weeks. With the success of "Hound Dog," Robey added his new star to his A-list tour of Johnny Ace, Junior Parker, and, when available, Bobby "Blue" Bland.

In September 1953, Robey left Houston to meet with Johnny Otis, who then signed on with Peacock Records. Afterward Robey returned to Houston to oversee a host of new recording sessions with Ace, Thornton, and Otis. One of the recordings from this session was Ace's "Saving My Love for You," which wasn't released until the end of the year, with Robey trying to catch the holiday market.

Cash Box previewed the record on December 12, 1953, in its "Rhythm 'n Blues Reviews" column, and it highlighted the song in its "Award o' the Week" box. The reviewer noted, "Johnny Ace's newest 'Saving My Love for You' is news 'cause it heralds another hit for the Duke Record 'ace.' Continuing in the same ballad vein that is his strong point, Johnny lends his warm and intimate styling to the lovely slow item with the result another extremely powerful disc. Ace sings the sentimental love tune tenderly against a soft and subdued instrumental backing."

> *"Saving My Love For You"*
> *You said you want me, baby, I'm glad.*
> *I feel so good now, 'cause you're not mad.*
> *Please believe me, I'm saving my love for you.*
> *We'll be together, and it won't be long,*
> *I'll make you love me from that day on.*
> *Please believe me, I'm saving my love for you.*
> *Can't you remember last September?*

We kissed and we said goodbye.

I pretended that I was happy.

But, darling, I wanted to cry.

We'll be together, and it won't be long,

I'll make you love me from that day on.

Please believe me, I'm saving my love for you.

[instrumental break]

We'll be together, and it won't be long,

I'll make you love me from that day on.

Please forgive me, I'm saving my love for you.

The song was written by Sherman "Blues" Johnson, who got full songwriting credit. Johnson wasn't a Houston soft touch who could be bought off for fifty dollars. He had been recording with his group, the Clouds of Joy, on the Trumpet Records label in Jackson, Mississippi. While short-lived, the independent label also recorded other great blues singers such as Elmore James and Sonny Boy Williamson.

The B-side behind of "Saving My Love For You" was "Yes, Baby." The *Cash Box* reviewer liked it, writing, "Johnny Ace surprises and etches a jump item 'Yes, Baby' with the aid of an unnamed fem. thrush [singer]. A good deck but not as potent as 'Saving My Love for You.' Definitely another biggie for Ace."

Billboard, which had previewed the record on December 5, 1953, said about "Yes, Baby": "Ace proves on this side that he can sell a rhythm tune as well as a ballad. He really comes thru with a powerful rendition on this jump effort, while the combo and unbilled singer swings out behind him."

That unbilled singer on "Yes, Baby" was Big Mama Thornton.

December 1953 was going to be a competitive market. Sharing the "Award of the Week" was another Willie Mabon number, "I Got to Go." *Cash Box* proved prescient when it picked for "Sleeper of the Week" the slow doo-wop number "A Sunday Kind of Love," by the Harptones, which would end up being one of the classic songs of the era.

There was no real downtime for Ace. Except for the recording session in September, he was consistently on the road from August to the end of the year in a coast-to-coast marathon, from the Shrine Auditorium in Los Angeles to the Apollo in New York. All of it arranged by Peacock-controlled Buffalo Booking Agency, run by another Houston go-getter, Evelyn Johnson.

SAVING MY LOVE FOR YOU

Born in 1920 in Thibodaux, Louisiana, where the waters were apparently entrepreneurial (recall Hosea Hill), Johnson moved with her mother to Houston in 1926. After high school she attended Houston College for Negroes (now Texas Southern University). When she was in her mid-twenties she took a job with Robey to be the office manager of the Bronze Peacock. After three years with Robey, she became his most trusted employee and in 1949 helped him form Peacock Records. One year later, she attained her license from the American Federation of Musicians to book and manage union artists, founding the Buffalo Booking and installing herself as president.

Buffalo Booking became a huge operation, and it helped to put order into the chitin' circuit. Then the agency came to dominate its Texas and Gulf Coast regions. As Lauterbach notes, "Don Robey and Evelyn Johnson's chitlin' circuit conglomerate had blossomed into the most elegantly functioning racket anywhere in the industry." Lauterbach's criticism was that the Johnson system carried weaker groups through the circuit riding on the coattails of the stronger groups, and that Johnson coerced promoters to book her lesser-known acts by threatening to withhold the sure moneymakers like Johnny Ace. That wasn't an original concept. Alan Freed had been doing something similar since his inaugural concert in Cleveland, the one that ended up as America's first rock 'n' roll riot. It became standard procedure, and Johnson had just smoothed out the wrinkles for the formerly unorganized southern loop of the chitlin' circuit.

"Johnson would put those tours together with numerous acts," Roger Wood said. "Johnson would place a really strong act first, followed by a mediocre act, a strong act and then a new act, etc. If you wanted to get the A-act then you would also get the other acts."

"Robey and Johnson did a heckuva job working those venues," said Al Bell. "They knew what artists to put in what venue that would attract the biggest crowds, so the owners and artists could make some money. Evelyn Jonson was a precious lady, very intelligent."

If there was a true complaint about Buffalo Booking Agency, it is that musicians would travel for months all over the circuit and come home with barely a dime in their pockets because they had been charged for laundry, required outfits, and other assorted tabs. When they got back to Houston, these expenses wiped out what musicians were supposed to be paid.

As Milton Hopkins observed, "there wasn't any money made by the sidemen although the main acts got paid pretty good."

Roy Head gave a nod to Johnson, saying, "Evelyn took me over, and she booked me all over the country. I worked with everyone from Etta James and Bo Diddley to James Brown and Four Tops."

After the success of "3 O'Clock Blues," B. B. King formed a small revue similar to what Johnny Otis had been doing. Although not King was not a Duke-Peacock musician, Evelyn Johnson took over the booking for the show. King recalled, "There were tiny clubs and big barns, nice black theaters and nasty roadhouses. . . . Most of our work, though, was in the South, especially Texas. Texas had more juke joints than rattlesnakes . . . We drained the South dry – Louisiana, Alabama, Mississippi, Georgia."

The genius of Robey and Johnson, Wood stressed, was that they helped create the post–World War II chitlin' circuit and then made a tremendous profit booking Peacock acts on that circuit.

Almost anyone who worked with Johnson proclaimed she was one of the nicest people in the company and that this was part of the way the Robey-Johnson team worked, like bad cop and good cop. "After talking with Robey and getting all the threats and the .45 on the table, they would go to Johnson, who would patch things up and create a compromise for everyone," said Wood. "They all seemed to like her, and her people skills seemed to be impeccable."

Lavelle White remembered Johnson with affection. "She took care of my business. She's the one who put me out there. Don Robey came into the studio once or twice when I was recording, but he didn't hang around too much. Joe Scott, a good engineer and director, did the recording sessions."

Peacock was managing the artists, booking the artists, recording the artists – in short it was handling every phase of the money-making operations, and Robey did quite well. As for Johnson, how did she fare? Robey was married. He had a family all that time he was having an affair with Evelyn Johnson. He would tell her that once his kids were raised he would leave his wife and share all his holdings with her. Robey did leave his wife, but he married another woman.

Wood got to know Johnson very well in her later years and even spoke at her funeral. She would always say to him, "Just don't ask me about my relationship with Robey."

She would, however, speak about the personalities she worked with in those years with Robey. It turns out that the warm and fuzzy Johnson didn't like the performers very much, but think about having to herd musicians nearly every day for years. That would have gotten old very fast. She called Big Mama Thornton "a female thug."

SAVING MY LOVE FOR YOU

As for Johnny Ace, Johnson said, "He was a fool. He drank recklessly and . . . played with his gun recklessly." In 1985 interview, she said, "You could go down the block and find ten boys who could sing better than Johnny, but he had that certain something."

That was the consensus on Ace. Success came suddenly, and he partied too much and behaved badly.

Nick Tosches wrote, "Fame and fortune [were] instantly his, not for a moment, but for every moment since ["My Song"]. No rise to lasting fame had ever been so sudden, nor would any other ever be. It was uncanny. His records were fine, but not so fine as all this."

Milton Hopkins, who traveled with Ace, added, "He was a nice guy, but he liked to horse around. As to women, Johnny Ace was no different from the rest of us. Most of the musicians had a lot of women. There was no getting away from that." In another interview, Hopkins was more specific. "He was always horse-assing around. He liked to wrestle – four, five guys at a time. He had knives and guns, he'd talk about your mama and shit. He got a little too loose when drunk."

Fame came at Johnny Ace too fast. He drank heavily and screwed around with the women, wrote Lauterbach, who also claimed Ace developed a highly disturbing but safely rigged, good-luck ritual of spinning his revolver's empty cylinder, cocking the hammer, placing the barrel against his head, and pressing the trigger, which was either a frightening attention-getter or a cry for help or both.

Wood, who interviewed musicians that played with Ace, pointed back to his immaturity and irresponsibility, noting that he drank too much, met up with too many women, and bought himself an Italian .22 handgun that he waved around like a water-pistol. Milton Hopkins, who toured with Ace, said, "He was a guy who liked to joke around. Johnny had his own gun that went with him everywhere."

And everywhere is where Ace went.

With Thornton's "Hound Dog" success, Johnson teamed the two, which is when they met. Thornton was the opening act. By the autumn, the tour was playing the A-circuit in the Northeast, including the Royal Theater in Baltimore and the Howard in Washington, where were they joined on the tour by Junior Parker and His Blue Flames and the Harptones.

An article in the *New York Age* early in October 1953 blasted the headline "Johnny Ace and 'Big Mama' Thornton Are Headliners in New Apollo Revue." The story read: "Two of the hottest recording personalities in the country, Willie Mae ('Hound Dog') Thornton and Johnny ('The Clock')

Ace making his first local appearance, headline the new show coming to the 125th St. Apollo Theater this Friday, October 23. The Bill Johnson and Tab Smith orchestras, George Holmes, The Wallace Brothers, 'Crackshot' Hamilton and his comedy group, and Princess Tall Chief round out the show."

The newspaper ads for the show updated the lineup. An ad headline read: "Week Only Beg. [beginning] Fri. Oct. 23rd." Underneath: "The Nation's Newest Recording Star Johnny 'The Clock' Ace, Bill Johnson and band with Junior Parker, co-starring Willie Mae 'Hound Dog' Thornton [and then the remainder of the performers as mentioned in the article].

On Thanksgiving night, B. B. King joined up with old friends Ace and Parker, along with Thornton, for a show back in Houston.

Variety, which was more conservative than the other trade publications for the entertainment industry, was still not on board with the growing strength and attraction of rhythm and blues music. Johnny Ace was the hottest thing on the R&B record charts, but *Variety* wasn't buying in. Tosches dug up *Variety*'s review of Ace's first Apollo appearance, and it asserted that Ace was "too stiff and wooden." It conceded that Ace possessed a smooth baritone voice, but the bottom line was negative: "His song salesmanship isn't commensurate with the quality of his voice."

Variety was on a different planet because the Johnny Ace–Big Mama Thornton show was such a big hit that they would be invited back at Apollo. On April 23, 1954, the tour's second appearance at the Apollo, the trade publications raved about the tour making a "smashing appearance." This time *Variety* agreed, and its review was all accolades: "Miss Thornton and Ace split the vocalistics with support from a driving seven-man combo/ four rhythm, two reed and a bass. Femme is a heavy rhythm & blues thrush while Ace is a mellow crooner. The contrast is effective and sustains interest and excitement all the way."

The *Cash Box* "Rhythm and Blues Ramblings" column of January 24, 1954, mentioned the second concert months in advance, reversing the order of the stars: "Willie Mae 'Big Mama'" Thornton and Johnny Ace, the big Don Robey duo, working one-nighters in the east, go into the Apollo Theater, Harlem, on April 23. This marks Willie Mae's fourth and Johnny's second time on the boards of the Palace of R&B."

At the start of 1954, Duke-Peacock announced some new signings and shows. Little Junior Parker, who originally had success with Sun Records, decided being on a Buffalo Booking tour was a good thing for his career and tightened that tie by signing with Peacock Records. At the same time, Robey

SAVING MY LOVE FOR YOU

brought into the fold Texas bluesman Lester Williams and assigned him to Duke Records, which was now a subsidiary label of Peacock. There were also mentions of Peacock performers on tour, including Al Grey, Gatemouth Brown, and Rosetta Perry recently playing in Baton Rouge, and a new entertainer in the group, Little Richard, with his combo The Upsetters, playing in his hometown of Macon.

The charts at the start of the year were dominated by Clyde McPhatter's "Money Honey" and Joe Turner's "Honey Hush." Johnny Ace's "Saving My Love for You" was not yet a national best seller, but it was the fifth-most-played record on jukeboxes. On January 23, "Saving My Love for You" joined *Billboard*'s top ten list of best sellers for the first time, at number ten. It would eventually reach number two. At the same time, Guitar Slim's "The Things I Used to Do" began to be played across the country. On January 30, *Billboard* ran a listing of what it called "Territorial Best Sellers," which were the top ten about a dozen selected cities. Here's how the Johnny Ace versus Guitar Slim battle was turning out: In Atlanta, "Saving My Love for You" was number two, and "The Things I Used to Do" was number seven. Charlotte was similar, with "Saving My Love for You" at number three and "The Things I Used to Do" at number seven. In St. Louis, it was "The Things I Used to Do" at number one and "Saving My Love for You" at number ten. While "Saving My Love for You" was in the top ten in Los Angeles and Philadelphia, Guitar Slim's record was in the top ten in New York, Chicago, and New Orleans (number one in the last city).

Going into March, Guitar Slim and Johnny Ace were still slugging it out across America. The *Cash Box* "Hot" column on March 6, 1954, showed "Saving My Love for You" outdoing "The Things I Used to Do" in New York and Newark but the positions reversed in Chicago, New Orleans, and San Francisco. The magazine, in that issue, inserted a bit of boasting in its "Stars over Harlem" column, which led with this item: "Can't help but think about how there just seems to be no stopping that Johnny Ace, Don Robey–Irv Marcus combine. Their big one at this scribbling is the soothing "Saving My Love for You," which was picked by this column many, many weeks ago as a sure bet to tug away and away at the very heartstrings."

In *Billboard*'s January 30, 1954, gossip column "Rhythm & Blues Notes," Peacock got a few mentions, including Irving Marcus being on the West Coast to sign a new gospel group called the Paramount Singers, and Gatemouth Brown forming his third orchestra. The bigger news was that the Johnny Ace and Willie Mae Thornton tour was now being backed by the C. C. Pinkston orchestra and had returned to the Southern chitlin' circuit, playing in Alabama and Georgia. The added feature on this tour was Little Junior Parker playing as a separate act backed by Bill Johnson's Blue Flames. It was a new year and time to get back on the road.

While on the West Coast to sign new talent, Marcus was corralled by a *Billboard* writer in Hollywood. The chatty Marcus revealed that the company had moved to a new headquarters building in Houston that would house offices, recording studios, and a pressing and processing plant. The pressing and processing plant, Marcus bragged, was the most modern factory of its kind in the South, where Peacock could turn recorded tapes into finished discs. In addition, the company would have its own printing department, enabling it to print its own labels and promotional materials.

The expansion, said Marcus, was to accommodate "ambitious plans for the further growth of the indie rhythm and blues firm."

Marcus had every reason to be optimistic because the combined Peacock and Duke labels hit peak sales the year before, racking up an estimated sales of 1.5 million records, mostly due to Willie Mae Thornton's "Hound Dog" and Johnny Ace's three hits, "My Song," "Cross My Heart" and "The Clock." That haul didn't even include Robey's gospel catalog, which added another half a million records sold.

Unfortunately for Duke-Peacock or Peacock-Duke, whatever it was calling itself, 1954 would prove to be a different kind of year for the company and its performers. Bad blood was brewing, although that was not unusual at a company often run by intimidation and sleight of hand.

Roger Wood made an offhand comment about Evelyn Johnson: that she never married and never had kids, intimating that she had patiently waited for that day when Robey would divorce his wife and marry her. Lauterbach had a different view, saying that she yearned for children of her own, but the turmoil at Peacock pretty much exhausted her maternal resources. Some of the performers couldn't read or were educated in a limited way, some struggled with substance abuse, and all wanted for better grooming if not better behavior. Lauterbach wrote, "They all fought with each other and with Robey, mostly over money."

When the former Beale Streeters got to Houston, Robey immediately started making money off them. On the plus side, he kept them in clothes and in cars, and, if they needed help with women, he could help them that way as well. He knew how to pamper his moneymakers. When they realized their records sold by the thousands, they thought, "Well, I'm going to make a lot of money." It didn't happen. Robey owned the publishing. If they wrote songs, they didn't own all of the songwriting credits, and all those pampering expenses got billed back to them.

SAVING MY LOVE FOR YOU

Money and theft of songwriting credits were standard complaints in the 1950s and into the 1960s. Ace would have other grievances too. He missed the gentler ways of David Mattis, who pretty much discovered him.

Ace was a free spirit, while Robey was a disciplinarian. Little Richard called him a dictator and said, "He was so possessive he would control every breath that you breathed. I resented him for being so mean. He had artists like Clarence 'Gatemouth' Brown, Bobby Bland and Johnny Ace. He controlled all of them."

Not quite. Like a pouty child, Johnny Ace misbehaved, bridling and bucking at Robey's constraints.

Roy Head, who came Peacock years after Johnny Ace was dead, eventually heard all the scuttlebutt about their relationship, and he affirmed, "Johnny Ace didn't like Don Robey." From the stories Head had listened to from the other musicians, he added, "Johnny Ace and Don Robey got into a little 'squat' that night of Johnny Ace's last show."

Whatever Ace and Robey's differences were, the obvious conflicts were between Ace and Evelyn Johnson, who as the head of Buffalo Booking was the person from Duke-Peacock who Ace had to deal with continually since he was forever touring. They fought all the time, said Milton Hopkins, who toured with Ace and was onstage the night Ace died. Years later, Roger Wood asked Evelyn about Johnny Ace's death, and she was coy in her response, deflecting to Ace's unsatisfactory behavior.

Hopkins also said he didn't remember seeing Robey at the auditorium that night, which would make for a good cover. After the gun went off and Ace fell to the floor, the Duke-Peacock executive first to be fetched was Johnson, who was at the auditorium working that night.

Writer Ed Ward claimed that rumors had been running strong that Johnny Ace had found a way to break his contract and had already signed with another record company. Although a Robey contract was seemingly forever, he didn't pay his lawyers well enough: "Robey was less than meticulous when it came to contracts and more than likely Ace's would have been easy to break."

No doubt Ace didn't trust Robey after the Marie Adams "My Song" record. And their personalities didn't jibe with Ace the perennial juvenile and Roby the somewhat strict disciplinarian. Whatever was going on with Ace and Robey, Ace staying on the road kept them apart. It was odd that once Ace came under Robey management he rarely stepped into a recording studio, and when he did it was never big sessions, just a couple of recordings and it was over. In two years at being at the top of his game, Ace's oeuvre was less than twenty songs.

Robey could punish his contract performers in numberless big and petty ways. For example, on April 24, 1954, *Billboard* did a quick review of the "Best Selling Rhythm and Blues Records" from 1949 through 1953, which included "My Song" in 1952 and "Hound Dog" and "The Clock" in 1953. Robey took the whole bottom half of the same page to promote Peacock and Duke, again as two separate labels. The prime position on the left was all about Peacock, with the lead being "Coming Soon!!!! Willie Mae Thornton's record of '54 "I Smell a Rat" b/w "I've Searched the Whole World Over." On the right, Duke Records was the focus, first "Hound Dog" by Willie Mae "Big Mama" Thornton, then a vertical listing of five of Robey's gospel performers listed, then the names of Johnny Otis, Marie Adams, Gatemouth Brown, and Little Richard, followed by those of all the former Beale Streeters. Johnny Ace's name was in smaller type than the names of everybody else in the whole ad. It looks like that happened because all his hits were included, but if someone took a quick glance at the ad they might well not have seen Ace listed.

Out in the so-called real world beyond Duke-Peacock, the bigger phantasmagoria of people, places, and events, was Johnny Ace himself. And Ace had by this time become more than simply famous. Since the introduction of the radio and then formatted play early in the twentieth century, the phenomenon of the teen idol had become part of the mass American culture. Basically "teen idol" means celebrity with a fan base of teenagers. Although the term was not in existence in the 1930s, Bing Crosby and Rudy Vallee fit the model. Then, in the 1940s, Frank Sinatra was the object of affection for the bobby-soxers (teenager girls who wore white bobby socks). By the time the 1950s rolled around, it looked like Johnnie Ray was going to be the next big thing with teenagers, but he was a quick flash before the coming of Elvis. That's the general outline. However, between Johnnie Ray and Elvis Presley was Johnny Ace.

But one of the rarest things to find is a recorded or printed interview with Johnny Ace. Outside of his music, it would appear now that he didn't even exist. Partly that was because of the continued separation of American music into categories of pop (mostly white singers) and rhythm and blues (mostly black singers). It was also because neither the record companies nor the print media wanted to challenge segregation in the South by making too much of black performers. No one wanted to be assaulted, as Nat King Cole was during a concert in Birmingham.

SAVING MY LOVE FOR YOU

The success of Johnny Ace was due to his popularity with African American teenagers, both in the South and in much of urban America. Middle-class teen boys on the streets of New York, Philadelphia, Los Angeles, and other big cities even copied his look and laid-back "cool" demeanor as they understood it. Since he was the first African American teen idol, that was like being part of a secret society because the mass media didn't cover black teenage culture, which was a far cry from white teen culture. Take a look at Eddie Fisher, who was a year older than Ace and was popular with white teens exactly at the same time. Fisher had as many records charting in 1952 as Ace did in his entire career. Over the period of 1952–53, Fisher had three number one records to Ace's two. It seemed like Fisher's handsome face was on every teen magazine in the early 1950s. He got to appear in movies and dated the A-list of Hollywood actresses, including three of whom he would wed: Debbie Reynolds and Elizabeth Taylor in the fifties and Connie Stevens in the sixties.

There's no record of Johnny Ace hooking up with a Lena Horne, Dorothy Dandridge, or Eartha Kitt.

Being a teen idol, Johnny Ace didn't have to have the best voice or have the wildest stage presence – all he had to do was be Johnny Ace, and black teenage girls swooned. If Ace's next records weren't as good as his prior recordings, the young ladies still swooned, but they also bought less records.

In the spring of 1954, Duke unleashed a new single by Johnny Ace, "Please Forgive Me," with "You've Been Gone So Long" on the B-side. The latter was written by Johnny Ace, who once again fought off Robey for full songwriting credit. The jaunty tune has Ace effectively mixing jump blues and pop. It has fine orchestration, which is because Johnny Otis and his ensemble backs him up nicely.

"You've Been Gone So Long" had the possibility of being the A-side, which is how *Cash Box* played it out in its "Award of the Week" box for May 22, 1954. The review was almost an appraisal of Ace's career, which still seemed to stun the entertainment press:

> In the short time Johnny Ace has been with Duke, the young artist has risen to the point [that] today he's one of the top wax sellers and steady money makers. Ops and dealers all remember "My Song," "The Clock," and "Saving My Love for You." New Ace disk makes a strong bid for a two-sided contender with a sensational vocal and solid rhythm number

dubbed "You've Been Gone So Long." The socko Johnny Ace backing and Ace's vocal should have the boxes [jukeboxes] jumping. Johnny is tops on the flip side as puts his heart and soul into a romantic lament tagged "Please Forgive Me." Both sides may go up hand in hand. Watch the top of the lists.

It seems the reviewer was actively lobbying for a change in Johnny Ace offerings. That was not going happen. "Please Forgive Me" was a fine song, just not much different from anything he had done before. It was written by Joseph August, with Don Robey stealing half the songwriting credits.

Joseph August was a New Orleans singer with a local hit, "Poppa Stoppa's Be-Bop Blues." Columbia Records bought his contract, and he played with a number of jazz musicians in the Northeast, including Al Hibbler and Charlie Parker. Johnny Otis met him in New York and talked him into signing with Duke, which is how he came to write "Please Forgive Me" for Johnny Ace. He didn't last too long with Duke as bad deals and resulting financial problems left him broke – no surprise there, as he was used and let loose by Robey. In 1955, he split for California.

Robey and Irv Marcus went back to working their magic on the trade publications. In the same issue as the review of "Please Forgive Me," Bob Rolontz's gossipy "Rhythm and Blues Notes" in *Billboard* noted: "Key releases include a new Louis Jordan waxing on Aladdin, and a Johnny Ace cutting on Duke." The payback was a quarter-page ad headlined "The History of Johnny Ace." The add promoted these statistics: "My Song" was said to have had 53,000 sales in eight days; "Cross My Heart," 51,000 sales in six days; "The Clock," 49,000 sales in five days; "Saving My Love for You," 46,000 sales in four days; and "Please Forgive Me," 100,000 sales in two days.

The big difference with "Please Forgive Me" was that it was being released into a R&B market crowded with much better records than before. Clogging up the best-seller list were the Midnighters' "Work with Me Annie," the Clovers' "Lovey Dovey," Joe Turner's "Shake, Rattle and Roll," Guitar Slim's "The Things I Used to Do," and the Spaniels' "Goodnight, Sweetheart." On top of that, the Crows' "Gee" and Muddy Waters's "I'm Your Hoochie Koochie Man" were being played heavily on America's jukeboxes, while soon to come into the market was "Sh-Boom" by the Chords.

Two weeks later, Johnny Ace and Big Mama Thornton were back out on the road, this time on a string of one-nighters through North Carolina. Robey and Marcus moved on, taking an ad in *Billboard* on June 5, 1954,

SAVING MY LOVE FOR YOU

for Little Junior Parker and the Sultans. That week, "Please Forgive Me" was strong in about a dozen cities across the country, but not in New York or Chicago, which means it hadn't yet hit the best-seller list. The song would eventually reach number six on the R&B charts, which was good – just not as good as any Johnny Ace record prior to it.

The travel and the lack of recording were flattening Ace's career. His next record, "Never Let Me Go," was released about the first of October, six months after "Please Forgive Me."

Once again, an Ace record jumped out quickly, with strong performances in cities such as Philadelphia, Atlanta, Nashville, Dallas, St. Louis, Detroit, and Chicago. Nevertheless, the record's path to success had unseen roadblocks. In the past, Johnny Ace record buyers could always find a hidden gem on the B-side. Not so much with "Never Let Me Go," as the B-side was an instrumental ("Burley Cutie"). It's not that this was a bad song. It wasn't. "Burley Cutie" was an early rave-up, with Johnny Ace on the piano playing off a dominant Johnny Board saxophone. But it was an instrumental, almost as if it were a filler for the A-side although the tune was written by Johnny Ace. On both the A-side and B-side, Ace was playing with a new band, Johnny Board and his orchestra. As for A-side, Ace's voice is deeper than in the past, either because of maturity or constantly singing for two years running. It's a good song, leaning more toward pop and slightly away from the blues.

The problem was that his being on the road so much put the Johnny Ace release in a difficult position. Back in May, when "Please Forgive Me" hit the market, among the performers with top ten records were the Midnighters, Roy Hamilton, the Clovers, and Clyde McPhatter. When "Never Let Me Go" hit the market, those acts had already released follow-up records that were again bestsellers. Roy Hamilton went from "You'll Never Walk Alone" to "Ebb Tide"; Clyde McPhatter rolled from "Such a Night" to "Honey Love"; and the Clovers easily slid from "Lovey Dovey" to "I've Got My Eyes on You." In a real coup, the Midnighters had the number one best seller "Work with Me Annie" when "Please Forgive Me" was released," and six months later, when "Never Let Me Go" came out, they had the number one record with a follow-up song, "Annie Had a Baby," plus the group's "Sexy Ways" was still a bestseller after thirteen weeks on the chart. Incredibly "Work with Me Annie" was also still a best seller after twenty-four weeks on the chart.

Against tough competition, "Never Let Me Go" managed to climb to number nine on the best-seller chart. So, after barnstorming for two years, everything Johnny Ace did was a still top ten best seller. The newer records just didn't reach number one or number two. Of *Billboard*'s top twenty-five records R&B records of 1954, a popularity vote by the magazine's readers, published December 4, "Work with Me Annie" was number one, "The Things I Used to Do" was number five, and further down the list were "Saving My Love for You" and "Please Forgive Me." Johnny was once again the second-most-popular R&B male performer behind Joe Turner, beating out Roy Hamilton.

With the weakness – and that's a relative term – of Ace's last two records, there was consternation back in Houston. Was Johnny Ace, Duke-Peacock's cash cow, slipping?

Pledging My Love

C
H
A
P
T
E
R

14

Who killed Johnny Ace – Conspiracy theories abound – "Pledging My Love" skyrockets – Tribute songs – After "Anymore," no more

For the last *Billboard* issue of 1954, on December 25, Robey and Marcus put together another promo. At the time, the best-selling record was the Charms' "Hearts of Stone," with "Earth Angel" coming up fast, making its first appearance on the best-selling R&B record chart. On the jukeboxes, the most played song was "You Upset Me, Baby," by Ace's old Memphis buddy B. B. King. The ad put together by Robey and Marcus was another Peacock and Duke twofer. Again, Peacock got the A-position, here at the top left corner of the page, with the main promotion being for Gatemouth Brown's "Midnight Hour" and then gospel records by the Spirit of Memphis Quartet and the Dixie Hummingbirds. Duke Records got the B-position below Peacock. The main promotion was for Johnny Ace's new record "Pledging My Love," with "No Money" on the B-side. Also promoted were the Sultans and the Southern Tones. Why Johnny Ace's record didn't get the main promotion is a good question. Did it entail something between Robey and Ace?

On Christmas Day, Johnny Ace and Big Mama Thornton had a big show at the City Auditorium in Houston. The Saturday night concert attracted twenty-five hundred fans. Generally, Big Mama was the opening act when they played together, and she opened here. Milton Hopkins, who was in the band that night, remembers it this way: "We did her whole set, and her last number was 'Hound Dog.'"

Before the big "Hound Dog" climax to the Big Mama set, Ace joined her for their duo "Yes, Baby." Afterward, Ace returned to his dressing room. "We were on the stage, still closing out the first act, and playing Big Mama's theme song," Hopkins recalled. "Then Big Mama came running onstage, screaming, hollering, and waving her arms. I couldn't make out what she was saying. Quickly we learned something happened in the dressing room. It turned out Johnny Ace had shot himself."

The next day, the *Houston Post* ran a few paragraphs about the incident under the headline "Russian Roulette Fatal to Band Leader at Auditorium." The key paragraphs quoted witnesses as saying Ace "whipped out a .22 caliber, seven-shot revolver with one live cartridge in the cylinder."

Paraphrasing witnesses, the story went on to say that Ace had placed the barrel of the gun against the heads of each of his four companions, spinning the cylinder and pulling the trigger each time. Then, while his twenty-two-year-old girlfriend Olivia Gibbs sat on his lap, "he placed the gun against his own head and fired. He fell dead with a wound in the eye."

The *Houston Chronicle* ran a much fuller story under the headline "Negro Singer Dies in Roulette Game." The story begins by identifying Johnny Ace as "27-year-old Johnny Alexander, a well-known singer." It appears that the *Chronicle* staff had doubts about readers knowing who Johnny Ace was. The story quoted Don Robey explaining that Johnny Alexander, billed as Johnny Ace, was one of the top rhythm and blues singers in the country and that the "blues ballad baritone" was *Cash Box* magazine's top rhythm and blues singer in 1953 and wrote many of his own songs.

The article also quoted a Mary Margaret Carter (sister of Houston singer and guitarist Goree Carter), who was one of five people sitting and drinking in the singer's dressing room. Ace was playing with a .22 caliber revolver, Carter said, when Big Mama Thornton (identified as "another entertainer") told him to put the gun down. When he continued to play with the pistol, Thornton took it away from him and removed the single bullet in the cylinder.

"Put it back," Ace demanded. "Nothing will happen."

Thornton acceded to Ace's request but told him to put the gun away. Instead, "as the little group watched in horror, Alexander [Ace] spun the cylinder of the gun, put it up to Miss Gibbs' ear, and pulled the trigger. There was a click. Nothing happened. 'There's nothing to it,' smiled Alexander, according to Mrs. Carter. 'Watch this,' Alexander said."

The paper reported: "He spun the cylinder again, put the gun to his right ear. This time there was an explosion. Alexander slumped to the floor. Police said he died instantly."

Judging from witness interviews, the story appears very cut and dry. Johnny Ace was playing with a gun, put it to his head, and the one bullet in the cylinder went off as he pressed the trigger.

Not everyone believes the reportage – for good reason, as there are inherent problems in that storyline.

The action was between sets, so even if they had drinks in the dressing room, Ace didn't have time to get fully inebriated, meaning he would have been aware of his actions. And if he knew there was a bullet in the gun, why would he first have put the gun to his girlfriend's head – or anyone else's – and pulled the trigger? He put another person's life at risk – and risked his own career. If he was suicidal (and there is no reason to believe he was), he would have just put the gun to his own head.

Johnny Ace had already sung a duet with Big Mama Thornton, and he was the closing act, so he ought to have been preparing to go back onstage. Was he so sure of his invincibility that he would play Russian roulette? It's doubtful.

The more likely scenario is that Johnny Ace did not know there was a bullet in the gun. There are many stories about Johnny Ace shooting his gun at signs and inanimate objects. Also, stories abound about Johnny Ace traveling with his pistol and mock-firing with an empty cylinder. And if he didn't know there was a bullet in the cylinder, how did it get there? That's the mystery.

A little over a month later, a different take on the facts appeared. Originally a wire service story out of Houston but appearing in many African American newspapers, such as the *Pittsburgh Courier* on February 5, 1955, was an article about one of the principals in the Johnny Ace drama, Olivia Gibbs. Now calling herself Johnny Ace's fiancée, although he never divorced, she said that of the morning of the shooting Johnny had been drinking and playing with a gun. She had made him stop. Then, she claimed, he had displayed a diamond ring she had given him. But Gibbs was a waitress at one of Robey's Houston clubs and couldn't afford to be giving away diamond rings.

Gibbs she told the journalist:

He went around snapping it [his pistol] at people. . . . Willie Mae Thornton, a blues singer, said she prevailed upon Ace to give her the gun and he had snapped it at herself, Miss Gibbs and Joe Hammond, another singer. Miss Thornton said she turned the chamber and a bullet fell out. Johnny Ace continued to snap the gun at others in the dressing room. Finally, Joe Hammond said, "You snapped it at everyone else, try it on yourself." "Now watch me," said Johnny, "I'll show you it won't shoot." With his arm around Olivia Gibbs, Johnny placed the gun to his temple. Crack! went the gun. Ace fell to the floor mortally wounded.

Gibbs also told the reporter that she had loved Ace and he had loved her and that he had been separated from his wife since 1952. She hoped for a divorce by June 1955. "Then we would have married," she said. "He called me every night when he was on the road, as if he wanted to hear me for inspiration."

None of the stories about the night Johnny Ace killed himself mention Robey, although by some accounts he saw Ace that day, and according to one source they quarreled.

Lauterbach interviewed a man named Sax Kari, who worked for Robey in the 1950s, and his story was that even if Robey didn't pull the trigger, it happened under his direction. In Sax Kari's telling, Robey coerced Big Mama Thornton into slipping a bullet into Johnny's gun. In exchange, he would continue his work making her a star.

Thornton would have only needed to fabricate the story she told police about Ace telling her to put the bullet back in the gun, because if Johnny knew about the bullet, he would have been responsible for its consequences, his own death or someone else's. That's a key point because if he did *not* know about the bullet, then he was being set up. Olivia Gibbs, wrote Lauterbach, told the police she didn't know thing about the gun being loaded.

Lauterbach concluded, "For Robey, Russian roulette was a beneficial ruling from the county authorities, implying that Johnny knew there was a bullet in the gun when he pulled the trigger. Closing the case immediately cancelled any further investigation." A county coroner's inquest ruled that Ace's death was self-inflicted.

Roy Head once referred to Robey as black mafia. While not truly mafia, Robey dealt with New Orleans quite a bit in the music business, and the Crescent City was a mafia town. Robey knew how the mafia worked. If the mafia did something for you, it expected something in return, and that's how Robey operated. If he did something for you, say awarded you a Cadillac and thousand-dollar check, then you would accept him taking 50 percent of songwriting credits, which could end up as a hundred-thousand-dollar bonus to him. He took care of Big Mama in her early days at Peacock, and he probably gave money to Olivia Gibbs as well. A couple of years later it was time to collect on that payment. Someone needed to slip the bullet into Johnny Ace's gun.

While Robey setting up Johnny Ace for a death through Big Mama's or Olivia Gibbs's complicity falls into realm of conspiracy theory, a lot of people who knew Robey thought him quite capable of murder.

PLEDGING MY LOVE
191

Years later, when Roy Head was under Robey management, he said, "Everyone who worked at Duke-Peacock still thought Robey had him killed, although by that time there was no way to prove it."

Lavelle White was in Houston but not at the show when Johnny Ace died. "It was the saddest thing I ever heard. I don't think he shot himself. It was someone evil who killed him."

Even Roger Wood, who thought highly of Don Robey and what he did for the Houston music scene, admitted there were a lot of people who believed Robey had planted the bullet.

One thing is fairly certain: Robey showed no grief for Johnny Ace's death. What he did exhibit was a cold efficiency for promotion in the wake of the death. This only fueled the second part of the Robey conspiracy theory. Johnny Ace's sales were slipping, and he put in place a scheme for the Hank Williams effect. As Wood observed, some folks suggest Robey caused the death of Johnny Ace because of what he had seen when the twenty-nine-year-old country singer Hank Williams died on January 1, 1953. About six months prior, Williams recorded a song called "I'll Never Get Out of This World Alive." Soon after Williams's death it went to number one on *Billboard*'s country chart.

Like commanding troops before a major battle, Robey swung into action, arranging publicity, orchestrating a funeral worthy of a potentate, and getting Ace's last record, "Pledging My Love" played and available to a waiting public.

The funeral on January 2, 1955, was set held at the beautiful and historic Clayborn Temple, then an AME church, within walking distance from Beale Street. Pallbearers, including Beale Streeters of yore – B. B. King, Rosco Gordon, Little Junior Parker, toasted their comrade at the Mitchell Hotel and walked through the throngs to the church. A Memphis photographer named Ernest Withers documented it all, and Robey made sure photos went out to the African American press, including the Associated Negro Press Wire. An estimated five thousand people attended the funeral, although crowd size reports may have been boosted by Robey's grander estimation. Johnny Ace was buried at Memphis's New Park Cemetery.

"Pledging My Love" took off like a rocket to the stars.

The always-on-the-ball "Rhythm 'n Blues Ramblings" in *Cash Box* led off its January 15, 1955, column with this reportage: "One of the quickest take-offs in memory is the new Johnny Ace 'Pledging My Love' on Duke. While there is no doubt the tragic death of Ace is playing a big part in the surging demand for his new record, it is a coincidence (and ironic twist) that 'Pledging My Love' is also his best record. We have spoken to distributors, retail stores and juke box operators and the conversations all run the same. The gist of it being that it is Ace's biggest and the demand is far outrunning the supply."

"Pledging My Love" is a simple song about romantic love. The lyrics showcase a subtle, interior rhyme scheme throughout: the word "forever" is repeated, twice pared with "I'll love you." Otherwise it's just a long ramble about the singer's commitment to a woman. The strongest lyrics end the song. It's a two-line repeat from the middle of the song: "Just promise me, darling, / your love in return / May this fire in my soul, dear, / forever burn."

Robey doubled down on promotions. In *Billboard* on January 22, 1955, Robey's quarter-page ad read: "His Songs Will Always Live, Duke's Greatest Recording Artist, the Late Johnny Ace." In smaller letters: "First nationwide hit in 1952 was 'My Song' – Duke #102. Since then, he has had eight national hits in a row." The promotion included a listing of all his big hits plus "Angel," which was the B-side of "Cross My Heart."

With all the noise about "Pledging My Love," Robey thought small, only about the record's African American market. The world was changing, and white teenagers were buying R&B records almost as fast as they were Joan Weber's "Let Me Go, Lover," number one on the pop charts mid-January. He needed to read the trade magazines in which he was so ardently spending money. *Billboard*'s column "Talent Corner" on January 29, 1955, was an unabashed paean to Johnny Ace, crediting him with the rise of the soulful slow tune, which by the next decade would be mainstreamed into the wider genre called soul music. The columnist wrote, "Ace's simple and unaffected style of singing, his evident sincerity and heart, actually started the R&B field on a type of song that has come to be known as a 'heart-ballad.'"

Robey seems to have missed reading the line that read "with its current sales in the pop markets, many observers expect ["Pledging My Love"] to soon jump into the pop charts." Crossover was the coming revolution, but Robey didn't see it. He didn't trust Johnny Ace's "Pledging My Love" to cross over, and, in what was probably his worst deal ever, he agreed to split the publishing revenue from the song with a company called Wemar Music if Wemar could convince a well-known pop singer to record the song. It did, getting Teresa Brewer to cover "Pledging My Love." Ironically, both songs reached as high as number seventeen on the pop charts.

Robey didn't give it all away. "Pledging My Love" was written by Fer-

PLEDGING MY LOVE

dinand "Fats" Washington, a paraplegic who had been wounded in the Second World War and had a blues show on Memphis radio. He was one of the first DJs to play Elvis Presley's "That's All Right." Robey took half the songwriting credits, which was worth a small fortune because everybody and their brothers and sisters covered the song, including Elvis Presley. Brown and Friedrich's *Encyclopedia of Rock 'n Roll*, published in 1970, noted in its Johnny Ace entry: "Ace's death stunned the R&B world as well as many of his newly-found pop fans – and it also helped to make his record, 'Pledging My Love,' one of the year's biggest hits. And, as time passed by, the Ace waxing of the song became a classic. It still is one of the heaviest selling oldies but goodies on the market."

Like money in the bank!

What Robey also didn't foresee, although he eventually tried to push into the craziness, was the first tribute record phenomenon. No one could have predicted a flood of songs in encomium to the late, great Johnny Ace.

It all happened quickly. The in-the-know writer of *Cash Box*'s "Rhythm 'n Blues Ramblings" wrote first about it in their February 12, 1955, column. From New York, the columnist wrote, "The Johnny Ace memorial race is on. So far Varetta Dillard, Johnny Fuller, Linda Hayes and Frankie Ervin [have] entered the derby." The Los Angeles columnist also observed, "Several diskeries [record companies] are releasing tunes immortalizing the late Johnny Ace. Hollywood Records recently released 'Johnny Ace's Last Letter' with Frankie Ervin backed by "Why Johnny Why" with Linda Hayes. Both sides feature Johnny Moore's Blazers. . . . Aladdin is also hitting the market with 'Last Letter' by Johnny Fuller. Lyrics imply that Ace's death was a suicide."

Not mentioned were the Rovers' "Salute to Johnny Ace" on the Music City label and "Johnny's Still Singing," by the Five Wings, on the King label. In an effort not to be outdone, Robey's Peacock label brought back Ace nemesis Marie Adams to sing "In Memory (A Tribute to Johnny Ace)." If you are thinking these songs came and went in a flash, you would be right – except for one, Varetta Dillard's "Johnny Has Gone" for the Savoy record company. The Harlem-born singer was a veteran of the music business, having a few hits early in 1950s, most importantly "Mercy, Mr. Percy" in 1952. In November 1955, when *Billboard* published its popular vote for "Best Rhythm and Blues Record of 1955," "Pledging My Love" was number three and 'Johnny Has Gone" number six.

"Pledging My Love" ended the year with what Lauterbach called the "triple crown": the year's top R&B seller and leader in both jukebox and radio plays. A Peacock-Duke ad in *Billboard* read: "Thank you DJs for your overwhelming votes . . . and our thanks to all of our distributors, juke box operators, and retail stores for making 'Pledging My Love' the big record of the year."

Robey had a couple more tricks up his sleeve to cash in on the death of Johnny Ace. First he signed St. Clair Alexander, Ace's brother, to perform as "Buddy Ace." When that didn't succeed, he signed Jimmie Lee Land to the Peacock label on the condition that *he* perform as Buddy Ace, again in an effort to capitalize on the late singer's popularity. An item in *Jet* magazine on March 24, 1955: "Don Robey, owner of Peacock records, has found a successor to the late blues singer Johnny Ace (who blew his brains out). It's Ace's brother Buddy, who's just out of the Army."

He also rushed out a greatest hits LP, called *Memorial Album*, which was the wording on the jacket (above "Johnny Ace" in a much larger cursive font). There were twelve songs on the album, beginning on side one with "Pledging My Love" and ending on side two with a song called "Anymore."

In July, about seven months after Ace's death, Duke records released the last Johnny Ace single, "Anymore," with "How Can You Be So Mean" on the B-side. "How Can You Be So Mean" was a Johnny Ace composition, and he got full credit in this case for the songwriting, under his real name, John Alexander. The A-side was another "Fats" Washington song, with Robey taking half the songwriting credits. (Other old Johnny Ace tunes were discovered and released by Duke the following year, but, with little promotion and the Johnny Ace story now ancient history, these records died on the vine.)

On July 16, 1955, "Anymore" was the *Cash Box* "Award o' the Week," and the reviewer pretty much summed it up in terms of Ace's career, writing: "Here's another money maker for the trade[.] Johnny Ace's long-awaited follow-up to 'Pledging My Love' is another slow blues ballad titled 'Anymore' that has all the qualities that made 'Pledging' a hit. As with all of Ace's previous hits, the format is similar. It is a slow, pretty song with sentimental lyrics and the Ace individually stylized vocal. The band accompaniment is soft and permits the artist to handle the soft offering with just the proper degree of support. The story is one of breaking off of a romance."

The songwriter really stressed the concept of "anymore," meaning "any longer." So the listener hears such phrases as "believe you anymore" and "trust you anymore." Despite these gloomy turns, the song is one of optimism because the singer has moved on, found another lover, and won't be "blue no more." The singer feels so good about himself that he tells his ex-lover that she will never have to worry again.

By the second week in August, "Anymore" was hot in New York, Chicago, New Orleans, and Newark, competing against some fine songs: Fats Domino's "Ain't It a Shame," Chuck Berry's "Maybellene," dueling "Unchained Melody" versions by Al Hibbler and Roy Hamilton, and the Nutmegs' "Story Untold."

"Anymore" would be another top ten record. Over a two-year period, Johnny Ace released eight major records, all of which went top ten, with three going all the way to number one. Ace was so popular he created a whole genre of musician, sometimes called the blues crooner, and, equally important, he forced open the pop records charts to R&B music.

On November 12, 1955, *Billboard* magazine summed up the music scene: "The year 1955 was the year rhythm and blues virtually took over the pop field. The trend continues strong and, despite covers by top pop artists [Georgia Gibbs reworking LaVern Baker's "Tweedle Dee," the McGuire Sisters' redoing the Moonglows' "Sincerely," the Crew-Cuts recording the Penguins' "Earth Angel," and many others] more and more original versions of tunes by R&B artists are making it in all the markets. Ironically, the pacesetter spins-wise is the late Johnny Ace."

The most appropriate summation in the most inappropriate publication about the meaning of Johnny Ace's death was written by Gary Herman in his macabre book *Rock 'n' Roll Babylon*: "Bob Dylan once commented that 'singers and musicians I grew up with transcend nostalgia – Buddy Holly and Johnny Ace are just as valid to me today as then.' It was not merely clever talk to say that Johnny Ace and Hank Williams parenthesize rock 'n' roll. It's all there in their lives and deaths – sweetness and bitterness, darkness and light, black and white, anger and joy, success and failure, above all, the tragedies and pleasure of youth."

Under the headline "Johnny Ace Fan Dies Like Idol at Russian Roulette," an item in *Jet* magazine, September 15, 1955, read: "A 14-year-old admirer of the late singer Johnny Ace, Theodore Madison of West Palm Beach, followed his hero's path to death when a day-long game of Russian roulette ended with a bullet crashing through his right temple. A second youth, William Hollis, 16, said he and young Madison had taken a .32 caliber pistol, loaded it with a single bullet, and taken turns spinning the cylinder, placing the barrel against their heads and pulling the trigger. Both boys were avid fans of Ace, who died in a Christmas day game of Russian roulette last year."

Finally, writer Ed Ward put Johnny Ace's death in a cultural context: "Nine months later, a young actor named James Dean would die, and since the phenomenon would occur among white teenagers, it would get some attention in the press. To have achieved death became something of an honor, a point of fascination, among teens. There wasn't anything particularly ghoulish about it, either; death, being inevitable, became somehow 'cool,' for after all, two of the hippest people around, Johnny Ace and James Dean, had already crossed to the other side."

Epilogue

Sometimes authors get lost in small grove of trees and forget about the forest. That's what happened to me with this book. My idea was to write about three super-talented R&B pioneers, who came to fame in the early 1950s and then died young under sometimes controversial circumstances. Since they passed away before rock 'n' roll conquered the world, they were forgotten, as were their significant contributions to popular music. Oldies stations rarely dipped into the deep bucket of R&B tunes before the rock 'n' roll break-out year of 1956, so their songs were no longer heard, and, to make matters worse, those institutions that should know better, such as the Rock 'n' Roll Hall of Fame, have completely disregarded them, even though what they added to the collective sound of popular music in the past seventy years was so much more important than the contributions of three-quarters of the performers in that august hall.

My focus was narrow at the start—to bring foster awareness about the lives and deaths of these wonderful musicians. But as I was writing the book I came to realize that bigger historical issues abounded.

When looking at the life of Jesse Belvin, a couple of important sociological and historical trends arose of which I became cognizant. When it comes to the origins of rock 'n' roll, musicologists tend to focus on the southern rockabilly influence or the urban sounds of New York and Chicago. Completely lost in the discussion is the importance of what was happening in Los Angeles from the 1930s through the 1950s.

Historically, "the Great Migration" refers to the years from 1916 to 1960 when over six million African Americans migrated from the rural South to the cities in the North, Midwest, and West. One subset of this vast and lengthy migration was that of African Americans who resided in Texas and Oklahoma. Many of the families from this region, instead of going north, went west to California, not just to work the agricultural regions of central California but also to Los Angeles and other points in Southern California that were rapidly growing in population. Industrial and urban-service employment jobs continued to become available there to all.

"As a result of housing tension, many Black residents ended up creating their own cities within big cities, fostering the growth of a new urban, African-American culture," a History Channel documentary on the Great Migration reported. The most obvious example is Harlem, a section of northern Manhattan. However, an equally good representation would be South Central Los Angeles.

During World War II, thousands of soldiers and sailors came through Southern California heading to the Pacific Theater. Before being shipped out, during their days and weeks in the region, they wanted to be entertained, and the places to go were the increasing number of nightclubs in Los Angeles, many of which featured the hippest jazz and blues singers in the country. Musicians from many of these former Texas families now living in South Central played the clubs and by the 1940s attracted a second wave of Texans, upcoming singers, musicians, and songwriters who could get better-paying nightclub work and also record. During the World War II years and into the early 1950s, more independent record companies that specialized in jazz and rhythm and blues were started in Los Angeles than anywhere else in the country.

The culmination of this surge of musicianship and recording capabilities was one of first R&B nodes in the country, South Central Los Angeles. Probably as much doo-wop and blues came out of this area as from New York and Chicago. Not all of these bluesman, songwriters, and smooth-singing Jesse Belvin type of singers had Texas roots, but many of them did. A parallel development to the rise of the creative nodes in places such as South Central Los Angeles and Texas was the unheralded phenomenon of African-American entrepreneurship.

Business-minded African American men and women owned juke joints, clubs, and hotels for black musicians in the Jim Crow world of the 1950s. A newer generation opened recording studios, started their own record companies, and became artist managers and tour bookers. Just like their white counterparts, while performing a great service in regard to popularizing an American art form, many of the black entertainment businesspeople of this era were sharp-elbowed and borderline unscrupulous, financially taking advantage of the artists they were helping to make successful, if not famous. Before Berry Gordy created Motown Records in Detroit, the most successful African American entrepreneur in the music business was Don Robey, who operated out of Houston. Besides creating Peacock Records, he owned a record store, the most popular nightclub in Houston for black performers, controlled the chitlin' circuit throughout Texas, and, along with Evelyn

EPILOGUE

Johnson, ran a successful artist management and booking agency. Deep in the segregated and hostile South of the early 1950s, Robey pulled off an unlikely coup: he bought a record company, Memphis-based Duke Records, which was owned by a white man. Black men business just didn't buy white businesses in the South.

Robey was as feared as he was esteemed. The contentious relationship between Robey and his top performer, singer Johnny Ace, may have had something to do with the performer's sad, sudden, and self-inflicted demise. All that unhappy business is the more well-known backdrop to the unsung historical and sociological movements that transformed the all-American genres of rhythm and blues, blues, and country into rock 'n' roll, a music form that conquered the world.

Acknowledgments

I want to thank all those individuals who took time out from their busy days to respond to my phone calls requesting an interview for this book. Some of the people mentioned below had to be interviewed more than once, which probably bordered on harassment, but they were all game and very interested in the subject. With appreciation to:

Billy Allen
Rodney Glenn (Guitar Slim Jr.) Armstrong
Al Bell
Linzie Butler
Carlo Ditto
Roy Head
Clarence "Frogman" Henry
Gaynel Hodge
Milton Hopkins
Freddie King
Chester Jones
Gloria Jones
Gary Levingston
Rebecca Miller
Woody Sistrunk
Billy Vera
Adam Wade
Justine "Baby" Washington
A C Wharton Jr.
Lavell White
Roger Wood
Wade "Wacko" Wright

Appendix
Selected R&B Hits, 1952–1955

Compiled with data from Playback.fm (https://playback.fm) and Rate Your Music (https://www.rateyourmusic.com).

1952

#2: "My Song," Johnny Ace

1953

#5: "The Clock," Johnny Ace
#18: "Saving My Love for You," Johnny Ace
#22: "Dream Girl," Jesse & Marvin
#43: "Cross My Heart," Johnny Ace
#84: "Baby Doll," Marvin & Johnny

1954

#2: "The Things That I Used to Do," Guitar Slim
#17: "Saving My Love for You," Johnny Ace
#18: "Earth Angel," The Penguins
#46: "Please Forgive Me," Johnny Ace
#60: "Never Let Me Go," Johnny Ace
#61 "Tick Tock/Cherry Pie," Marvin & Johnny

1955

#4: "Pledging My Love," Johnny Ace
#5: "Earth Angel," The Penguins
#53: "Anymore/How Can You Be So Mean," Johnny Ace

Discography

Compiled with data from 45Cat (45cat.com) and Rate Your Music (https://rateyourmusic.com).

JESSE BELVIN, SINGLES 1950–1960 (AND *MR. EASY*)

Jesse Belvin, "Dream Girl" / "Hang Your Tears Out to Dry," Recorded In Hollywood, #120-45, 1950

Jesse & Marvin, "Dream Girl" / "Daddy Loves Baby," Specialty, #447-45, 1952

Jesse Belvin, "Trouble and Misery" / "I'm Only a Fool," Money, #208-45, 1955

Jesse Belvin, "One Little Blessing"/ "Gone," Specialty, #550-45, 1955

Jesse Belvin, "Love, Love of My Life" / "Where's My Girl," Specialty, #550-45, 1956

Jesse Belvin, "Betty My Darling" / "Dear Heart," Hollywood, #45-1059, 1956

Curley Williams (pseudonym), "This Heart of Mine" / "Be Mine," Modern, #45x1004, 1956

Jesse Belvin, "Goodnight My Love" / "I Want You with Me Xmas," Modern, #45x1005, 1956

Jesse Belvin, "Goodnight My Love" / "Let Me Love You Tonight," Modern, #1005, 1956

Jesse Belvin, "I Need You So" / "Senorita," Modern, #45x1003, 1957

Jesse Belvin, "By My Side" / "Don't Close the Door," Modern, #45x1015, 1957

Jesse Belvin, "I'm Not Free" / "Sad and Lonesome," Modern, #1020, 1957

Jesse Belvin, "You Send Me" / "Summertime," Modern, #45x1025, 1957

Jesse Belvin, "Beware" / "Dry Your Tears," Cash, #1056, 1957

206   DISCOGRAPHY

Jesse Belvin and His Space Riders, "My Satellite" / "Just to Say Hello," Modern, #45x1027, 1957

Jesse Belvin and the Sharptones, "Sugar Doll" / "Let Me Dream," Aladdin, #45-3431, 1958

Jesse Belvin, "Volare" / "Ever Since We Met," RCA Victor, #47-7310, 1958

Jesse Belvin, "Funny" / "Pledging My Love," RCA Victor, #47-7387, 1958

Jesse Belvin, "Guess Who" / "My Girl Is Just Enough for Me," RCA Victor, #61-7469, 1959

Jesse Belvin, "Little Darling" / "Deacon Dan Tucker," Knight (Imperial), #X2012, 1959

Jesse Belvin, "Sentimental Reasons" / "Senorita," Kent, #45x326, 1959

Jesse Belvin, "It Could've Been Worse" / "Here's a Heart," RCA Victor, #47-7543, 1959

Jesse Belvin, "Give Me Love" / "I'll Never Be Lonely Again," RCA Victor, #47-7596, 1959

Jesse Belvin, "Goodnight My Love" / "My Desire," Jamie, #1145, 1959

Jesse Belvin, Mr. Easy, RCA Victor, VLP 2105, 1960

Jesse Belvin, "The Door Is Always Open" / "Something Happens to Me," Class, #267, 1960</LIST>

EDDIE "GUITAR SLIM" JONES, SINGLES 1951–1958

Eddie "Guitar Slim" Jones and His Playboys, "Bad Luck Is on Me" / "New Arrival," Imperial, #IM-299, 1951

Eddie "Guitar Slim" Jones and His Playboys, "Standin' at the Station" / "Cryin' in the Morning," Imperial, #IM-301, 1951

Eddie "Guitar Slim" Jones, "Feelin' Sad" / "Certainly All," J-B, #603, 1952

Guitar Slim, "The Things That I Used To Do" / "Well, I Done Got Over It," Specialty, #XSP-482, 1953

Guitar Slim, "The Story of My Life" / "A Letter to My Girl Friend," Specialty, #XSP-490, 1954

Guitar Slim, "Woman Troubles" / "Cryin' in the Mornin'," Imperial, #IM-299, 1954

Guitar Slim, "Later for You Baby" / "Trouble Don't Last," Specialty, #XSP-527, 1954

DISCOGRAPHY   207

Guitar Slim, "Sufferin' Mind" / "Twenty-Five Lies," Specialty,
#XSP-536, 1954

Guitar Slim, "Our Only Child" / "Stand by Me," Specialty, #XSP-542, 1955

Guitar Slim, "I Got Sumpin' for You" / "You're Gonna Miss Me,"
Specialty, #XSP-551, 1955

Guitar Slim, "Think It Over" / "Quicksand," Specialty, #XSP557,
1955

Guitar Slim, "You Give Me Nothin' but the Blues" / "It Hurts to
Love Someone," Specialty, #XSP-569, 1956

Guitar Slim, "If I Should Lose You" / "It Hurts to Love
Someone," ATCO, #6097, 1957

Guitar Slim, "When There's No Way Out" / "If I Had My Life to
Live Over," ATCO, #6120, 1958

JOHNNY ACE, SINGLES 1952–1956 (AND TWO ALBUMS)

Johnny Ace, "My Song" / "Follow the Rule," Duke, #R-102,
1952

Johnny Ace, "Cross My Heart" / "Angel," Duke, #R-107, 1953

Johnny Ace, "The Clock" / "Aces Wild," Duke, #112, 1953

Johnny Ace, "Mid Night Hours Journey" / Earl Forrest, "Trouble
and Me," Flair, #45x1015, 1953

Johnny Ace, "Saving My Love for You" / "Yes, Baby," Duke,
#118, 1953

Johnny Ace, "Please Forgive Me" / "You've Been Gone So Long,"
Duke, #128, 1954

Johnny Ace, "Never Let Me Go" / "Burley Cutie," Duke, #132,
1954

Johnny Ace, "Pledging My Love" / "No Money," Duke, #136,
1954

Johnny Ace Sings, Duke, EP80, 1955

A Tribute Album to Johnny Ace, Duke, EP81, 1955

Johnny Ace, "Anymore" / "How Can You Be So Mean," Duke,
#144, 1955

Johnny Ace, "So Lonely" / "I'm Crazy Baby," Duke, #148, 1956

Johnny Ace, "Still Love You So" / "Don't You Know," Duke,
#154, 1956

Sources

CHAPTER ONE

"Artists' Biographies for Jockey Programming: *Guess Who* Penned by Belvin's Wife." *Billboard*, April 6, 1959.

"Big Jay McNeely, R&B's 'King of the Honkers, Dies at 91." *Boston Globe*, September 20, 2018.

"Billboard Year-end Top 30 Singles of 1953." Wikipedia.

Birnbaum, Larry. *Before Elvis: The Prehistory of Rock 'n' Roll*. Scarecrow Press, 2013.

Cash Box.

"Deacon's Hop—Big Jay McNeely and Detroit Gary Wiggins." *Bman's Blues Report*, April 29, 2012, www.bmansbluesreport.com/2012/04/deacons-hop-big-jay-mcneely-and-detroit.html.

The Dead Rock Stars Club, 1990–1991. www.thedeadrockstarsclub.com.

Electric Earl. www.electricearl.com.

Ennis, Philip. The Seventh Stream: The Emergence of Rocknroll in American Popular Music. Wesleyan University Press, 1992.

George, Nelson. The Death of Rhythm and Blues. Pantheon Books, 1988.

James, Etta, and David Ritz. *Rage to Survive: The Etta James Story*. Da Capo Press, 1995.

Komara, Edward, and Peter Lee. "Jessie Mae Robinson." In *The Blues Encyclopedia*. Taylor and Francis, 2004.

Larkin, Colin. The Virgin Encyclopedia of Fifties Music. Virgin Books, 2002.

"Marvin Phillips." TIMS: This Is My Story. tims.blackcat.nl/.

Osborne, Jerry, and Bruce Hamilton. Record Collectors Price Guide: Blues/Rhythm and Blues/Soul. O'Sullivan, Woodside, 1980.

https://playback.fm.

Propes, Steve, and Galen Gart. *LA R&B Vocal Groups, 1945–1965*. Big Nickel Publications, 2001.

Rate Your Music. https://rateyourmusic.com/.

Shaw, Arnold. *Honkers & Shouters: The Golden Years of Rhythm and Blues*. Collier Books, 1978.

CHAPTER TWO

"Best Sellers in Stores, Most Played in Juke Boxes." *Billboard*, December 25, 1954; February 26, 1955; April 2, 1955.

Birnbaum, Larry. *Before Elvis: The Prehistory of Rock 'n' Roll*. Scarecrow Press, 2013.

Black, Johnnie. *Singles: Six Decades of Hot Hits and Classic Cuts*. Thunder Bay Press, 2006.

Dawson, Jim. "The Penguins and Earth Angel." Electric Earl, https://www.electricearl.com/dws/penguins.html.

The Dead Rock Stars Club, 1990–1991. www.thedeadrockstarsclub.com.

Gart, Galen. *The American Record Label Directory and Dating Guide*. Big Nickel Publications, 1989.

Gillett, Charlie. *The Sound of the City: The Rise of Rock and Roll*. Outerbridge & Dienstfrey, 1970

Goldberg, Marv. "The Penguins." Unca Marvy's R&B Page. https://www.uncamarvy.com/Penguins/penguins.html.

Goldberg, Marv. "The Platters." Unca Marvy's R&B Page. https://www.uncamarvy.com/Platters/platters.html.

Larkin, Colin. The Virgin Encyclopedia of Fifties Music. Virgin Books, 2002.

"R&B Territorial Best Sellers." *Billboard*, December 25, 1954; February 12, 1955; February 26, 1955; April 2, 1955.

Sullivan, Steve. *Encyclopedia of Great Popular Song Recordings*. Scarecrow Press, 2013.

Warner, Jay. *American Singing Groups: A History from 1940s to Today*. Hal Leonard, 2006.

Williams, Richard. "Cleve Duncan Obituary." *Guardian,* November 15, 2012.

Chapter Three

"American Musician George Motola." https://peoplepill.com/people/george-motola.

Birnbaum, Larry. *Before Elvis: The Prehistory of Rock 'n' Roll*. Scarecrow Press, 2013.

"The Cash Box Hot." *Cash Box*, December 8, 1956.

"The Cash Box Rhythm and Blues Reviews." *Cash Box*, April 23, 1955.

Dawson, Jim. "Jesse Belvin Discography." Electric Earl. electricearl.com/dws/belvin.html.

Eder, Bruce. "Jesse Belvin Biography." AllMusic. https://www.allmusic.com/artist/jesse-belvin-mn0000333175/biography.

James, Etta, and David Ritz, *Rage to Survive: The Etta James Story*. Da Capo Press, 1995.

Marsh, Dave. *The Heart of Rock and Soul: The 1001 Greatest Singles Ever Made*. New American Library, 1989.

"R & B Reviews." *Cash Box*, October 27, 1956.

"Rhythm & Blues Ramblings." *Cash Box*, May 21, 1953.

Ricard, L. "Tragic Loss for the Music World." https://www.prweb.com/releases/2005/10/prweb303295.htm.

"This Week's R&B Best Buys." *Billboard*, December 1, 1956.

SOURCES

CHAPTER FOUR

Callahan, Mike, and David Edwards. "The Early Years: 1950–1955." In *Randy Wood: The Dot Records Story*. Both Sides Now Publications. http://www.bsnpubs.com/dot/dotstory3.html.

Corcoran, Michael. "Little Indie Label Domino Laid Down Austin Sounds before Scene's Heyday." *Austin American-Statesman,* June 5, 2010.

Hamilton, Andrew. "The Slades Biography." AllMusic. https://www.allmusic.com/artist/the-slades-mn0000502447.

Karp, Kate, and Marv Goldberg. "They Cheated, They Lied—The Story of Frankie Ervin." Unca Marvy's R&B Page. http://www.uncamarvy.com/FrankieErvin/frankieervin.html.

Kramer, Gary. "On the Beat: Rhythm and Blues-Rock 'n' Roll." *Billboard,* February 23, 195.7

"R&B Ramblings." *Cash Box,* March 9, 1957.

"R & B Reviews." *Cash Box,* April 6, 1957.

"The Shields." Tom Simon Home Page. www.tsimon.com/shields.htm

"R & B Disk Jockey: Regional Record Reports." *Cash Box,* September 27, 1958; October 4, 1958; October 10, 1958.

"R& B Retail Outlets: From Coast to Coast." *Cash Box,* October 4, 1958; October 10, 1958.

CHAPTER FIVE

"Believe Slashed Tires Caused Death of Jesse Belvin, Wife." *Jet,* March 10, 1960.

"The Billboard Hot R & B Sides." *Billboard,* April 30, 1959; June 1, 1959.

"The Billboard Reviews This Week's Singles." *Billboard,* October 27, 1958.

Bronson, Fred. *The Billboard Book of Number One Hits.* Billboard Publications, 1985.

"Distributor News." *Billboard,* April 30, 1959; June 1, 1959.

Eder, Bruce. "Jesse Belvin Biography." AllMusic. https://www.allmusic.com/artist/jesse-belvin-mn0000333175/biography.

"4 Killed in 2-Car Crash Near Hope." *Arkansas Democrat,* February 6, 1960.

"Four Persons Die in Crash Near Hope." Texarkana Gazette, February 7, 1960.

"4 Persons Die in 2-Car Wreck Near Hope Sat." *Hope (AR) Star*, February 8, 1960.

James, Etta, and Ritz, David. *Rage to Survive: The Etta James Story.* Da Capo Press, 1995.

"Jesse Belvin." Recording Academy. https://www.grammy.com/artists/jesse-belvin/1179.

"Ku Klux Klan (after 1900)." *Encyclopedia of Arkansas.* https://encyclopediaofarkansas.net/entries/ku-klux-klan-2755.

Motley, W. "West Coast Roundup." *Jet,* January 1, 1960.

"Reviews of New Pop Records." *Billboard,* February 23, 1959.

Richmond, Norman. "Jesse Belvin: The Most Gifted of All." Pan-African News Wire, February 11, 2010.

Robinson, Major. "New York Beat." *Jet,* March 3, 1960.
"Slashed Tires on Belvin's Auto Probed." *Los Angeles Sentinel,* February 18, 1960.
"Tonight Only." *Arkansas Gazette,* February 5, 1960.

CHAPTER SIX

Bentley, Chris. "Elko—The Old House of Music." *Juke Blues,* July 1985.
Berry, Jason, Jonathan Foose, and Tad Jones. *Up rrom the Cradle of Jazz: New Orleans Music since World War II.* University of Georgia Press, 1986.
Birnbaum, Larry. *Before Elvis: The Prehistory of Rock 'n' Roll.* Scarecrow Press, 2013.
"Buddy Guy on Guitar Slim" (video). YouTube, July 31, 2008. https://www.youtube.com/watch?v=wyfcGqKtOeo.
Charters, Samuel. *The Poetry of the Blues.* Avon, 1963.
Dance, Helen Oakley. "Walker, Aaron Thibeaux [T-Bone]." *Handbook of Texas.* https://www.tshaonline.org/handbook/entries/walker-aaron-thibeaux-t-bone.
Erlewine, Stephen Thomas. "*Stone Down Blues* Review." AllMusic. https://www.allmusic.com/album/stone-down-blues-mw0000866073.
"Gatemouth Brown Dead at 81." CBS News, September 11, 2005. https://www.cbsnews.com/news/gatemouth-brown-dead-at-81.
Gillett, Charlie. *The Sound of the City: The Rise of Rock and Roll.* Outerbridge & Dienstfrey, 1970.
Guitar Center. "Legendary Blues Guitarist Buddy Guy at Guitar Center" (video). YouTube, February, 28, 2014. https://www.youtube.com/watch?v=un-OXLWhvDc.
Hannusch, Jeff. *I Hear You Knockin': The Sound of New Orleans Rhythm and Blues.* Swallow Publications, 1985.
"Kal Mann." Wikipedia. https://en.wikipedia.org/wiki/Kal_Mann.
Keil, Charles. *Urban Blues.* University of Chicago Press, 1968.
Lauterbach, Preston. *The Chitlin' Circuit and the Road to Rock 'n' Roll.* W. W. Norton, 2011.
"Lead Belly." *Guitar Player,* August 1996.
Motley, W. "West Coast Roundup." *Jet,* January 1, 1960.
Myrus, Donald. *Ballads, Blues and the Big Beat.* MacMillan, 1966.
Obrecht, Jas. "'Black Snake Moan' / 'Match Box Blues'—Blind Lemon Jefferson (1927)." Library of Congress, 2014. https://www.loc.gov/static/programs/national-recording-preservation-board/documents/Blind-Lemon-Jefferson.pdf.
Osborne, Jerry, and Bruce Hamilton. *Original Record Collectors Price Guide: Blues/Rhythm and Blues/Soul.* O'Sullivan Woodside, 1980.
Palmer, Robert. "The Church of the Sonic Guitar." *Guitar World,* June 1995.
Palmer, Robert. *Deep Blues.* Penguin Books, 1981.
Ritz, David. *The Brothers Neville.* Little, Brown, 2000.
"Rolling Stone's 100 Greatest Guitarists of All Time." IMDb, November 28, 2016. https://www.imdb.com/list/ls066632618.
Shaw, Arnold. *Honkers and Shouters: The Golden Years of Rhythm and Blues.* MacMillan, 1978.

SOURCES

"Sunnyland Slim." Encyclopaedia Britannica. https://web.archive.org/web/20150912182258/https://www.britannica.com/biography/sunnyland-slim.

"T-Bone Walker." All About Jazz. https://www.allaboutjazz.com/musicians/t-bone-walker.

"Victoria Spivey." The Blues Trail. http://www.thebluestrail.com/artists/mus_vspiv.htm.

"Willie Egan." Last.fm. https://www.last.fm/music/Willie+Egan/+wiki.

"Worried Blues." *Chicago Defender*, May 19, 1928.

CHAPTER SEVEN

arwulf arweulf. "Larry Darnell Biography." AllMusic. https://www.allmusic.com/artist/larry-darnell-mn0000781226/biography.

"B. B. King: Miss Martha King / When Your Baby Packs Up and Goes." Discogs.com. https://www.discogs.com/BB-King-Miss-Martha-King-When-Your-Baby-Packs-Up-And-Goes/release/7031392.

Benner, Amelia. "Number One with a Bulleit." *Illinois Wesleyan University Magazine*, issue 2, 2009.

Birnbaum, Larry. *Before Elvis: The Prehistory of Rock 'n' Roll*. Scarecrow Press, 2013.

"Bullet, 'Always a Smash Hit.'" https://web.archive.org/web/20210227061119/https://www.bopping.org/bullet-always-a-smash-hit-the-grandaddy-of-nashville-indie-country-labels-600-755-

cou try-serie-1946-1952/ "Voo-Doom53,"https://www.bopping.org/bullet-always-a-smash-hit-the-grandaddy-of-nashville-indie-country-labels-600-755-country-serie-1946-1952/#more-6400.

Cash Box, December 6, 1952.

"The Cash Box Hot." *Cash Box*, December 13, 1952; January 17, 1953.

"The Cash Box Rhythm 'n Blues Reviews." *Cash Box*, December 13, 1952.

Coleman, Rick, *Blue Monday: Fats Domino and the Lost Dawn of Rock 'n' Roll*. Da Capo Press, 2006.

Cusic, Don. "Nashville Recording Industry." *Tennessee Encyclopedia*. https://tennesseeencyclopedia.net/entries/nashville-recording-industry.

"45 Discography for Imperial Records—5000 Series." "http://www.globaldogproductions.info/i/imperial-5000-series.html.

"Guitar Slim." Mississippi Blues Trail. http://www.msbluestrail.org/blues-trail-markers/guitar-slim.

Hannusch, Jeff. "Eddie 'Guitar Slim' Jones 1926–1959." *Guitar Player*, March 1984.

Hannusch, Jeff. *I Hear You Knockin': The Sound of New Orleans Rhythm and Blues*. Swallow Publications, 1985.

Havers, Richard. "The Englishman, Blues and Country Music History." Udiscovermusic. https://www.udiscovermusic.com/stories/the-englishman-blues-and-country-music-history.

King, B. B., and David Ritz. *Blues All around Me: The Autobiography of B. B. King*. Avon Books, 1996.

Kunian, David. "The Things I Used to Do Legend of Eddie Guitar Slim Jones." YouTube. https://www.youtube.com/watch?v=D66npz599FQ.

Osborne, Jerry, and Bruce Hamilton. *Original Record Collectors Price Guide: Blues/Rhythm and Blues/Soul*. O'Sullivan Woodside, 1980.

Palmer, Robert. *Deep Blues*. Penguin Books, 1981.

Pavlow, Big Al. *Big Al Pavlow's The R&B Book: A Disc-History of Rhythm and Blues*. Music House, 1983.

"Reviews of New R&B Records." *Billboard*, October 9, 1954.

Ritz, David. *The Brothers Neville*. Little, Brown, 2000.

Wirt, John. *Huey "Piano" Smith and the Rocking Pneumonia Blues*. Louisiana State University Press, 2014.

CHAPTER EIGHT

Birnbaum, Larry. *Before Elvis: The Prehistory of Rock 'n' Roll*. Scarecrow Press, 2013.

"The Cash Box Hot." Cash Box, December 26, 1953; May 29, 1954.

Coleman, Rick. *Fats Domino and the Lost Dawn of Rock 'n' Roll*. Da Capo Press, 2006.

Dahl, Bill. *"Guitar Slim Biography." AllMusic*, https://www.allmusic.com/artist/guitar-slim-mn0000654490.

Ennis, Philip. *The Seventh Stream: The Emergence of Rocknroll in American Popular Music*. Wesleyan University Press, 1992.

"The Final Count." Cash Box, December 4, 1954.

Hannusch, Jeff. "Eddie 'Guitar Slim' Jones 1926–1959." *Guitar Player*, March 1984.

Hannusch, Jeff. *I Hear You Knockin': The Sound of New Orleans Rhythm and Blues*. Swallow Publications, 1985.

Hannusch, Jeff. *The Soul of New Orleans: A Legacy of Rhythm and Blues. Swallow Publications, 2001.*

Hannusch, Jeff. "Thibodaux' Sugar Bowl." *Beat Magazine*, May 1, 1999.

Hirshey, Gerri. Nowhere To Run: The Story of Soul Music. Penguin Books, 1984.

James, Etta, and David Ritz. Rage to Survive: The Etta James Story. Da Capo Press, 1995.

"Most Played In Juke Boxes." Billboard, January 23, 1954; March 13, 1954; March 20, 1954.

"National Best Sellers." Billboard, January 23, 1954; March 13, 1954; March 20, 1954.

"The Nation's Rhythm & Blues Top 15." Cash Box, March 20, 1954; April 3, 1954.

Palmer, Robert. *Deep Blues*. Penguin Books, 1981.

"R&B Territorial Best Sellers," Billboard, March 13, 1954; March 20, 1954.

"Review of New R&B Records." Billboard, November 13, 1954.

"Rhythm & Blues Notes." Billboard, June 5, 1954.

"Rhythm and Blues Ramblings," Cash Box, April 24, 1954; November 20, 1954.

"Rhythm 'n Blues Reviews." Cash Box, July 10, 1954.

SOURCES

Slaven, Neil. *Electric Don Quixote: The Definitive Story of Frank Zappa.* Omnibus Press, 2003.

"Stars over Harlem." *Cash Box*, December 26, 1953; April 3, 1954; April 24, 1954.

"Top 67 R&B Songs in 1954." Playback.fm. https://playback.fm/charts/rnb/1954.

Ward, Ed, Geoffrey Stokes, and Ken Tucker. *Rock of Ages: The Rolling Stone History of Rock and Roll.* Rolling Stone Press/Summit Books, 1986.

CHAPTER NINE

Birnbaum, Larry. *Before Elvis: The Prehistory of Rock 'n' Roll.* Scarecrow Press, 2013.

Burley, Dan. "Talking About." *Jet*, March 24, 1955.

Coleman, Rick. *Fats Domino and the Lost Dawn of Rock 'n' Roll. Da Capo Press,* 2006.

Gart, Galen. *First Pressings: The History of Rhythm and Blues: Special 1950 Volume.* Big Nickel, 1993.

Gart, Galen. *First Pressings: The History of Rhythm and Blues*, vol. 5, *1955.* Big Nickel, 1990.

Gart, Galen. *First Pressings: The History of Rhythm and Blues*, vol. 6, *1956.* Big Nickel Publications, 1991.

Gart, Galen. *First Pressings: The History of Rhythm and Blues*, vol. 7, *1957.* Big Nickel Publications, 1987.

Govenar, Alan. *Meeting the Blues. Taylor Publishing, 1988.*

"Guitar Slim Dies." *Cash Box*, February 21, 1959.

"Guitar Slim Signs with Atlantic." *Billboard, March 17, 1956.*

Hannusch, Jeff. "Eddie 'Guitar Slim' Jones 1926–1959." *Guitar Player*, 1984.

Hannusch, Jeff. *I Hear You Knockin': The Sound of New Orleans Rhythm and Blues.* Swallow Publications, 1985.

Hannusch, Jeff. "Thibodaux' Sugar Bowl." *Beat Magazine*, May 1, 1999.

Horowitz, Is. "RIAA Report Spotlights Expansion of '55 Record Biz," Billboard, March 17, 1956.

Palmer, Robert. "The Church of the Sonic Guitar." *Guitar World*, June 1995.

"Portrait of a Philosopher." *Cash Box, January 18, 1958.*

"Reviews of New R&B Records." *Billboard, June 16, 1956.*

"Reviews of R&B Records, Billboard, January 29, 1955; October 15, 1955.*

"Review Spotlight On." *Billboard, June 16, 1956.*

"Rhythm-Blues Notes," *Billboard, March 31, 1956; April 23, 1955.*

Ward, Ed, Geoffrey Stokes, and Ken Tucker. *Rock of Ages: The Rolling Stone History of Rock and Roll.* Rolling Stone Press/Summit Books, 1986.

Wirt, John. *Huey "Piano" Smith and the Rocking Pneumonia Blues.* Louisiana State University Press, 2014.

CHAPTER TEN

Birnbaum, Larry. *Before Elvis: The Prehistory of Rock 'n' Roll.* Scarecrow Press, 2013.

216 SOURCES

Cantor, Louis. *Wheelin' on Beale*. Pharos Books, 1992.

Dahl, Bill. "Percy Mayfield Biography." AllMusic. https://www.allmusic.com/artist/percy-mayfield-mn0000309328/biography.

Garland, Phyl. *The Sound of Soul*. Pocket Books, 1971.

George, Nelson. *The Death of Rhythm and Blues*. Pantheon Books, 1988.

Gillett, Charlie. *The Sound of the City: The Rise of Rock and Roll*. Outerbridge & Dienstfrey, 1970.

Jones, LeRoi. Blues People. William Morrow, 1963.

King, B. B., and David Ritz. Blues All around Me: The Autobiography of B. B. King. Avon Books, 1996.

McKee, Margaret, and Fred Chisenhall. *Beale Black and Blue: Life and Music on Black America's Main Street*. Louisiana State University Press, 1981.

Rolontz, Bob. "Rhythm & Blues Notes." Billboard, October 16, 1954.

Shaw, Arnold. Honkers and Shouters: The Golden Years of Rhythm and Blues. Collier Books, 1978.

"Top 100 R&B Songs in 1948." Playback.fm. https://playback.fm/charts/rnb/1948.

"Top 100 R&B Songs in 1949." Playback.fm. https://playback.fm/charts/rnb/1949.

Tosches, Nick. Unsung Heroes of Rock 'n' Roll: The Birth of Rock in the Wild Years before Elvis. Harmony Books, 1984.

Ward, Ed, Geoffrey Stokes, and Ken Tucker. *Rock of Ages: The Rolling Stone History of Rock and Roll*. Rolling Stone Press/Summit Books, 1986.

Chapter Eleven

"Best-Selling Retail Rhythm and Blues Records." Billboard, August 9, 1952; August 16, 1952; August 23, 1952; September 27, 1952; November 1, 1952.

"The Cash Box Hot." Cash Box, December 6, 1952.

Ennis, Philip. The Seventh Stream: The Emergence of Rocknroll in American Popular Music. Wesleyan University Press, 1992.

"Jazz 'n Blues Reviews." Cash Box, September 6, 1952.

King, B. B., and David Ritz. Blues All around Me: The Autobiography of B. B. King. Avon Books, 1996.

Lauterbach, Preston. *The Chitlin' Circuit and the Road to Rock 'n' Roll*. W. W Norton, 2011.

McKee, Margaret, and Fred Chisenhall. *Beale Black and Blue: Life and Music on Black America's Main Street*. Louisiana State University Press, 1981.

"Most Played Juke Box Rhythm and Blues Records." Billboard, September 27, 1952; November 1, 1952.

"1952's Top R&B Records." Billboard, December 27, 1952.

Palmer, Robert. Deep Blues. Penguin Books, 1981.

"Peacock Adds Duke to Fold." Billboard, August 2, 1952.

Raichelson, Richard M. Beale Street Talks: A Walking Tour down the Home of the Blues. 2nd ed. Arcadia Records, 1999.

"Rhythm and Blues Notes." Billboard, August 9, 1952; August 16, 1952; August 23, 1952; September 27, 1952.

"Rhythm and Blues Ramblings." Cash Box, December 6, 1952.

SOURCES

"Rhythm and Blues Record Reviews." Billboard, August 23, 1952; September 27, 1952.

"Round the Wax Circle." Cash Box, August 16, 1952.

"Success Story: Peacock Makes the Grade under Leadership of Don Robey and Irv Marcus." Cash Box, July 18, 1953.

Tooms, Robert "Nighthawk." "A Real Beale Streeter: Earl Forest." American Blues News, July 30, 2009. http://americanbluesnews.blogspot.com/2009/07/memphis-real-beale-streeter-earl-forest_30.html

Tosches, Nick. Unsung Heroes of Rock 'n' Roll: The Birth of Rock in The Wild Years before Elvis. Harmony Books, 1984.

CHAPTER TWELVE

"Another Terrific Hit." Billboard, January 3, 1953.

"Award o' the Week." Cash Box, June 20, 1953.

"Billboard Review." Billboard, September 19, 1953.

Brown, Ruth, and Andrew Yule. Miss Rhythm: The Autobiography of Ruth Brown, Rhythm and Blues Legend. Donald I. Fine Books, 1996.

Cash Box, October 3, 1953.

Corcoran, Michael. "The Sacred Music of Houston Record Mogul Don Robey." Houston Press, April 14, 2015.

Farley, Charles. Soul of the Man: Bobby "Blue" Bland. University of Illinois Press, 2011.

Hogan, Ed. "Don Robey Biography." https://www.allmusic.com/artist/don-robey-mn0000192354/biography.

"The Hollywood Antitrust Case: aka The Paramount Antitrust Case." Hollywood Renegades Archive. http://www.cobbles.com/simpp_archive/1film_antitrust.htm.

Jackson, John. Big Beat Heat: Alan Freed and the Early Years of Rock and Roll. Schirmer Books, 1991.

Kirby, David. Little Richard: The Birth of Rock 'n' Roll. Continuum, 2009.

Lauterbach, Preston. The Chitlin' Circuit and the Road to Rock 'n' Roll. W. W Norton, 2011.

McKee, Margaret, and Fred Chisenhall. Beale Black and Blue: Life and Music on Black America's Main Street. Louisiana State University Press, 1981.

"Most Played in Juke Boxes." Billboard, January 31, 1953.

"New Records to Watch." Billboard, January 10, 1953.

"Our Thanks To." Billboard, February 28, 1953.

"Reviews of This Week's New Records." Billboard, January 17, 1953.

"Rhythm and Blues Notes." Billboard, January 31, 1953.

"Rhythm 'n Blues Ramblings." Cash Box, July 4, 1953.

Sporke, Michael. Big Mama Thornton: The Life and Music. McFarland, 2014.

"Territorial Best Sellers." Billboard, January 17, 1953.

"Top R&B Records." Billboard, July 18, 1953.

Ward, Ed, Geoffrey Stokes, and Ken Tucker. Rock of Ages: The Rolling Stone History of Rock and Roll. Rolling Stone Press/Summit Books, 1986.

"The Week's Best Buys." Billboard, June 27, 1953.

White, Charles. *The Life and Times of Little Richard, the Quasar of Rock.* Harmony Books, 1984.

Chapter Thirteen

Ankeny, Jason. "Mr. Google Eyes Biography." *AllMusic.* https://www.allmusic. com/artist/mr-google-eyes-mn0000512032/biography.

"Award o' the Week." *Cash Box,* December 12, 1953; May 22, 1953.

Birnbaum, Larry. *Before Elvis: The Prehistory of Rock 'n' Roll.* Scarecrow Press, 2013.

"The Cash Box Disk Jockey Poll." *Cash Box,* July 18, 1953.

"The Final Count." *Cash Box,* December 4, 1954.

George, Nelson. *The Death of Rhythm and Blues.* Pantheon Books, 1988.

Guralnick, Peter. *Last Train to Memphis: The Rise of Elvis Presley. Little, Brown,* 1994.

"The History of Johnny Ace." *Billboard,* May 22, 1954.

"Introducing Peacock Records, Inc. and Duke Records." *Billboard,* April 24, 1954.

"Johnny Ace and 'Big Mama' Thornton Are Headliners in New Apollo Revue." *New York Age,* October 24, 1953.

King, B. B., and David Ritz. *Blues All around Me: The Autobiography of B. B. King.* Avon Books, 1996.

Lauterbach, Preston. *The Chitlin' Circuit and the Road to Rock 'n' Roll.* W. W Norton, 2011.

"National Best Sellers." *Billboard, January 9, 1954.*

"Most Played in Juke Boxes." *Billboard, January 9, 1954.*

"Peacock, Duke to Houston." *Billboard, January 30, 1954.*

"Reviews of This Week's New Records." *Billboard, December 5, 1953.*

"Rhythm and Blues Notes." *Billboard, September 12, 1953; January 9, 1954; January 30, 1954; June 5, 1954.*

"Rhythm 'n Blues Ramblings." *Cash Box, July 23, 1954.*

"Sleeper of the Week." *Cash Box, December 12, 1953.*

Sporke, Michael. *Big Mama Thornton: The Life and Music.* McFarland, 2014.

"Territorial Best Sellers." *Billboard, January 30, 1954.*

"This Week's Best Buys." *Billboard,* June 5, 1954.

Tosches, Nick. *Unsung Heroes of Rock 'n' Roll: The Birth of Rock in The Wild Years before Elvis. Harmony Books, 1984.*

Ward, Ed, Geoffrey Stokes, and Ken Tucker. *Rock of Ages: The Rolling Stone History of Rock and Roll.* Rolling Stone Press/Summit Books, 1986.

White, Charles. *The Life and Times of Little Richard, the Quasar of Rock.* Harmony Books, 1984.

Wood, Roger. "John, Evelyn Joyce." *Handbook of Texas.* https://www.tshaonline. org/handbook/entries/johnson-evelyn-joyce.

SOURCES

Chapter Fourteen

"Ace Died Because He Loved to Play Pranks, Says Girl." *Pittsburgh Courier*, February 5, 1955.

"Award o' the Week." Cash Box, July 16, 1955.

"Best Sellers in Stores." *Billboard*, December 25, 1954.

Brown, Len, and Gary Friedrich. *Encyclopedia of Rock and Roll*. Tower, 1970.

"The Cash Box Hot." Cash Box, August 13, 1955.

Guralnick, Peter. *Last Train to Memphis: The Rise of Elvis Presley. Little, Brown, 1994.*

Herman, Gary. *Rock 'n' Roll Babylon. Perigee, 1982.*

"His Songs Will Always Live." *Billboard*, January 22, 1955.

Jet, March 24, 1955.

Johnny Ace: The Best of the Blues. Creative Concepts, 1979

"Johnny Ace Fan Dies Like Idol at Russian Roulette." Jet, September 15, 1955.

"Merry Christmas and New Year to the Operators and D.J.'s." *Billboard*, December 25, 1954.

"Most Played on Juke Boxes." *Billboard*, December 25, 1954.

"Last Chance." *Cash Box*. November 26, 1955.

Lauterbach, Preston. *The Chitlin' Circuit and the Road to Rock 'n' Roll*. W. W Norton, 2011.

"Negro Singer Dies in Russian Roulette Game." *Houston Chronicle*, December 26, 1954.

Orbock, Joseph A. "Land, Jimmy Lee [Buddy Ace]." *Handbook of Texas*. https://www.tshaonline.org/handbook/entries/land-jimmy-lee-buddy-ace.

"Rhythm 'n Blues Ramblings." *Cash Box*. January 15, 1955; February 12, 1955.

"Russian Roulette Fatal to Band Leader at Auditorium." *Houston Post*, December 26, 1954.

"Thank You DJs for Your Overwhelming Support." *Billboard*, July 16, 1955.

"Talent Corner." *Billboard*, January 29, 1955.

"Virtual Surrender: 1955, the Year R&B Took Over Pop Field." Billboard, November 12, 1955.

Ward, Ed, Geoffrey Stokes, and Ken Tucker. *Rock of Ages: The Rolling Stone History of Rock and Roll*. Rolling Stone Press/Summit Books, 1986.

Index

"3×7=21," 91, 92
"3 O'Clock Blues," 104, 141, 144, 150, 158, 176
5–10–15 Hours," 104

Abramson, Herb, 125, 126
Ace, Johnny (John Marshall Alexander Jr.), 19, 23, 3, 52, 53, 56, 104, 112, 114
Ace Records, 95, 120
"Ace's Wild," 167
Adams, Faye, 138, 169
Adams, Marie, 155–57, 165, 166, 172, 181, 182, 193
"Africa," 56
"After Sunset," 85
"Ain't Got No Home," 116
"Ain't I the Lucky One," 53
Aladdin Records, 50, 85, 104, 141, 142, 184, 193
Albert, Don, 82
Alexander, Alger "Texas," 140, 141
Alexander, St. Clair, 194
Allen, Billy, 14, 37, 59, 60, 63, 66
"All She Wants to Do Is Rock," 10, 145
"All That Wine is Gone," 18
Ames Brothers, 18
American Record Company, 87
Am I Asking Too Much," 144
Andrews, Ernie, 100
"Angel," 165, 192
"Angel In My Life," 36
"Ain't It a Shame," 195
Anka, Paul, 42
"Annie Had a Baby," 185
Anthony, Ray, 18
"Anymore," 194

Archilbald (John Leon Gross), 91
"Are You Lonesome Tonight," 51
Argo Records, 126
Armstrong, Albertine, 129, 130
Armstrong, James, 129, 130
Armstrong, Louis, 86
"As If I Didn't Know," 58
Atlantic Records, 108, 109, 119, 125, 126, 168
Atlas Records, 21
Atco Records, 126, 127, 131
Atkins, Chet, 101
August, Dan, 54
August, Joseph, 184
Augustine, Victor, 108
Austin American-Statesman, 47, 49
Austin City Limits, 46

Backbeat Records, 160
"Baby," 46
"Baby Doll," 22
"Baby, Don't Do It," 19, 20
"Baby, I Don't Care," 44
"Baby Please Come Home," 39
"Bad Luck Is Upon Me," 100
"Bad, Bad Whiskey," 141, 166
Baker, LaVern, 31, 195
Baker, Lee, 144
Ballad, Blues and the Big Beat, 76
Ballard, Julius, 88
Bartholomew, David, 79, 81, 83, 84, 90–92, 94, 99, 100, 103–6, 109
Basie, Count, 147
Bass, Ralph, 11
Baugh, Richard, 57, 58
Baxter, Les
Beach Boys, 26

Beale Black and Blue: Life and Music on Black America's Main Street, 143

"Beale Street Blues," 143

Beale Street Blues Boys (Group), 149

Beale Streeters (Group), 149–53, 166, 167, 180, 182, 191

"Bear Cat," 172

Beatles, 79, 160

Beamon, B.B., 159

Before Elvis: The Prehistory of Rock 'n' Roll, 27, 41

"Believe in Me," 17

Bell, Al, 137, 143, 151, 159, 162, 163, 1678

Bells of Joy (Group), 153, 164

Belvin, Jack, 13

Belvin, Jesse, 72, 124, 138, 140

Belvin, Jesse Jr., 13, 14, 16, 17, 52, 64

Belvin, Jo Ann, 9, 10, 37, 44, 45, 50, 52, 53, 55, 59, 60, 62, 63, 65, 66

Belvin, Jonathan, 52

Belvin, Selena Allen, 13, 14

Bennett, Tony, 21, 40

Bentley, Chris, 71, 72

Benton, Brook, 54

Berry, Chuck, 53, 121, 125, 195

Berry, Richard, 12, 13, 15, 26, 27, 38, 39, 46

"Beware," 44

Big Al Pavlow's The R&B Book: A Disc-History of Rhythm and Blues, 92

Big Jay McNeely's Blue Jays, 10

Bihari Brothers, 17, 23, 34, 38, 39, 43, 149, 150, 165, 166, 167

Bihari, Joe, 17, 23, 24, 34, 38, 167

Bihari, Jules, 17, 22, 38

Biahri, Lester, 156

Bihari, Saul, 17, 34

Bill Haley and His Comets, 114

Birnbaum, Larry, 27, 41, 73, 74, 81, 88, 141

Blackboard Jungle, 10

The Black Elvis, 62

"Black Snake Blues," 78

"Black Snake Moan," 77, 78

Black Swan Records, 77

Blackwell, Bumps (Robert Alexander), 16, 120–22

Bland, Bobby, 141, 148–52, 155, 157, 161, 166, 173

Bleyer, Archie, 113

Blossoms (Group), 12

"Blueberry Hill," 41

"Blue Moon," 28

"Blue Monday," 81, 99

Blue Monday: Fats Domino and the Lost Dawn of Rock 'n' Roll, 90

Blue Records, 13, 29

"Blue Suede Shoes," 121

Blues All Around Me, 148

Blues People, 136

BMI, 47

Board, Johnny, 185

Bocage, Spider (Eddie Bo), 96, 120

Bob and Earl, 26

Bolden, Buddy, 130

Bolden, Oscar Jr., 94, 96

"Boogie Woogie Cha-Cha," 54

"Boogie Chillin,'" 10

Boone, Pat, 47, 51, 79

"Booted," 158

Booth, Charles, 161

"Bossa Nova Baby," 51

Both Sides Now Publications, 13

"Brazil," 126

Brewer, Teresa, 51, 192

Brinson, Ted, 29

Bronze Records, 16, 142

Brooks, Hedda, 156

Brown, Charles, 42, 112, 125, 127, 139, 140, 145, 158

Brown, Clarence "Gatemouth," 73–75, 81–85, 95, 98, 115, 131, 152, 153, 165, 166, 179, 182, 187

Brown, Nappy, 58

Brown, Roy, 90, 101

Brown, Ruth, 20, 40, 104, 112, 125, 126, 138, 151, 159, 171

Brown, Texas Johnny, 161

Brown and Friedrich, 193

Brunswick Records, 87

INDEX

Bulleit, Jim, 101, 102, 146
Bullet Records, 101, 142, 146
Burbank, Charles, 109
Burch, Don, 47
"Burley Cutie," 185
Burley, Dan, 124
Busker, Ernie, 126
"But I Do," 116
Butler, Linzie, 144
"Butterfly," 79
"Buzz, Buzz, Buzz," 13, 26
"By My Side," 45, 46

Caddy Records, 44
Cadillacs (Group), 126
"California Hop," 13
"Call It Stormy Monday (But Tuesday Is Just As Bad), 81
Campi, Ray, 48
Cane, Marvin, 57, 58
Canned Heat (Group), 10
Capello, Lenny, 54
Campbell, Choker, 119
Carroll, Jack, 47
Carter, Doug Saint, 60
Carter, Goree, 188
Carter, Mary Margaret, 188
Cash Records, 35, 39, 44
Castelles (Group), 126
"Catch a Falling Star," 55
"C. C. Rider," 45, 46
"Certainly All," 71, 102
Chantones (Group), 53
Charles, Bobby (Robert Charles Guidry), 115, 166
Charles, Ray, 31, 56, 65, 73, 103, 109, 110, 112, 113, 117, 119, 120, 121, 124–27, 140, 141, 158
Charms (Group), 23, 30, 114, 187
Charters, Samuel, 78
Checker, Chubby, 79
Chenier, Clifton, 127
Cherry, Don, 12
"Cherry Pie," 14, 23, 24
Chess Records, 115, 117, 119, 171
Chess, Leonard, 115, 116

Chess, Marshall, 115
Chess, Phil, 115
Chords (Group), 23, 31, 114, 184
Chudd, Lew, 71, 83, 84, 90–92, 99, 104–6, 155
Church, Eugene, 12, 15, 36, 37, 38, 50, 54
Clayton, Merry, 12
"Clean Up Your Own Backyard," 51
Cliques (Group), also the Klock Klicks, 37, 38
"The Clock," 19, 167–70, 177, 178, 180, 182–84
Clouds of Joy (Group), 174
"Christmas Blues," 103
Clovers (Group), 103, 104, 112, 113, 125, 155, 166, 168, 169, 184, 185
Coasters (Group), 13, 126
Cochrane, Eddie, 39
Coed Records, 57, 58
Cole, Dick "Cane, 158
Cole, Nat King, 42, 52, 56, 92, 109, 113, 139, 143, 182
Coleman, Rick, 90, 91, 99
Collins, Al, 120
"Come Back," 141
"Come Back Baby," 141
"Come Dance With Me," 55
"Come On," 131
"Come Prima," 53
Como, Perry, 18, 55, 118
"Contented," 102
Cooke, Sam, 15, 42, 44, 56, 60
Copeland, Johnny, 163
Coral Records, 51
Cotton, Lawrence, 128
Craig, Francis, 101
Crawford, Sugar Boy, 97
Crew-Cuts (Group), 30, 32, 118, 195
Criss, Sonny, 10
Crosby, Bing, 29, 182
"Cross My Heart," 165–67, 170, 180, 184, 192
"Crossroad Blues," 86
Crows (Group), 23, 29, 114, 184
"Crying In the Chapel," 18, 19, 169

"Crying In the Morning," 100, 115
Cullum (McCullum), Ann, 141

"Daddy Loves Baby," 20
Dahl, Bill, 113
"Dance With Me Henry," 119
Dandridge, Dorothy, 183
Darin, Bobby, 126
"Darling You Know I Love You," 102
Darnell, Larry, 11, 19, 45, 46, 92, 97, 103, 145
Dave Clark Five, 25
"Daughter of the Desert," 54
Davenport, Ethel, 100
Davis, Kirk 27, 38, 59, 63, 64, 66
Davis, Maxwell, 38, 45
Dawn, Billy, 53
Dawson, Jim, 35, 39
Day, Bobby (Robert James Byrd), 14, 26–28
Day, Margie, 126
"Day In-Day Out," 22
De Heer, Dick, 19
Dean, James, 16
The Death of Rhythm and Blues, 16
Debonairs (Group), 13
Decca Records, 51, 89, 101
"The Deacon Hop," 10, 11, 13
Dean, James, 196
"Deep Blues," 92
Dells (Group), 41
Deluxe Records, 90, 91, 104
"Depression Blues," 115
"Devil or Angel," 125
Dick Lewis and His Harlem Rhythm Boys, 17
Diddley, Bo, 126, 176
Dillard, Varetta, 31, 193
"Dim, Dim the Lights," 114
Dinkins, Curlee, 25, 27
Ditta, Carlo, 107, 109, 129, 130
Dixie Humming Birds, 119, 153, 187
Doggett, Bill, 41
Dolphin, John 20, 21, 33, 34, 44
Domino, Fats, 41, 48, 75, 79, 81, 91,
92, 98, 99, 104–6, 113, 115, 116, 121, 122, 127, 128, 138, 195
Domino Records, 46–49
Dominoes (Group), 104, 155
"Don't Be Cruel," 41
"Don't Close the Door," 44, 46
"Don't Cry Baby," 18
"Don't Worry 'Bout Me," 113
"Don't You Just Know It," 95
"The Door Is Always Open," 56
Dootone Records, 12, 13, 29
Dootones (Group), 12
"Do The Clam," 51
Dot Records, 47, 48, 51
Dots (Group), 39
Doucette, Salvador, 91
"Down Through the Years," 131
"Dragnet Blues," 43
"Dream Baby," 158
Dream Boogie: The Triumph of Sam Cooke, 62
"Dream Girl," 19–21, 26, 27, 1645"Dream House Blues," 72
"Dreamy Eyes," 39
Drifters (Group), 23, 114
"Drifting Blues," 139
"Dry Your Tears," 44
Duke (Duke-Peacock) Records, 150–55, 157–61, 163–67, 169, 172, 173, 176, 178–84, 186, 187, 190, 192–94
Duke Ellington Band, 21
Duncan, Adolph "Billy," 148–50
Duncan, Cleve, 12, 27, 31, 32
"Drinkin' Wine Spo-Dee-o-Dee," 18, 19, 125

"Earth Angel," 9, 11, 12, 21, 26–28, 30–33, 39, 40, 42, 114, 117, 187, 195
Easter, Monte, 100
"Ebb Tide," 138, 185
Eckstein, Billy, 56
Eddie "Guitar Slim" Jones and His Playboys, 100
Eder, Bruce, 39, 56

INDEX

Edwards, Tommy, 21
Eisenhower, President Dwight, 60
Elko Records, 71
Ellington, Duke, 147
"El Mambo," 103
Empire Records, 39
Encyclopedia of Rock 'n Roll, 193
England, Ernie, 125
Ennis, Philip, 18, 105
Ertegun, Ahmet, 109, 125, 126
Ertegun, Nesuhi, 125
Ervin, Frankie, 43, 44, 47–49, 193
Ervin, Jessie, 43
Ervin, Willie (Charlie), 43
Esquerita, 97
Eugene Church and the Fellows, 38
"Ever Since We Met," 52
"Every Day I Have the Blues," 141
Excelsior (Exclusive) Records, 13, 16

Fadely, Imogene, 49
Faith, Percy, 18
Farmer, Art, 12
"The Fat Man," 92
Faubus, Governor Orval, 60
Federal Records, 32, 35, 36
"Feelin' Good, 172
"Feelin' Sad," 71, 102, 103, 109, 113
Fellas (Group), 12
Ferguson, Burt, 145
Fidelity Records, 26
Fiestas (Group), 36, 54
First Pressings: The History of Rhythm
    and Blues, Special 1950 Volume,
    125
Fisher, Eddie, 18, 47, 113, 183
Five Blind Boys of Mississippi (Group),
    153, 155
Five Pearls (Group), 118
Five Keys (Group), 114
Five Royales (Group), 19, 20
Five Wings (Group), 193
Flair Records, 167
Flames, 25, 26, 27
Flares (Group), 1332

Fleetwoods (Group), 42, 46
"Flip," 22
Foley, Red, 89
"Follow the Rule," 152
Fontenette, Gus, 109
Ford, Charles, 59, 63, 64
Ford, David, 25, 27, 65, 66
Ford, Frankie, 95
"Foot Stompin,' Part 1," 13
"Forever," 17
Forest, Earl, 148–50, 153, 166–68
"For You My Love," 11, 19, 45, 92,
    97, 145
Four Aces (Group), 113
Four Flames (Group), 26
Four Star Records, 16, 142
Four Tops, 176
Frankie Marshall and His Band, 126
Freed, Alan, 56, 110, 111, 162, 163,
    175
Freeman, Bobby, 58
Freeman, Ernie, 48
Frizzell, Lefty, 87
Fulbright, J. l., 71
Fuller, Johnny, 193
Fulson, Lowell, 84, 119, 140, 141, 144
"Funny," 52, 55

Gaines, Roy, 126
Gant, Cecil, 101, 135–38, 140, 141,
    146
Gassers (Group), 39
"Gatemouth Boogie," 83, 85, 98
Gay Notes (Group), 125
Gayten, Paul, 115, 116
"Gee," 23, 114, 184
Gehrig, Lou, 82
George, Nelson, 16, 140, 142
Gene (Forrest) and Eunice (Russ), 31,
    118
Gershwin, George, 34
Gibbs, Georgia, 119, 195
Gibbs, Olivia, 188–90
Gillett, Charlie, 25, 74, 140
Gilt Edge Records, 137

INDEX

"Girl of My Dreams," 37, 38
"Gitarro," 54
"Goin' Home," 104, 106
"Gold," 54
Goldberg, Marv, 29, 33, 44, 49
"Good Lovin,'" 168, 169
"Good Luck to You," 39
Goodman, Shirley, 104, 105, 115
"Goodnight My Love," 9, 39–42, 44, 45, 112
"Goodnight Irene," 156
"Goodnite Sweetheart Goodnite," 23, 41, 184
Gondoliers (Group), 109
"Gone," 35
"Good Rockin' Tonight," 51, 90
Gordon, Dexter, 12
Gordon, Rosco, 125, 148–51, 154, 155, 158, 166, 191
"Got the Blues," 146
"Gotta Find My Baby<" 166
Grace, Charlie, 79
Grammer, Billy, 53
Grant, Gogi, 122
Green, Carl, 17, 19, 22, 23, 30, 33
Green, Norman (Guitar Slim Green)," 72
Grey, Al, 179
Gribble, Jim Moder
Grissom, Dan, 100
Grissom, Jimmy, 21
"Guitar In My Hands," 85
Guitar Slim (Eddie Jones), 23, 179, 184
Guitar Slim Jr. (Rodney Glenn Armstrong), 97, 122, 129, 130
Guitar Slim Green, 72
"Guess Who," 9, 53–55, 64
"Guitar Slim," 83
Guralnick, Peter, 62
Gunter, Cornell, 12, 13, 27, 30, 32
Gunter, Shirley, 12, 138
Guy, Buddy, 73, 74

Haley, Bill, 115
Hall, Gerry, 93

"Hallelujah, I Lover Her So," 127
Hamilton, "Crackshot," 178
Hamilton, Fat Man, 84, 92
Hamilton, Roy, 112, 114, 138, 185, 195
Hammond, John P., 77
Handy, W.C., 143
"Hang Your Tears Out To Dry," 21
Hannusch, Jeff, 84. 90, 94, 98, 100, 102, 106, 109, 123, 128, 129
Hardy, Solomon, 148
"Harlem Shuffle," 26
Harptones, (Group), 174, 177
Harris, Peppermint (Harrison Demotra Nelson Jr.), 21
Harris, Thurston, 25
Harris, Wynonie, 10, 145, 1645Harrison, Wilbert, 22, 54
Harvey, Bill, 165
"Have Mercy Baby," 104, 155
Hawkins, Screamin' Jay, 84
Haws, Hampton, 10
Hayes, Linda, 193
Head, Roy, 160, 161, 176, 181, 189–91
Hendrix, Jimi, 73, 74, 131
The Heart of Rock and Soul: The 1001 Greatest Singles Ever Made, 42
"Heartbeat," 53
Heartbeats (Group), 41
"Heartbreak Hotel," 51, 121
"Hearts Can Be Broken," 36
"Hearts of Stone," 23, 30, 36, 41, 114, 187
"Hello, How Ya Been, Goodbye," 127, 131
"Help Me Somebody," 19
Henry, Clarence "Frogman," 116
Herman, Gary, 195
"He's My Man," 155
"Hey, Miss Fannie," 103, 104
"Hey Senorita," 29, 30
Hibbler, Al, 184, 195
Hill, Hosea, 107, 108, 122, 129, 175
Hill, Jessie, 101, 161
Hill, Thurston, 122, 129

INDEX

Hilltoppers (Group), 18
Hirshey, Gerri, 117
Hitchcock, V.C., 101
Hite, Les, 80
"Hit The Road Jack," 158
Hodge, Alex, 12, 13, 15, 22, 30, 32, 40, 50
Hodge, Gaynel, 11–18, 21, 22, 26–33, 39, 40, 50, 93
Holiday, Billie, 44
Holly, Buddy, 51, 53
Hollywood Flames, 13, 14, 26, 3
Hollywood Four Flames, 26–28
Hollywood Records, 35, 43, 44, 193
Holmes, George, 178
"Honey Hush," 109, 179
"Honey Love," 114, 185
Honkers and Shouters: The Golden Years of Rhythm and Blues, 12, 17
"Honky Tonk," 41
Hooker, John Lee, 10
Hopkins, Lightnin,' 73, 141
Hopkins, Milton, 161, 162, 175, 177, 181, 187
Horne, Lena, 183
Hosea Hill's Serenaders, 108
"Hound Dog," 19, 34, 51, 171, 173, 177, 180, 182, 187
Houston Chronicle, 188
Houston Informer, 83, 127
Houston Post, 188
Houston Press, 160
Houston, Joe, 36
"How Can You Be So Mean," 194
"How Much Is That Doggie in the Window," 18
Huey Piano Smith and the Clowns, 93, 94
Huff, Jimmy, 17
Huggy Boy (Dick Hugg), 30, 44
Hunt, Pee Wee, 18
Hunter, Ivory Joe, 41, 92, 139, 140, 143

"I Almost Lost My Mind," 92, 139

"I Care," 45
"I Cried," 166
"I Cried for You," 103
"I Don't Know," 20, 103, 104, 171
"If I Had My Life to Live Over," 128
"If I Should Lose You," 127
"I Got A Woman (I've Got A Woman)," 31, 117, 141
"I Got Loaded," 21
"I Got Stung," 53
"I Got To Go," 174
Ike Turner and his Kings of Rhythm, 149
"I Know," 27
"I Know Your Wig Is Gone," 81
"I'll Never Get Out of This World Alive," 191
"I'll Never Love Again," 18
"I'm Gone," 104
"I'm Gonna Play the Honky Tonks," 157
"I'm In Love (With a Girl)," 38
"I'm In Love Again," 127
"I'm Mad," 171
"I'm Not a Fool," 22
"I'm Only a Fool," 34
Imperial Records, 13, 16–18, 71, 90, 91, 99, 100, 104, 114, 155
"I'm Sorry," 50
"I'm Walking Behind You," 18
"I'm Your Hoochie Koochie Man," 112, 184
Ink Spots, (Group), 137
"In Memory (A Tribute to Johnny Ace), 157, 193
"In the Still of the Night," 56
"I Need You So," 45
"I Smell a Rat," 182
"It Could Have Been Worse," 64
"It Hurts to Love Someone," 127
"It May Sound Silly," 41
"It's A Shame," 72
"It's Midnight," 22
"It's Just a Matter of Time," 54
"It Should Have Been Me," 112

228 INDEX

"I've Got My Eyes on You," 185
"I've Searched the Whole World Over,"
182
"It Was Just a Summer Love," 53
"I Wanna Know Why," 38
"I Want You with Me Xmas," 40
"I Went to Your Wedding," 27
"I Wonder," 135, 136, 152
"I Won't Hold You Back," 56
"I Won't Mind at All," 127

J-B (Jim Bulleit Records), 71, 102
Jacquet, Illinois, 44
Jackie Brentson and his Delta Cats, 149
Jackson, John, 162
Jackson, Willis, 58
"Jailhouse Rock," 34, 51, 172
James, Elmore, 75, 174
James, Etta, 12, 15, 17, 22, 37, 38, 46,
64, 65, 67, 113, 119, 124, 127, 176
"Jealous Lies," 102
"Jeanie, Jeanie, Jeanie," 39
Jefferson, Lemon Henry "Blind
Lemon," 75–81, 84, 131
Jefferson, Joe, 13
Jesse and Marvin, 14, 19–21, 26, 27
Jesse Belvin and the Sharptones, 50
Jesse Belvin: Mr. Easy, 61
Jessie Hill's House Rockers, 101
Jewels (Group), 36
"Joe Joe Gun," 53
John, Little Willy, 40, 53
"Johnny Ace's Last Letter," 44, 193
"Johnny Has Gone," 31, 193
Johnny Moore's Three Blazers, 43, 44,
47, 139, 144, 145, 156, 193
Johnny Otis Band, 11
"Johnny's Still Singing," 193
Johnson, Bill, 178
Johnson, Evelyn, 174–76, 181
Johnson, Marv, 58
Johnson, Robert, 85–87, 108
Johnson, Sherman "Blues," 174
Johnson, Theard, 91
Jones, Annie Lee, 129

Jones, Barry, 129, 130
Jones, Chester, 37, 59, 66
Jones, Daisy (Bowdre), 129
Jones, Gloria, 12
Jones, LeRoi (Amiri Baraka), 136
Jones, Quincy, 120
Jones, Sam, 87
Jones, Sarah May, 129
Jones, Tom, 82
Jordan, Louis, 136, 184
Joy Jumpers, (Group), 95
"Juanita," 40
"Juke," 103, 158
Jukebox Records, 21
"Junker's Blues," 92

Kallen, Kitty, 113
"Kansas City," 22, 34, 54, 172
Kari, Sax, 190
"K. C. Loving," 54
Karp, Kate, 44, 49
Kay, George, 54
Keil, Charlie, 75, 81
Kern, Don, 151
King, B. B. (Riley), 73, 75, 96, 98, 101,
104, 113, 141, 144, 145, 147–51,
153, 156, 158, 164–66, 173, 176,
178, 187, 191
King, Ben E., 118
King, Earl, 74, 84, 93, 97, 108, 114,
120, 123, 128, 131
King, Little Freddie, 97
King, Jewel, 91, 92
King, Pee Wee, 101
King Records, 90, 154
Kingsmen (Group), 46
Kitt, Eartha, 183
"Ko Ko Mo," 31, 118
Knowles, Raymond, 54
Kramer, Gary, 44
Kunian, David, 88, 103

Lambert, Lloyd, 73, 108, 109, 123,
126, 128, 129
Lance, Major, 44

INDEX

Langloise, Eddie Lee (Eddie Lang, Little Eddie), 98, 101, 102
La Rosa, Julius, 18
"Last Night's Dream," 178
Lastie, David, 102
"Last Letter," 193
"Last Time I Saw My Heart," 53
"Later," 26
"Later Baby," 103
"Later for You Baby," 115
Laurie, Annie, 90
Lauterbach, Preston, 82, 83, 150–52, 154, 158, 170, 175, 177, 190, 193
"Lawdy, Miss Clawdy," 104, 106, 107, 155
Law, Don, 87
Ledbetter, Huddie William "Lead Belly," 76
Leiber (Jerry) and Stoller (Mike), 34, 172
Lee, Arthur, 11, 12
Lee, Leonard, 105, 115
"Lemon's Worried Blues," 76
Les Hite Orchestra, 80
"(Let Me Be Your) Teddy Bear," 79
"Let Me Dream," 50
"Let Me Go, Lover," 192
"Let Me In," 126
"Let's Do It," 18
"Let The Good Times Roll," 105
"A Letter to My Girlfriend," 11
Levingston, Gary, 34, 35, 42, 44, 52, 61, 64
Lewis, Bobby, 58
Lewis, Furry, 144
Lewis, Harold, 36, 159
Lewis, Richard, 17, 19, 22, 23
Lewis, Smiley, 81, 99
"Ling Ting Tong," 114
Little Anthony and the Imperials, 53
"Little Bitty Pretty One," 25
Little Milton, 141
Little Richard, 21, 97, 121, 124, 127, 163, 179, 182
Little Walter, 103, 124, 126, 138, 158

Littlefield, Little Wille, 22, 106
Lockwood, Robert Junior, 146, 152
"Lonely Teardrops," 53
Los Angeles Sentinel, 61
"Lost Wandering Blues," 78
"Louie, Louie," 12, 46
Louisiana Weekly, 74, 98, 99, 100, 109
Louis Jordan and His Tympany Five, 145
Love (Group), 11
"Love Is Here To Stay," 55
"Love Me," 53
"Love Me Baby," 166
"Love of My Life," 53
"Love, Love of My Life," 124
"Love Potion No. 9," 169, 172
"Lovers Never Say Goodbye," 53
"Lovey Dovey," 112, 184, 185
"Lovin' Blue," 166
Lowe, Bernie, 79
Lubinsky, Herman, 11

Mabon, Willie, 20, 103, 104, 171, 174
Madison, Theodore, 195
"Makin' Whoopee," 56
"(Mama) He Treats Your Daughter Mean, 20, 151
Mann, Kal (Kalman Cohen), 79
Marascalco, John, 39, 41
Marcello, Carlos, 107
Marchan, Bobby, 94, 95, 120
Marcus, Irving, 154, 156, 170, 179, 180, 184, 187
Marsh, Dave, 42
Marsmen (Group), 22
Martin, Dean, 122
Marvin & Johnny, 14, 22, 23, 30, 34, 36
Marvin Philips and His Men from Mars (Group), 19
Matassa, Cosimo, 89, 90, 104–6, 110, 116, 120
"Matchbox," 78
"Match Box Blues," 78
Matthews, Fat Man, 103

230 INDEX

Mathis, Johnny, 57, 58
Mathis Johnny (not singer of "Chances Are"), 102
Mattis, David James, 150–56, 158, 163, 164, 166, 167, 169, 170, 172, 181
"Maybellene," 195
Mayfield, Curtis, 140
Mayfield, Percy, 44, 139, 140, 158, 165
Mays, Willie, 114
McCann, Les, 15
McCarthy, Joe, 82
McCracklin, Jimmy, 166
McDaniels, Gene, 15
McDonald, Cliff, 137
McGee, Sticks, 18, 19, 125
McGuire Sisters, 40, 41, 51, 117, 195
McNeely, "Big" Jay (Cecil), 10, 11, 13, 15, 17, 18, 54, 72, 99, 165
McNeely, Bob, 10
McPhatter, Clyde, 25, 125, 127, 179, 185
McShann, Jay, 1645
Meaux, Huey, 161
Medallions (Group), 13
Memorial Album, 194
"Memories Are Made of This," 122
"Memphis Blues," 143
Memphis Slim, 141
Mercury Records, 32, 142, 156
"Mercy Mr. Percy," 193
"Merry Christmas Baby," 139
Mesner, Eddie, 85, 104, 105
Mesner, Leo, 85, 104
Meteor Records, 16
MGM Records, 139
"Miami," 38
Midnighters (Group), 23, 112, 113, 114, 184, 185
"Midnight Hours," 187
"Mid Nigh Hours Journey," 166, 167
Milburn, Amos, 36, 112, 141, 145
Miller, Rebecca, 44, 59, 64, 65
Millinder, Lucky, 1654
Mills Brothers (Group), 136, 137

Milton, Roy, 21
"Miss Martha King," 101, 146
Mitchell, Andrew "Sunbeam," 153, 158
Mitchell, Frank, 109, 110
Modern Records, 16, 17, 22, 23, 34, 37–39, 43, 45, 149, 150, 166, 167
Modugno, Domenico, 52, 53, 55
Monday, Paul, 164
Money Records, 34, 35, 45
"Moonglow," 122
Moonglows (Group), 31, 41, 117, 195
Moore, Oscar
"Mona Lisa," 92, 156
"Money Honey," 179
"More Than You Know," 144
Moroccos (Group), 125
"A Mother's Love," 114
Motola, George, 39–42, 44, 47, 48
"Mr. Blue," 46
Mr. Easy, 54, 56
Murphy, Matt, 166
Musical Chairs, 58
Music City Records, 193
"My Baby Left Me," 102
"My Desire," 38
"My First Date," 71, 72
"My Girl Is Just Enough Woman for Me," 54
"My Lean Baby," 167
"My Prayer," 127
"My Song," 104, 151, 152, 154–57, 164–67, 170, 180–84, 192
"Mystery Train," 172
"My Story," 104, 164
"My Time Is Too Expensive," 98
Myrus, Donald, 76

Nat King Cole Trio, 139
Nathan, Syd, 90
"Nature Boy," 49, 143
"Near You," 101
"Nel Blu Dipinto Di Blu (Volare)," 52, 53, 55
Nelson, Earl, 26

INDEX

Nelson, Ford, 148
"Never Let Me Go," 185
"Nervous Man Nervous," 13
Nettles, Willie, 96, 99, 100–102
"Never, Never," 167
Neville, Arthur, 74, 93
"New Arrival," 100
Nohl, Max, 63, 64
"no Money," 187
"No More Doggin.'" 158
Norfolk Journal and Guide, 62
Nowhere to Run: The Story of Soul
    Music, 117
Nutmegs (Group), 195

Obrecht, Jas, 77
Ogden, Bob, 82
"Oh What a Night," 41
Oh Yeah," 53, 126
Okeh Records, 78, 156
The Okey Dokey Radio Show," 105
"Okie Doke Stomp," 115
Oliver, Paul, 138
"Ol' Man River," 55
"Ooh Poo Pah Doo," 101, 161
"Oop Shoop," 12
"Once There Lived a Fool," 21
"One Kiss Led to Another," 126
"One Little Blessing," 35, 36
"One Mint Julep,"' 104, 155
"One Night," 53
"One Scotch, One Bourbon, One Beer,"
    141
Orioles (Group), 18, 29, 138, 144, 145,
    169
Osborne (Jerry) and Hamilton (Bruce),
    18, 72, 85
Otis, Johnny, 11, 17, 22, 30, 36, 37,
    38, 43, 54, 72, 82, 165, 171–73,
    176, 182–84
Otis, Shuggie, 72
"Our Father," 155
"Our Only Child," 118
"Over and Over," 25

Pacini, Angelo, 147
Pacini, Lorenzo, 147
Page, Patti, 18, 27
Page, Rickie, 39
Paich, David, 56
Paich, Marty, 55, 56
Painia, Frank, 97, 107, 108, 110, 122,
    123
Palmer, Earl, 91
Palmer, Robert, 74, 77, 81, 92, 102,
    123, 131, 147, 149, 155
Pankey, Dwight, 63, 64
Paramount Pictures, 47
Paramount Singers, 179
Parker, Charlie, 103, 184
Parker, Herman "Little Junior," 148,
    155, 166, 172, 173, 177, 178, 185,
    191
Parker, Robert 93–95
Parker, Sonny, 166
Paxton, George, 57, 58
Peacock Records, 119, 153, 154–56,
    159, 164, 166, 168, 171, 174, 175,
    179, 180, 182, 187, 193
Penguins (Group), 12, 29–33, 114, 117,
    195
Pepper, Art, 55
Pepper, John, 145
Perkins, Carl, 78, 79, 121
Perkins, George, 79
Perry, Emory (Johnny), 14, 19, 23
Perry, Rosetta, 179
Philco-Aladdin, 16
Phillips, Dewey, 158
Phillips, Marvin, 12, 14, 15, 17, 19, 20,
    22, 23, 72
Phillips, Sam, 149–52, 154, 173
Pierce, Dick, 55, 56
Pierce, Don, 34, 43
Pinkston, C.C., 179
Pipp. Wally, 82
Pittsburgh Courier, 189
Platters (Group), 13, 30, 32, 127
"Please Forgive Me," 183–86
"Please Let Me Know," 118

"Please Send Me Someone to Love," 140

"Pledging My Love," 31, 52, 53, 56, 187, 191–94

The Poetry of the Blues, 78

Poison Gardner and his All Stars, 84

"Poppa Stoppa's Be-Bop Blues," 184

Presley, Elvis, 41, 44, 51–53, 74, 79, 121, 141, 172, 173, 182, 193

"Pretty Girls Everywhere," 38, 54

"Pretty Mama Blues," 143

Price. Lloyd, 21, 91, 104, 106, 112, 155, 165

Price, Ray, 101

Price, Sammy, 77

Princess Tall Chief, 178

"Problems," 53

Puente, Tito, 103

Prysock, Arthur, 58, 60–62, 165

"Quicksand," 124

R&B Records, 36

"Rag Mop," 92, 156

Rage to Survive: The Etta James Story, 12

Rainey, Ma, 78, 147

Rainey, Ma II Lillie Mae Glover), 144

Ram, Buck (Samuel), 32, 33

"Raunchy," 48

Ravens (Group), 104, 125, 138, 144

Rawls, Lou, 15, 56

Ray, Johnnie, 182

"Reconsider Baby," 141

RCA Records, 44, 45, 47, 51, 52, 54–56, 66, 67

Recorded In Hollywood Records, 20, 21, 34

Red, Piano, 144

Redhead, 54

Redding, Otis, 141

Reed, Herb, 13

Reed, Jimmy, 127

Reif, Bobby (Bob), 26

Reinhardt, Django, 75

Reynolds, Debbie, 183

Richard Berry and the Dreamers, 30

Richard Lewis and the Barons, 17

Richardson, Laura Jane, 46

Richmond, Norman, 62

Ridgely, Tommy, 91

"Rip It Up," 127

"Rising High Water Blues," 79

"The Rising Sun," 71

Rituals (Group), 54

Rivers, Johnny, 95

"The River's Invitation," 165

Robbins, Marty, 53

Robey, Don, 79, 82, 83, 85, 119, 121, 152–55, 157, 159, 160–65, 167, 171–73, 175, 178–82, 184, 187–94

Robi, Paul, 32

"Rocket 88," 149

Rockets (Grouop), 36

"Rock Me All Night Long," 104

Robbins, Marty, 87

Robins (Group), 29, 124

Robinson, Jessie Mae, 21, 27, 29, 141

Robinson, Major, 60

Rock 'n' Roll Babylon, 195

Rock of Ages: The Rolling Stone History of Rock and Roll, 106

"Rockin' Pneumonia and the Boogie Woogie Flu Part 1," 94, 95, 120

"Rock-in Robin," 14, 25

Rockwell, Willie Ray, 25, 27

Rodgers (Richard) and Hart (Lorenz), 28

Rogers, Pauline, 126

Rogers, Shorty, 55

"Rollin' Like a Pebble in the Sand," 158

"Roll Over Beethoven," 121

"Roll With Me Henry," 119

Rolontz, Bob 138, 184

"Roomin' House Boogie," 141, 145

"Rosanna," 56

Rovers (Group), 193

Royal Jokers (Group), 126

RPM Records, 149, 150, 152

INDEX

233

Rupe, Art (Arthur Goldberg), 20–23, 34–36, 105–7, 110–12, 117, 119–22, 140, 142, 155

Rydell, Bobby, 52, 79

"Saddle the Cow," 150

"Sad Hours," 103

"Sad Story," 18

Sahl, Mort, 55

Salk, Dr. Jonas, 56, 58

"Salute to Johnny," 193

Sanders, Richard, 146, 150

"Saturday Night Fish Fry," 145

"Saving My Love For You," 19, 23, 112, 114, 173, 174, 179, 183, 184, 186

Savoy Records, 11, 13, 193

"Sea Cruise," 95

"Searchin,'" 34

"See You Later Alligator," 115

"Send For Me If You Need Me," 144

"Senorita," 45

Sensations (Group), 126

"Sentimental Heart," 36

"Seven Days," 125

Seward, Alex (Slim Seward, Georgia Slim), 72

"Sexy Ways," 185

Shaw, Arnold, 12, 17, 137

Sheiks (Group), 36, 37

Seventh Stream: The Emergence of Rocknroll in American Popular Music, 18

"Shake A Hand," 169

"Shake, Rattle and Roll, 23, 112, 114, 184

"Shame, Shame, Shame," 105

Shaw, Arnold, 80, 136

"Sh-Boom," 23, 31, 114, 184

Sherman, Dick, 52

Sherman, Robert 52

Shields (Group), 43, 49

Shirley Gunter and the Queens, 12

Shirley and Lee, 104, 105

"Signed, Sealed, Delivered," 130

Simon, Bill, 119

Sinatra, Frank, 55, 56, 113, 182

"Since I Fell For You," 90

"Sincerely," 31, 41, 117, 195

"Since I Met You Baby," 41, 139

Sinegal, Willie Norman (Bill), 94, 108

"Sinner, Sin No More," 119

Sistrunk, Woody, 81, 11

"Sittin' and Wonderin,'" 124

Skip and Flip, 23

Slades (Group), 47, 49

Smith, Bessie, 147

Smith, Huey "Piano," 92, 94–96, 99, 100, 102, 108, 119, 120

Smith, Lloyd "Fatman," 164

"Smokey Joe's Café," 124

"Smooth Operator," 40

"So Fine," 36, 54

"Song Bird Records, 160

"So Long," 151, 152

"Some Day Some Where," 166

"So Much," 53

"Song From Moulin Rouge," 18

The Sound of the City, 25

Southern Tones, 187

Spades (Group), 46, 47

Spaniels (Group), 23, 41, 112, 184

Specialty Records, 16, 20–22, 26, 34–36, 104, 105, 107, 108, 111–13, 116–18, 120–22, 124, 140, 142, 155

Spirit of Memphis Quartet, 187

Spivey, Victoria, 78

Sporke, Michael, 163

"Stack-A-Lee," 91

Stafford, Jo, 113

"Stagger Lee," 91

"Stand By Me," 118, 172

"Standin' In the Station," 100

Stax Records, 137, 163

Stevens, Connie, 183

Stevie Wonder, 130

"St. Louis Blues," 143

Stoloff, Morris, 121

Stone, Cliffie, 53

"Stone Down Blues," 72

"The Story of My Life," 111, 113, 114, 130, 131
"Story Untold," 195
Stovall, Percy, 98, 101
"Such a Night," 185
Sure Shot Records, 160
"Sufferin' Mind," 116, 117
"Suffering the Blues," 40
"Sugar Doll," 50
Sugar Lumps (Group), 97
"Sugar Mama," 34
Sultans (Group), 185, 187
"A Sunday Kind of Love," 174
Sun Records, 51, 101, 151, 154, 172
Sunny Guitar Slim (Guitar Slim Green?), 71
Sunnyland Slim, 72
Super Disc Records, 16, 142
"Sweet Little Rock 'n' Roll," 53
Swing Time Records, 27, 109, 140, 141

"Tabarin." 26
Bruce Tate, 28, 29
"Take Good Care of Her," 58
Tan Town Records, 151
Taylor, Elizabeth. 183
"T-Bone Blues," 80
"Teach Me Tonight," 31
"Teddy Bear Blues," 79
"Tell Me," 39
"Tell Me Pretty Baby," 165
"Tell Me So," 145
Tender Records, 48
"Tennessee Waltz, 157
Texarkansas Gazette, 64
"That's All Right," 51, 193
"That's How Heartaches Are Made," 61
"That's the Way It's Gonna Be," 48
"Thinking and Drinking," 141
"Think It Over," 124
"The Things That I Used to Do," 23, 84, 97, 100, 108–13, 115, 117, 119, 122, 130, 131, 179, 184, 186
"There's Something on Your Mind," 54, 94

Thomas, Rufus, 147, 149, 151, 172
Thomas, Carla, 141
Thornton, Willie Mae "Big Mama," 19, 153, 160, 163, 166, 171–74, 176–80, 182, 184, 187–90
"Those Lonely, Lonely Nights," 120
"A Thousand Miles Away," 41
Three Dots and a Dash, 17, 18, 20
Tibbs Brothers, 126
"Tico Tico," 103
"Tik Tock," 23, 24
"Ting-a-Ling," 104, 156
Tisby, Dexter, 12, 28–30
"Too Many Women," 166
"Too Soon to Know," 138, 144
"Tootles," 54
Tosches, Nick, 146, 150, 151, 177, 178
Toto (Group), 56
Traits (Group), 161
Trammel, Charles, 30
"Tramp," 141
"Treasure of Love," 127
"Treat Her Right," 160
"Trouble and Me," 167
"Trouble and Misery," 34
"Trouble Blues," 145
"Trouble Don't Last," 115
Trumpet Records, 174
"Tryin' to Fool Me," 115
Tubb, Ernest, 89
Turner, Ike, 149, 150, 166
Turnero, Joel, 126
Turbans (Group), 126
Turks (Group), 12, 50
Turner, Joe, 23, 36, 73, 109, 112, 114, 125, 126, 138, 179, 184
Turrentine, Stanley 140
"Tutti-Frutti," 121
"Twenty-Five Lies," 115
"Two Steps From the Blues," 161
Tyler, Red, 91, 95
"Tweedle Dee," 31, 195

"Unchained Melody," 195
Upsetters (Group), 179
Urban Blues, 75

INDEX

Valino, Joe, 54
Vallee, Rudy, 182
Valli, June 18
Vaughan, Stevie Ray, 113
Verdon, Gwen, 54
Vera, Billy, 15, 34, 42, 56, 71, 81, 84, 99, 100, 103, 107, 112
"The Very Thought of You," 56
Vidalia, Patsy, 97
Vincent, Johnny (John Vincent Imbragulio), 95, 107–11, 119, 120
Vinson, Mose, 144
"Viva Las Vegas," 51

Wade, Adam (Patrick Henry), 56–58
Walker, Mel, 11
Walker, Aaron Thibeaux "T-Bone," 72–75, 79–84, 93, 119, 123, 131, 138, 156
"Walking the Dog," 147
Wallace Brothers, 178
Ward, Ed, 137, 138, 160, 167, 181,
Warren, Willie D., 88, 89
Washington, Baby (Justine), 58, 61
Washington, Bettye (Betty) Jean, 17
Washington, Dinah, 31, 103, 113, 138, 144, 156, 157, 167
Washington, Ferdinand "Fats," 193, 194
Waters, Muddy, 112, 131, 138, 184
Watson, Johnny Guitar, 12, 15, 48, 74
"Wayward Wind," 121
Webb, Joyce, 49
Weber, Joan, 192
"Weeds of Hate," 102
Welch, Lenny, 90
Welk, Lawrence, 51
"Well . . . All Right," 53
"Well, I Done Got Over It," 11
"(We're Gonna) Rock Around the Clock," 10
West, Bob, 102
Wexler, Jerry, 109, 125, 126
Wharton, A.C., 142, 168
"What a Diff'rence a Day Makes," 55

"Wheel of Fortune," 26
"When There's No Way Out," 127
"When the Sun Goes Down," 114
"When You Dance," 126
"Whipped Cream," 72
White, Barry, 12, 42
White, Bukka, 144
White, Lavelle (Lillia Lavell White), 128, 152, 163, 176, 191
"White Christmas," 23
"Who Drank the Beer While I Was in the Rear," 103
"Whoopin' and Hollerin'," 166, 167
"Why Don't You Head Off," 53
"Why Johnny Why," 193
"Wild One," 79
"Wild Wig," 11, 13
Williams, Buster, 48, 50
Williams, Curtis, 12, 21, 26–33
Williams, Hank 191, 195
Williams, Lester, 179
Williams, J. Mayo "Ink," 77
Williams, Mel, 36, 37, 48
Williams, Nat. D., 147
Williams, Tony, 32
Williams, Walter (Dootsie), 12, 13, 29–33
Wiliamson, Sonny Boy, 174
Willie Evans (Willie Egan?) and the Night Owls, 71
"Willie's Boogie," 72
Willis, Chuck, 40, 45, 46, 104, 1634
Wills, Bob, 87
Wilson, Brian, 26
Wilson, Carl, 26
Wilson, Carole, 102
Wilson, Dennis 26
Wilson, Jackie 51, 53, 58, 60–65, 67
Wilson, Murry, 26
Wilson, Nancy, 56
"Wine," 26
"Wine Woogie, 19
Winn, Henry, 159
Wirt, John, 96, 100, 101
Withers, Ernest, 191

INDEX

"Without Me Baby," 85
Wolf, Howlin,' 125, 131, 138, 150, 173
"Woman Troubles," 115
Wood, Randy, 47, 49
Wood, Roger, 154, 160–62, 169, 170, 175–77, 180, 181, 191
Wooley, Sheb, 101
"Work With Me Annie," 23, 112–14, 119, 184–86
Wright, Wade (Wacko), 95
"Write Me a Letter," 144
"The Writing on the Wall," 58

"Yes Baby," 174, 187
"Yesterday," 160
"You Are My Sunshine," 46
"You Cheated, You Lied," 43, 46, 47

You Didn't Want Me," 156
"You Know I Love You," 156, 158
"You'll Always Hurt the One You Love," 116
"You'll Never Walk Alone," 112, 114, 138, 185
"You Mean Everything to Me," 46
"Young Rascals," 169
"You Upset Me, Baby," 187
"You, You, You," 18
Young, Al, 91, 99, 100
"You've Been Gone So Long," 183, 184
Youngsters (Group), 39

Zappa, Frank, 113
"Zing! Went the Strings of My Heart," 55

EARTH ANGELS